Reg Sutteridge

1·98

—REG—
GUTTERIDGE
UPPERCUTS AND DAZES

My Autobiography
with Peter Batt

BLAKE

Published by Blake Publishing Ltd,
3 Bramber Court, 2 Bramber Road,
London W14 9PB, England

First published in 1998

ISBN 1 85782 208 0

British Library Cataloguing-in-Publication Data:
A catalogue record for this book is available
from the British Library.

Typeset by BCP

Printed in Great Britain by
Creative Print and Design (Wales), Ebbw Vale, Gwent

1 3 5 7 9 10 8 6 4 2

Every effort has been made to contact the relevant copyright-holders, but some were
unobtainable. We would be grateful if the appropriate owners would contact us.

Muhammad Ali

Reg Gutteridge was a fellow traveler with me for seventeen years. He never asked for a favor. Whether it be Madison Square Garden, Las Vegas, London, Manila, Kuala Lumpur, Zaire or Zurich, he was there.

I once told Reg to interview me in between rounds when I was bored beating a bum in the Far East. He even had the nerve to say George Foreman could whup me.

Reg is forgiven for his criticism, because he is a class guy and a wonderful friend, though I should have whupped him when he tricked me for "This Is Your Life" in London.

I am anxious to read his book of stories and fights, because Reg always tells it like it is.

Muhammad Ali.

P. O. Box 187 · Berrien Springs, MI 49103

*To my wife, Connie, for putting up with me all these years.
And daughters, Susan and Sally-Ann, to show them where I was
when they grew up. They have now presented me with four fine
grandsons, Jacques, Robbie, Matthew and Alexander.*

*Thanks, also to my old mate, wordsmith Peter Batt
for putting me write.*

CONTENTS

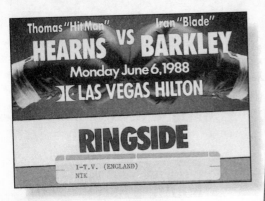

Thomas "Hit Man" vs Iran "Blade"
HEARNS vs BARKLEY
Monday June 6, 1988
LAS VEGAS HILTON
RINGSIDE
I-T.V. (ENGLAND)
NTK

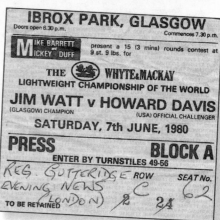

IBROX PARK, GLASGOW
Doors open 6.30 p.m.   Commences 7.30 p.m.
MIKE BARRETT and **M**ICKEY DUFF present a 15 (3 mins) rounds contest at 9 st. 9 lbs. for
THE WHYTE & MACKAY
LIGHTWEIGHT CHAMPIONSHIP OF THE WORLD
JIM WATT v HOWARD DAVIS
(GLASGOW) CHAMPION   (USA) OFFICIAL CHALLENGER
SATURDAY, 7th JUNE, 1980
PRESS   **BLOCK A**
ENTER BY TURNSTILES 49-56
REG. GUTTERIDGE   ROW   SEAT No.
EVENING NEWS
(LONDON)   C   62
TO BE RETAINED

THE SUPER FIGHT.
World Middleweight Championship
HAGLER vs. LEONARD
Presented by Top Rank, Inc. and Caesars Palace.
April 6, 1987

REG. GUTTERIDGE
ITV
SEC IV
ROW 1
SEAT 6
00/00/00   BROADCAST
CAESARS PALACE
LAS VEGAS

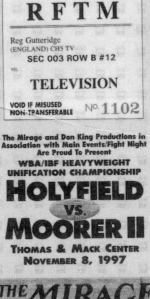

RFTM
Reg Gutteridge
(ENGLAND) CH5 TV
SEC 003 ROW B #12
YEL
TELEVISION
VOID IF MISUSED
NON-TRANSFERABLE   N⁰ 1102
The Mirage and Don King Productions in Association with Main Events/Fight Night Are Proud To Present
WBA/IBF HEAVYWEIGHT UNIFICATION CHAMPIONSHIP
HOLYFIELD vs. MOORER II
THOMAS & MACK CENTER
NOVEMBER 8, 1997
THE MIRAGE

WORKING PRESS
LADIES NOT ADMITTED
16   D   5
SECTION   ROW   SEAT
CONVENTION HALL   Monday Eve.
RAIN CHECK   MARCH
IMPORTANT   **13**
READ NOTICE BELOW   1961-8:30 P.M.
POSTPONEMENT STUB
WORKING PRESS
PATTERSON vs JOHANSSON
MON. EVE.   3:30 P.M.
MARCH **13** 1961
IF POSTPONED this RAIN CHECK will admit holder to this event on the postponed date. VOID IF STUB IS DETACHED FROM RAIN CHECK.

OFFICIAL CREDENTIAL
PRESS
CAESARS
ATLANTIC CITY
DeWITT vs BENN
APRIL 29, 1990
CAESARS ATLANTIC CITY WELCOMES
REG GUTTERIDGE
ITV
COMMENTATOR
SECT RINGSIDE ROW C SEAT 00

MONDAY   N⁰ 094   APRIL 15
Marvelous Marvin   Thomas "Hitman"
HAGLER vs HEARNS
WORLD MIDDLEWEIGHT CHAMPIONSHIP
ITV
AUG IV
ROW 1
SEAT 12
CAESARS PALACE

LE STADE DU PARC OLYMPIQUE MONTREAL
CHAMPIONNAT DU MONDE DES POIDS MI-MOYENS C.M.B.
SUGAR RAY LEONARD vs. ROBERTO DURAN
VENDREDI 20 JUIN 1980 A 19h00
PARTERRE EST
N⁰ E 06

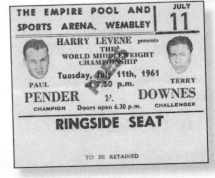

THE EMPIRE POOL AND SPORTS ARENA, WEMBLEY   JULY **11**
HARRY LEVENE presents THE WORLD MIDDLEWEIGHT CHAMPIONSHIP
Tuesday, July 11th, 1961 at 7.30 p.m.
PAUL   TERRY
PENDER v. **DOWNES**
CHAMPION   Doors open 6.30 p.m.   CHALLENGER
RINGSIDE SEAT
TO BE RETAINED

Some souvenirs from the years gone by.

ALI'S REVENGE??
THE BATTLE OF BROKEN JAW
12 MONDAY
ROUNDS SEPTEMBER 10
MUHAMMAD
ALI FORMER WORLD CHAMPION
vs.
KEN NORTON
NUMBER ONE CONTENDER

世界バンタム級 タイトルマッチ

WORLD BANTAMWEIGHT CHAMPIONSHIP

CHAMPION
FIGHTING HARADA
ファイティング・原田 〈15Rnd〉
CHALLENGER
ALAN RUDKIN
アラン・ラドキン 英

階 列 番
N A 17

主催 サンケイ新聞・サンケイスポーツ・フジテレビ 提供 篶崎ボクシングクラブ 特別リングサイド
後援 文化放送・ニッポン放送 認定 WBA・JBC ¥ 5,000
協賛 ライオン歯磨・ライオン油脂・サントリー株式会社

HOLMES
FRAZIER
PRESS
FRIDAY, NOVEMBER 25, 1983

CAESARS PALACE
LAS VEGAS · NEVADA

REG GUTTERIDGE
NAME
ENGLAND TV
AFFILIATION

II   BB   12
SEC   ROW   SEAT

BOXING AT THE FORUM
G BB 13
SEC ROW WORKING PRESS
PRESENTED BY GEORGE PARNASSUS PRODUCTIONS
Friday   Dec. 12, 1969   8 p.m.
15 ROUNDS · WORLD BANTAMWEIGHT CHAMPIONSHIP
RUBEN Vs. ALAN
OLIVARES RUDKIN
World's Champ   British Empire Champ
Mexico   Challenger
PRICE $35.00
Includes $1.75 State Tax
SAVE THIS COUPON FOR REFUND
IN CASE CONTEST DOES NOT TAKE
PLACE

FRANK BRUNO v JOE BUGNER
Saturday, 24th October, 1987
WHITE HART LANE
OFFICIAL PASS
Name   LWT
Nº   0275

Top Rank, Inc
AND
CAESARS PALACE
PRESENT
HAGLER
vs
DURAN
NOVEMBER 10, 1983

Reg Gutteridge (T)
World of Sports

SEC 4 ROW 1 SEAT 18

CAESARS
PALACE

TV

OFFICIAL   CREDENTIAL
don
PRESS
BLP
TYSON vs. SPINKS
TRUMP
PLAZA
ONCE AND FOR ALL · JUNE 27, 1988

TRUMP PLAZA WELCOMES:
Reg Gutteridge
Foreign TV
London TV
SECTION: W ROW: 1 SEAT:
Nº   0382

WORKING
PRESS
WORLD'S HEAVYWEIGHT CHAMPIONSHIP FIGHT
LISTON vs. CLAY
MIAMI BEACH CONVENTION HALL
TUE., FEB. 25, 1964, 8:45 P.M.
GUTTERIDGE
LONDON EVE NEWS
THIS IS YOUR ADMISSION TICKET
Non-Transferable
ENTER PRESS
GATE No. 2
Nº   288   — ONLY —
(Southeast Side of Convention Hall)
SEC E   ROW C   3

MIKE   FRANK
TYSON   BRUNO
Saturday · February 25, 1989
LAS VEGAS HILTON

LONDON
CLOSED
CIRCUIT
MEDIA
West
Row 2
Seat 18
Nº   2076

ARSENAL STADIUM, HIGHBURY, N.5
HARRY LEVENE   29
PRESENTS
Heavyweight Championship of the World
MUHAMMAD ALI   formerly
Champion of the World   CASSIUS CLAY
(U.S.A.)
V.
HENRY COOPER
Challenger   (GREAT BRITAIN)
15 — 3-minute Rounds
SATURDAY, MAY 21st, 1966
Doors open 6 p.m.   Commences 8 p.m.
Ringside PRESS
ROW A   SEAT 29
Enter via Stewards Entrance, Avenell Road

WANTED

Sportsmen of all grades to assist and support a GRAND TESTIMONIAL BENEFIT which is being organised on behalf of that respected Boxer and Second.

ARTHUR
GUTTERIDGE

The Greatest Boxing Programme ever is being fixed under the joint Direction of The Ring, N.S.C. and Jeff Dickson Promotions. Britain's Best Boxers will Compete in actual Contests under the personal supervision of L. F. Bettinson (N.S.C.), Victor Berliner (The Ring), Sam Russell (Stadium Club), Ted Broadribb (Jeff Dickson Promotions).

Supporting Patrons will include—The Right Hon. The Earl of Lonsdale, K.G., Lord Tweedmouth, C.M.G., M.V.O., D.S.O., The Right Hon. The Earl of Chesterfield, K.G., The Earl of Westmorland. Lord Hamilton of Dalzell, K.T., Sir George Prescott, Bart., Sir William Bass, Bart., Sir Humphrey De Trafford, Bart., M.C., Sir Walter De Frece, Brig.-Gen. Sir Norman Orr-Ewing, Bart., D.S.O., Brig.-Gen. C. R. De Crespigny, Col. The Hon. Henry C. Guest, Col. R. E. Myddelton, T.D., Major J. S. Courtauld, M.C., M.P., Major J. A. Morrison, Roland Oliver, Esq., K.C., M.C., J. O. Fane, Esq., Thomas Marlin, Esq., M.D., C. H. Douglas, Esq., Mrs. Dick Burge, L. F. Bettinson, Esq., Jeff Dickson, Esq.

Watch out for the Greatest Boxing Show ever staged at

WED. DEC. 16th
THE RING
WED. DEC. 16th

POPULAR PRICES: 2/- 3/- 5/- 7/6 & 10/-

THE PERFECTA PRESS (T.U.), 154, CAMBERWELL ROAD, S.E.

CHAPTER ONE

BUYING A BLIGHTY

'If you can keep your head when all about you
Are losing theirs and blaming it on you ...'
RUDYARD KIPLING

It was the noise of the explosion as my feet hit the ground that made me think, 'Oh dear, I shouldn't be doing this.' The first sensation to invade my senses was the smell of the cordite. The next was the pain.

I had experienced a similar combination of surprise and regret several times before when I had dropped my guard and walked into a wild swing from an opponent in the boxing ring.

But this was no mere haymaker I was encountering. It was a German Schu mine, which had just fractured every bone in my lower left leg and flung me more than three feet in the air and on to a flower bed.

To this day, I cannot hear a recording of that most haunting of war songs 'Where Have All The Flowers Gone?' without remembering those poor scorched petals in that garden in Normandy.

What I should not have been doing when my foot hit that mine was sliding down the side of a Sherman tank with a box of heavy signalling equipment on my back. The weight of the box meant that I had fallen rather than slid. I had been told often enough that, if you must jump off a tank you should do it from the front or the back, not the side, because if there were any mines around the tank, would already have run over them and saved you the job of setting one off personally.

However, I was only 20 at the time and suffering from the impetuosity of youth. My comrades in the tank were all around ten years older than me and kind, considerate and protective towards me.

They had a macho way of showing it, however. Particularly, the bald headed driver, Stan Stainer, whose first words to me after the blast were: 'You silly little sod. What did you go and do a stupid thing like that for?'

I could only mutter through clenched teeth that it wasn't my fault. 'Give Gerry an inch and he'll take a foot,' I groaned. This was a ludicrous conversation given the circumstances. But on hundreds of occasions since then I've seen and heard similar bizarre exchanges when a fighter has forgotten to duck and his concerned cornermen have relieved their own tension by giving the boy a good bollocking.

Fortunately, just like any second worth his salt, Stan was remembering to work on the cut. But it was more than he and the others dare do to enter this particular area of combat. Wisely, Stan took off his battledress jacket, told me to cling to its arm and they dragged me out of the flower bed on to the safety of a concrete path. On reflection, safety is perhaps not the right choice of words as there were enemy shells flying all around us and into the trees beyond.

We were in what was left of the garden of a badly damaged farm- house, which was still littered with empty sauerkraut tins and had been, until a few hours earlier, a front-line German infantry position. I have been told that an involuntary catchphrase I tend to use frequently in my boxing commentaries is: 'This is what is known in the trade as...' Well, in the words of the army trade I was then in, I had just 'bought myself a Blighty.' This was the soldiers' way of describing a wound that would get you sent back to hospital in Britain and away from the horrors of the D-Day invasion.

Eerily, only the night before, my mate, Bill 'Lobby' Lowe and I had been digging slit trenches. When we were finished, we lay down in them and, exposing only our feet which were dangling out at one end. I had joked to 'Lobby': 'I wouldn't mind copping a nice piece of shrapnel in the toes now and buying a Blighty.' There were, of course, Blighties and Blighties. And what, if you will pardon the expression, I had just bought myself was a 'right bastard of a Blighty.'

I had not helped my comrades much either by making sitting ducks of them as they hung around wondering what to do about this very dangerous situation. One of them, whose hands must have been shaking with fear for his own life as well as for my well-being, lit a cigarette and offered it to me.

I had never smoked because of the boxing training, so I instinctively replied through clenched teeth: 'What are you trying to do? Kill me?' My comrade had the grace to refrain from telling me that it was my naïvety that could well kill them.

These were old soldiers – some had served in the regular army in India and a couple of guys in our unit had been in the retreat from Dunkirk. As a conscript, I had already been nicknamed 'raw arse' in the barrack-room.

We were in The Royal Artillery and had been on an observation mission to locate the enemy infantry positions to prepare our future shell bombardment. We most definitely should not have been hanging around like this, fully exposed and stationary. Especially as the Germans had laughingly labelled our American-built Sherman tanks 'Tommy cookers' because of their propensity to burst into flames immediately they were hit by shell or mortar.

Like most other youngsters of my age, I had seen plenty of cowboy-and-indian films in my boyhood and secretly wondered what sort of courage I would be able to summon up if I were ever ambushed and in mortal danger. The answer turned out to be precious little. There is as much fear as courage in warfare – just as there is in the boxing ring. And I found myself truly terrified in that foreign field. I remember lifting my head and taking a peep. And, as I couldn't see my left boot, I instinctively knew the foot was gone. The pain was indescribable. But the fear was even more intense.

I was afraid that the lads would have to leave me here. Even if they didn't and managed to strap me to the top of the tank, there were so many ploughed fields to negotiate on the way back to our original position that I was convinced I would keep falling off.

It was not the Seventh Cavalry that came to my rescue but the Royal Lincolnshire Regiment. Suddenly, one of their jeeps appeared next to our tank. Its driver was picking up a couple of the regimental snipers who had just finished their deadly stint and he was returning them to base. The three of them wondered what this tank was doing out there in no man's land with its crew standing around smoking and they pulled up to investigate, thank God.

They decided to take over the rescue operation and take me back to the nearest casualty station. I waved a feeble goodbye to Stan Stainer and the others and I was off on the worst journey of my life. The Lincolnshire lads had put me on a stretcher and tied it on top of the jeep in the cab above their heads. Incidentally, Stan's daughter was to write to me on his death many years later asking me all about her Dad. I told her the truth – that he had been like a much-loved protective uncle to me.

As soon as the jeep engine revved into life, I was tossed up and down as if I were on a trampoline. To make matters worse, Gerry had spotted us so not only were shells whizzing over our heads, but bullets were ricocheting off the jeep. During that journey, I saw something that has periodically invaded my mind ever since. It pops into my consciousness like a faded photograph and seeps into my dreams giving me night sweats.

Earlier, on the way up to the farmhouse in the tank, I had been watching the shells bursting nearby, when I spotted one of our infantry men crouching in a hedgerow holding a Bren gun. During that jeep journey when I still had not received any pain killers, I caught sight of that young infantryman again. But by this time, his head had been blown off.

The effect this terrible sight had on me was to send a feeble message of gratitude to my brain – along the lines of 'there but for the grace of God, go I.' It often intrigues me, this human tendency to keep making comparisons with our fellow creatures even in the most dire circumstances. Perhaps it is something to do with hope and the survival instinct.

Maybe it was this compulsion for comparisons – one I have spent a lifetime indulging as a sportswriter and commentator – that made me keep the army issue tin box containing my spare spectacles. This was the only possession, apart from the compulsory dog tags, that the medics handed back to me after they cut the uniform from my body in casualty. It still lies rusting on my mantelpiece – 54 years on.

I would be hard put to explain why I stubbornly refuse every attempt my wife Connie makes to get rid of this unsightly ornament, except to venture that it acts as a reminder to take nothing for granted, least of all life itself. How could I have dreamed way back then that it would turn out to be a symbol of gratitude? For I am convinced that had I not lost that limb, I would have pursued my boxing dreams and not switched to writing and commentating – a course that has taken me around the world several times visiting places and witnessing events that I could never have dreamed of unless I had won the football pools.

However, the first plane journey of my life was to be in an RAF Dakota, lying flat on my back on a stretcher. My ticket to ride was an expensive one – not quite an arm and a leg, admittedly, but this particular 'Blighty' came pretty close. I would not be able to walk again for a while.

After an initial amputation under canvas in that casualty station in France, I was flown back to England for a further amputation and a period of recuperation in a military hospital.

Half a century later, after I had appeared on TV as the subject of *This Is Your Life*, one of our company officers wrote to me enquiring if I was the Gunner Gutteridge he thought I must be.

If so, he wrote, he was enclosing a page from a diary that had been kept by my old commanding officer, Captain Jack Hunter, describing the day I lost my leg – 7 August 1944 which was, incidentally, August Bank Holiday back home – as a 'thoroughly bad day all round for the company.' I cannot speak for the rest of the company, of course, but I couldn't have put it better myself.

CHAPTER TWO

HOSPITAL BLUES

'If you can wait and not be tired by waiting'
RUDYARD KIPLING

One of the first lessons I was taught as a budding boxer was never to lose my temper, in or out of the ring. Maybe that is why I bore no personal animosity towards the Germans who blew off my leg.

On the contrary, like so many of my comrades in arms, I had a sneaking respect for the average Gerry soldier. No matter what you threw at him, he came back for more.

However, when it came to the brass hats who were running the show on both sides, I was not overwhelmed with admiration. Especially when I was awarded the sum of 16 bob (shillings) a week, to compensate me for the loss of a limb, although inflation has, at least, seen that pension rise to £38 a week today.

In a class-conscious country like ours, it will come as no surprise to the reader that officers and NCOs were paid more. That kind of discrimination is beyond my understanding, as is racial discrimination, which, I am proud to say, no longer manifests itself in British boxing.

Another somewhat hilarious discriminatory factor in the lost legs department was the length of the stump. Pensions were calculated on the amount of wood needed to turn you into Long John Silver. An above-the-

17

knee job was worth a lot more than my puny below-the-knee offering. When I complained that there were a lot of knots in my first stump back in 1944, I was informed by the limb-fitters at Queen Mary's Hospital in Roehampton that there was a shortage of wood at the time because the best was being used to build our Mosquito aeroplanes.

However, when they stretchered me off that Dakota aircraft on my return from France, false legs were the last thing on my mind. I was still in shock after an emergency amputation in Normandy, and staying alive was the name of the game.

We landed at an airstrip somewhere near Oxford. Girls from the Womens' Auxiliary Air Force were waiting to look after us and their faces registered their shock at seeing all these young men, bandaged and bleeding. We all had a yellow card around our necks – a bit like the media accreditation discs I was to wear to so many sporting events later in life. The purpose of these cards was to ensure that we were given regular injections of penicillin to prevent incurable infections setting into our wounds – God knows how many young warriors' lives Alexander Fleming saved when he discovered that precious serum. One of these girls looked familiar and it turned out that we had danced together in Scotland, where I had been sent to train for the D-Day landing. As my old Grandad used to say: 'Dolly had done dancing' for a while.

The train that took us to hospital in Birmingham was truly terrible. The groans of the wounded, the incessant rattling of the wheels on the track and the smoke billowing out of the engine and in through the windows made it seem like a journey to Hell. We must have looked pretty hellish, too, because they unloaded us into a siding, at Selly Oak, instead of New Street Station, presumably because we were too gruesome a sight to inflict on a war-weary population.

However, the hospital, The Queen Elizabeth in Edgbaston, turned out to be first class. Every patient was a war casualty. I never did find out where they put the sick civilians. I had a second amputation there where a few more inches were lopped off what was left of my left leg, so that it could be prepared for a false limb.

The pretty young nurse who volunteered to push me around in a wheelchair was named Mavis Groves. I was to meet her again 50 years later. Mavis reappeared in my life, aged 79, as a guest on *This Is Your Life*. She had become a matron before retiring from the nursing profession, and as we chatted I learned that the years had given her more than her share of heartache. She had married twice and been widowed twice. As we were reminiscing, though, I couldn't keep the foolish thought from my mind that this was the first time I had ever seen her standing up and that she was much smaller than I remembered her.

When we were eventually allowed to leave the hospital, on crutches for a few hours at a time, we wore the famous hospital blues. Older readers will remember what they looked like – like blue pyjamas with a thin red tie. The blues we were issued with looked as though they had been leftovers from the First World War. Those blues seemed to be a symbol for heroism as far as civilians were concerned – they earned us respect, affection and a place at the front of the bus queue.

After I had recovered from my second amputation, half a dozen of us wore 'the blues' for an outing to see the famous radio show 'Itma', starring that marvellous comedian Tommy Handley, which was being recorded in a canteen at one of the big ammunition factories in Birmingham.

As we were being ushered down the aisle to what turned out to be a place of honour near the stage, I was larking about a bit on my crutches – yes, I suppose I've always been something of a show-off. But I suddenly froze as the warmest, most spontaneous and sustained round of applause rang out from the huge audience of workers. It sent shivers down my spine. None of us wounded squaddies could speak for half an hour or more we were so moved by the experience. I have never heard a tribute quite that sincere and emotional again in my life. Not even for the great Muhammad Ali.

I wore 'the blues' when I came home from hospital for my first convalescent leave and, again, they worked their magic.

My dad, Dick, said to me one day: 'Do you want to come out for a ride?' A ride in those austere times meant a bus trip, of course. Dad was going to the National Sporting Club to pick up some tickets for a boxing show. My family had been connected with the club since the turn of the century. It was in Old Compton Street, Soho, and is now The King Edward Theatre.

As we were standing in the foyer, I could hear magical big band music wafting out from the auditorium. It was so rhythmic that I swear it set even my missing toes tapping. It did not sound like a recording, so some instinct told me to look at the noticeboard. To my amazement, I discovered that none other than Glenn Miller and his famous orchestra were playing that music live at that very moment. Major Miller's American

Expeditionary Forces Band were doing regular BBC radio shows while they were based in London and they were rehearsing in, of all places, this old Gutteridge Family Baronial Boxing Seat. I was, needless to say, 'gobsmacked.'

In my teens I had fancied becoming a musician and saved up to buy a second-hand trumpet. Dad banished me to blowing in the backyard Anderson air-raid shelter. I was so serious that I asked an opponent I fought on a fund-raising show to try not to split my lip. Truth was I could blow my nose better than my trumpet.

'Dad!' I yelled like a star-struck schoolboy; 'my hero!' 'Who boy, me?' he replied. 'No, you silly old so-and-so,' I scolded him. 'Glenn Miller!'

'Really?' said Dad, 'I've heard of Mick The Miller, but who's this Glenn geezer?' Dear old Mick The Miller was, of course the most famous greyhound of all time and is to this day, stuffed and standing in the Natural History Museum.

After I had explained to my old man just what an icon Glenn Miller was to countless soldiers, sailors, airmen and their wives and sweethearts, he told me to stay and listen and off he scarpered. The music stopped suddenly and Dad returned with the great man at his side.

Dad, who was a natural born matchmaker, had explained that his boy was a wounded soldier on leave from the Front and would love to shake the distinguished band leader by the hand. Glenn was incredibly humble, solicitous and dignified. We shook hands and he invited me in to listen to the rehearsal. That experience was the thrill of a lifetime for me and it still hasn't been topped.

Taking great care with my crutches, Glenn sat me near the band and waved his baton to begin rehearsing again. What endeared me to the great man even more was that when the arranger asked what section he wanted, Glenn shouted, 'B, B for balls!' and then he gave me a great big wink, as if to say he could bandy barrack-room language about with the best of them.

He then proceeded to top the entire experience by telling me that, if I wanted to, I could come to the live performance tonight and that he would pick me up, personally, at the stage door.

That evening, ridiculously early, I was standing on my crutches outside the hall, clad in my hospital blues and looking, I suspected, like a forlorn soldier who had been stood up by his date. A taxi pulled up beside me and Glenn Miller opened the door. 'If you can manage to clamber aboard, we'll drive round the back to the stage door,' he announced.

Glenn took me into the dressing-rooms and, to my surprise, Mel Powell, the pianist, was messing about with a clarinet and the drummer was playing the piano. Perhaps this was their way of unwinding before the show – a bit like a boxer practising wrestling before a big fight. He positioned me on the stairs of the stage, just below the band. Then, at the end, he came down and sat beside me as the auditorium was being cleared.

Less than a month later, he was killed in a mystery plane crash over the English Channel and I was transferred from Birmingham to Roehampton to prepare for the limb fitting.

We were full of bravado on the wards when new patients were wheeled in. I would shout: 'Which one have you lost?' If the lad said it was the right, I would yell: 'That's handy, we need a new left winger for our blow football team.' This kind of banter usually helped the newcomers find their feet (if you'll pardon the pun).

I must confess that the banter turned bitter and the air turned blue whenever matron boomed: 'Stand to your beds for orderly officer's inspection.' We had to hop down to the foot of our beds and stand to attention without wobbling over.

In the case of one particular patient, the ward banter was pre-meditated. Between us, we had come up with a crude form of therapy, which seemed to help a brave Scots kid in the bed opposite mine. Young 'Jock' had a severely wounded back. He had charged a German gun position, single-handed, but when he reached the enemy his Sten gun had jammed and, as he turned to run away, a grenade was thrown at him, which missed, but splintered his back with shrapnel.

It meant that he had to lie face down all the time and whenever he wanted to get up, he had to raise himself on all fours like a cow. It sounds childish, in retrospect, but we used to give poor 'Jock' a chorus of 'moos' for encouragement as he struggled for what seemed an eternity to reach this unsightly position. We did it with love, not malice, of course.

This gentle mickey-taking never failed to bring a brave grin to 'Jock's' face. The rest of us one-legged, and in some cases limbless, guys figured we were much better off than him in as much as when our false limbs were eventually fitted, we would at least be able to take them off occasionally to ease the chafing on the skin. Poor 'Jock' is probably severely disabled to this day, that is if he hasn't gone to meet his Maker yet.

There was only one meeting on my mind as Christmas approached that fateful year – that was a confrontation at the quartermaster stores in Olympia, Earls Court, where I was to be issued with my demob suit. Incidentally, in keeping with that inflexible universal law of what goes round comes round, I was to revisit Olympia several times many years later when it was used as a venue for Chris Eubank fights.

In addition to the suit I was handed a so-called medical discharge certificate, which was nothing more than a slip of paper stating that Gunner Gutteridge failed to fulfill medical requirements. There was nothing about being a wounded hero that could be used as a calling card in civvie street and this pissed me off. It was obviously going to be a level playing field out there in the employment stakes for all ex-squaddies, disabled or not.

So, after a few training spins on my brand new leg using the hand rails in the fitting centre, nearly six months of recuperation came to a close and I went home. Home was only a bus and a tube train journey away from Roehampton in south-west London to Islington, north of the River. A mate, whose name I cannot even remember, was discharged with me. It was the first time during hospitalisation that we had been out without our crutches and we were issued with a walking-stick apiece.

As we neared the bus stop, a bus approached. When the bus was still a few yards away, the pair of us glanced at each other and, without speaking, threw our sticks on to the pavement in unison. I have never used a walking-stick again.

Fate has been kind enough to give me more than enough leg-ups in other areas of life's swings and roundabouts.

CHAPTER THREE
INHERITANCE

'Feed them silence when they say
Come with us an easy way...'
RUDYARD KIPLING

In retrospect, I can see that the kindest yet cruellest cut fate dealt me was my inheritance. I was almost literally born with a gumshield in my mouth. My paternal grandfather, Arthur, was a renowned bare-knuckle fighter, who incidentally taught Rudyard Kipling to box back in the 1890s. My father, Dick, and his identical twin brother, Jack, were the best known cornermen in the business in their heyday.

As I was to realise later in life, all this macho history placed a heavy subconscious responsibility on a boy – especially for an only child as I was. It was an intimidating masculine lineage to live up to. Jack's son, Jackie Junior, must have sensed this, too, because he grew up to be 'Jackie Pallo', the famous all-in wrestling star when that sport was so big on television in the 1960s and 1970s.

Jackie and I found ourselves sparring with each other on an almost daily basis in our teens and we boxed exhibition bouts in front of fairly big audiences, but, to this day, I am not sure how much either of us really wanted to do it. I suspect that we were both driven by inner forces that made us want to emulate our fathers. Following in father's footsteps was a much more acceptable thing to do in those patriarchal days than it is now in these more rebellious times.

Not that my dad ever demanded, or even openly desired me to fight. In fact, it was the reverse. He was overprotective towards me and when I did eventually take up boxing seriously, he used to whisper, out of my earshot, to anyone who would listen, that I had a weak heart – in the hope that this would reach the ears of my opponent who would then go easy on me. Sadly, it was not me who had the weak heart – it was Dad and his more fiery twin, Jack, who both died of heart attacks in their forties. Being gassed on the Somme in the First World War had obviously not helped either of them to achieve longevity, either.

So, when I threw that walking-stick away in the street as I was heading back home from the War, some emotion deep inside me was also registering relief that, although my dreams of boxing greatness had been blown away in France, so, too, had the pressures of living up to what I imagined were my father's hopes for me.

I worshipped the ground my dad walked on and I sensed the feeling was mutual. He may have been a boxer, but he was never a bully. Boxing, in those chivalrous times, was about personal dignity – being able to look the playground bully in the eye, not beating up a smaller boy for his dinner money. Never, dear Reader, confuse boxing with thuggery, as so many of today's abolitionists do.

I have always admired and respected boxers because, unlike so many contemporary tearaways and loud-mouthed lager louts, they know they have nothing to prove. Boxers have put their manhood to the test in the boxing ring. They have discovered, after plenty of admittedly painful practice, that once the brain really believed that attack was the best form of defence, taking action took away the fear. The worst thing you can do when confronted with violence is to spend too much time thinking about your reactions or the consequences or you will freeze like a rabbit in headlights. It is more about self respect and dignity than bravery. Bravery is an abstract concept. Self-respect and dignity are necessitites for peace of mind.

The first boxer I fell in love with was Grandfather Arthur Gutteridge. As a small boy, our family lived next door to him and I remember wanting to get as physically close to him as I could. In the cobbled cellar of his working-class flat he had a tin bath – that cellar now, in all probability, houses racks of expensive wine in a reconstructed Regency house in a highly fashionable part of Islington.

One day I asked him if I could take a bath with him so that we could have a good old splash around together. 'Course you can, me son,' said Grandad. 'But we'll have to go in after George.' George was a prize French bulldog. Grandad was a French bulldog breeder of note and showed them at the Royal Agricultural Hall. George was due to go on show the following morning. I took one look at the hairs in the bath after George was finished, made my excuses and left. So, I never did get to take a bath with the old boy, but I spent many hours at his knee, in the time-honoured tradition, listening to his tales of derring-do about the old bare knuckle fights. When we talk about hard men today, they must be wimps compared to old Grandad and his ilk.

They were men of granite. Old Arthur's main claim to fame was that he was the first professional ever to box at the famous old Sporting Club at the turn of this century.

Another tale he liked to tell was how he taught Rudyard Kipling to box back in the days when the gentry sent their sons to men like Arthur to teach them the noble art. Grandad also gave me my first piece of reading material when, unwittingly starting my literary education at the top, he gave me a copy of Kipling's wonderful poem which has been an inspiration to me ever since and is the reason why I quote my favourite writer at the beginning of every chapter in this autobiography.

Writing was the last thing I had on my mind as a nine-year-old, however. In 1933, the year Hitler achieved ultimate power in Germany and sowed the seeds for me to lose a leg and millions of others to lose their lives, relatives and homes, I felt leather in my face for the first time when I had my first tilt at boxing in a one-rope makeshift ring in the hall of my junior school.

When my eyes began to water, I wouldn't swear that I was falling in love with the fight game, but that smack in the mouth sparked something off in my psyche that I have come to believe must have been what that great American writer, Jack London, so vividly described in his world famous book, *The Call Of The Wild*.

His canine hero, Buck, had been a house-trained pet until he was kidnapped, sold and transported to the Arctic to join a pack of huskies. Once there, the hair stood up on the back of Buck's neck as he felt the pull of his ancestral genes and he went on to battle his way to the top of the pack.

I didn't have an instant urge to become top dog, but I did experience an overwhelming desire to hit the other boy harder than he had hit me. This may simply have been the survival instinct, of course, but my young mind figured out that fighting back was something my father would have done. And, just like all the other addictions on offer during life's journey, the more I boxed the more I wanted to.

Anyway, that's my excuse and I'm sticking to it.

The irony of all this is that my Dad never once got down on his knees in the kitchen and sparred with me as the Dads do in all the fight films. My mother may have had something to do with that. She claimed that I took after her and therefore was much too delicate and good-looking – she even nicknamed me Tyrone, after Tryone Power, the heart-throb film star of the time – to consider taking up boxing.

That settled, organised fisticuffs took second place to staying alive, which was never a doddle for any working-class family in those recession-hit pre-War days. I did not box again until I joined the Canonbury Boys Club when I was 16 and there rubbed shoulders with several lads who went on to become top professionals.

Dad and brother Jack were French polishers by trade, but always said they would rather earn one pound in the fight game than ten pounds polishing. Consequently, there was more than enough boxing in their lives but never much money.

Unlike the families in the East End who were crowded together in tiny terraced houses, very like those in the mining communities up north and in Wales, in Islington we lived in what were once elegant houses with corniche ceilings and great big restoration fireplaces. Each family had, at best, three roomst, however, and there were four families to a house.

I mention the fireplaces because ours is etched on my memory forever. When I was a kid, Dad regularly bought home all his boxers' kits from that day's training at the gymnasium. A more sweaty, unseemly bag of washing I've never clapped eyes on before or since. In addition to endless rolls of bandages for wrist strapping, there were shorts, singlets and, worst of all, jockstraps.

My mother, who was not the slightest bit interested in boxing, refused point blank to wash this horrible gear. Even though those were the days of the male chauvinists and the little woman in the kitchen, Mum was having none of it. So I got lumbered with the job.

Now, around that time, the biggest (in every sense of the word) name in world boxing was Primo Carnera. An Italian, Carnera – all 6ft 6ins and 19 stones of him – was dubbed by the newspapers 'The Ambling Alp.'

When he was in London for a fight to build up his growing reputation my dad and brother Jack got the job of training him. They did not know it at the time, but Carnera turned out to be a useless freak who was being manipulated to earn a fortune for his dubious American handlers. He became the subject of the best- selling book and film by Budd Schulberg, *The Harder They Fall*.

I never did get the dubious thrill of seeing poor old Carnera fall, which must have been like watching a chimney collapsing, but I was the boy who handled his dirty washing. I used to hang it out to dry on the iron fireguard in front of the fire – I can assure you that the sight of Primo Carnera's outsize jock strap steaming in front of your living-room fire is a sight once seen never forgotten.

Islington was a fascinating mixed area even in those days, long before parts of it started to become fashionable again in the 1960s.

During my boyhood and youth and up until I got married in 1953, as the twins became more and more successful in the fight game, we lived in three different flats in that area. One was next door to my grandad, then next door to uncle Jack and eventually we moved to Arundel Square, which is now very fashionable. In earlier days, however, some of the properties there had housemaids.

I knew this because I delivered the milk door-to-door when I was 12 years old. I got five shillings every weekend for pushing a wheel-barrow full of milk for Express Dairies. The only reason I got the sack was because they replaced the barrows with horses, and we kids were made redundant. We reported for work at Highbury Corner, near the Arsenal football ground, at 5.30 in the morning. It was hard work heaving those handbarrows up the hills, but the faster we pushed it the less milk we had weighing it down.

On the way back, I would sprint full pelt with my empty barrow to the old-fashioned workmans' café in Liverpool Road where they had those hard-backed cubicles such as you see in American gangster films. The big difference was that, instead of cookies, I got stuck into dripping on toast for breakfast.

I remember saving up for a pair of flash new boxing boots, but my dear old mum nicked them to wear indoors for the housework. She used to call herself Dan Leno, when she wore them – he was a music hall turn with a famous funny walk. These boots were flat with leather soles and she looked more like Old Mother Reilly than Dan Leno to me as she flapped around the kitchen.

My mother was a tiny lady with great big dark eyes and a wonderful sense of humour. She also loved to play the horses.

She used to have a daily bet, in coppers, and there were always complicated messages on the note listing the 'any back' instructions – 'any back' meant that if one or more of the earlier horses won she would play up the winnings. I know all this because I ran her bets for her on my way to school. Betting was illegal in those days, of course, and I can still recall my nervous tension as I handed the bookies' lookout the bet as he hid in the doorway while his guv'nor lurked in a nearby yard. All the kids where we lived were used to running errands, but this particular assignment always made me feel like a big-time gangster, although I could count on one hand the amount of times Mum won.

Anyway, I don't think it was money Mum was interested in so much as a bit of relief from the daily drudgery of life in those harsh times. However insignificant the amounts of money she lost it seemed to give her a guilty conscience and cause for anxiety.

Another reason I remember those particular errands so clearly is that they were to have bizarre repercussions years later.

Those repercussions came during the Blitz of London by the German *Luftwaffe* early in the war. Mum was visiting one of my aunts when a nearby blast brought the ceiling down and blocked the passage to the front door at my aunt's flat. The two women were trapped for hours and my mum suffered a minor nervous breakdown.

Equally unexpectedly, she was sent for counselling. Just to prove that old saying that there is nothing new under the sun, even psychobabble was freely available long before these so-called 'caring sharing 1990s'.

Even more unexpectedly, she claimed the shrink cured her by persuading her to uncover the dark secret of her gambling habit all those years later. It seemed that Mum had always been worried sick that Dad would find out about her little addiction. Maybe that is why she signed the betting slips 'Jack Hobbs' after the legendary England opening batsman. As a kid, I never could figure that one out and I could make even less sense of her reply, at that time, which was: 'Oh, it's just me *nom de plume*, son.'

When I eventually heard this little story, it baffled me. I never saw my dad strike, or even threaten to strike Mum or me. That was in the days when wife beating was a common occurrence in working-class London. Every morning we kids would count the number of women with black eyes as they made their way to the pawnshop to pop Dad's suit until next pay-day.

Most working-class cockneys reared clans rather than families. It was common in the 1930s to have flats full of kids sleeping four to a bed. There wasn't room for most of the men to swing a cat – many of them made up for this by swinging their fists when they got home from the pub. Whether it was the discipline of the boxing regime that made my dad and his brother Jack more responsible, or just Mother nature, I do not know, but cousin Jackie and I as only children were very much in the minority.

The only times Mum and me laid low when Dad was about was when he'd had his traditional few pints on a Saturday night. We could always tell by looking at our dog's face when the old man brought her home from the boozer. Trixie was a wire-haired fox terrier and I swear she would toss her head back in utter disgust and contempt if Dad had too many and started tugging her lead too hard.

Never once in his life did Dad ever tug on my lead too hard, though. I would have followed him anywhere and the happiest and most long-lasting memories of my boyhood were when I followed him and his famous wrestlers to halls all around London and sometimes even to St Leonards, a seaside resort in Sussex.

Dad and Jack were also seconds for professional wrestlers who were part of the end-of-the-pier-style showbiz scene before the war. All their bouts were well rehearsed as were those of their TV successors in the 1970s but they were tough, fit, athletic men and it would have been extremely inadvisable to infer that they were 'luvvies' or the like.

Household names such as Jack Pye and Izzy Van Dutch used to fling my 12-year-old five-stone body around the seashore like a beach ball. It was a 'come on' for the punters to roll up for the show that night. I loved it, as most kids like dangerous games, but the fact that it was a beach full of pebbles, rather than sand, made it painful when they dropped me occasionally to liven things up. Even more way-out, looking back, was the fact that I helped to look after the money whilst they were wrestling in case there were any foolhardy dressing-room thieves about.

The most hilarious of all these memories, even if it was a bit scary for a kid, occurred on a coach trip back to London from St Leonards one night. For some reason, which did not register with me at the time, the wrestlers still had their dressing-gowns on while they were dozing in the back.

I was in the front seat with my dad when the coach suddenly skidded violently and screeched to a halt. The driver explained that he had swerved to avoid a rabbit, but that he thought he had caught it a glancing blow and that, although the bunny was almost certainly dead, it was probably still intact.

Dad decided that rabbit pie would make a tasty supper and promptly got out of the still-moving coach to investigate. Unfortunately, he slipped on the step of the coach and fell into the road with enough force to split his head open. There was nothing else for it, but to rush him to a nearby hospital.

Two of the wrestlers took him to casualty and the sight of a couple of massive men in dressing-gowns, and boxing boots had the nurses screaming that two of their patients were attempting to do a runner and had bashed up a porter into the bargain.

Naturally, I used to leave my impressionable young schoolmates wide-eyed with wonder whenever I recounted inside stories of famous boxers and wrestlers. That may well have been the unwitting start of my career as a commentator.

CHAPTER FOUR

FALLING IN LOVE WITH FLEET STREET

'If all men count with you, But none too much.'
RUDYARD KIPLING

Perhaps, the desire to communicate for a living began at the London Evening News. If so, the seeds being sewn took a long time to come to fruition. From messenger boy to a best seat at the main event is a long and sometimes hazardous journey, especially when fate is laying booby-traps at your feet. Still, maybe the fact that there is not much demand for one- legged messengers worked in my favour.

To begin at the beginning, my love affair with Fleet Street, although it felt much more prosaic than poetic at the time, began when I was only a week into my first pair of long trousers. Dad stationed me outside the Old Bell Tavern one day, stuck a glass of lemonade in one hand, an arrowroot biscuit in the other and told me to wait. Incidentally, schoolboy boozers were rare animals in those days, so that explains the lemonade and the biscuit.

The same could not be said for Fleet Street journalists, however, and Dad, ever the fixer, knew he would find at least one or even several of his boxing writer pals partaking of their customary liquid lunch.

It so happened that the old man hit the jackpot. When he came out, he asked triumphantly: 'What do you fancy boy – *Star*, *News* or *Standard*.' I didn't know it then, but my dad was offering me the stars, the moon and the cosmos because getting regular work of any kind was an achievement in the Great Depression of the 1930s.

If this all sounds like a game of 'Find The Lady' Lady Luck smiled on me when I chose the *Evening News* and started my working life on 7 April 1938. I never did leave the *News* – it left me 42 years later by merging with the *Standard*. By the way, the watch I received as a leaving present was stolen inside a week. The Good Lord must have been hinting that time did not hang around for any man, least of all for one like me who was approaching retirement age. He was right – it didn't and neither did I. But that part of my story will have to wait till later, time permitting, of course.

For me to claim that I, or any other kid of my generation, had received an education by the time we left school at the ingenuous age of 14 would have been as great an exaggeration as today's teenagers trying to pretend that Oasis or The Spice Girls can actually sing. Still, at least I could spell, which is, from what I read about today's educational standards, more than some University undergraduates can do.

I was to receive my education in a newspaper office and the only serious qualification I would attain was a degree in cynicism. Yet, I must admit there are worse ways of protecting yourself in this world of hard knocks than by being cynical.

I soon discovered what a little softy I was at heart when, on my first day at the *News*, one of the first jobs I was given was opening some post. One of the first envelopes I tore asunder contained a copy of the previous day's lunch-time edition, which had been cut into strips and glued together so that it resembled a crushed toilet roll.

Scrawled all over it in pencil were slogans such as 'Who wants to listen to your troubles?' followed by 'Got enough troubles of my own'. I was told that this particular missive had been arriving at the paper on a daily basis for as long as most people there could remember. Naturally, my boyish imagination conjured up a vision of some poor old grey beard, all alone in his bedsit, spending every evening on this thankless task. It was the first time, I had ever given a moment's thought to human experiences like loneliness and despair and it sent a shiver down my spine. I was lucky enough to realise even then that this was what my dad must have meant when he had said proudly after he got me my job: 'I'm sending you to the university of life, boy.'

Many world-weary years later, my old writing colleague, the incomparable George Whiting of the *Evening Standard* topped this little tale of mine by telling me a funnier and, in some ways, sadder story of his own. George was a wizard of a descriptive sportswriter, right up there with the most eloquent in the world but he was, by his own admission, not the best judge of a boxer or even a boxing match.

One evening we were taking a nightcap together during one of our numerous and enviable all expenses paid trips to some exotic location when he brought us down to earth by telling me about the anonymous postcard he had received with unerring regularity for the past 30 years. Whenever dear old George had tipped a forthcoming fight the wrong way, which was often, the postcard would read: 'Wrong again, prick!'

The George Whiting of my boyhood days was C. E. Nash. Every word he wrote for the *Evening News* was scribbled in pencil and, to my amazement, the linotype operators managed to understand it. The kind of blanket coverage in today's newspapers came in with TV, because modern readers want more to read than they have already seen for themselves on the box.

In that age of innocence men like C E Nash and even later big time boxing writers such as Frank Butler of the *News Of The World* and Peter Wilson of the *Daily Mirror* simply reviewed a boxing match in the same way that a contemporary theatre critic reviews a play.

Even right up until the advent of package holidays for the so-called masses, colourful sportswriters like Desmond Hackett of the *Daily Express* wrote up their visits to boxers' training camps as if they were penning travelogues, too. In pre-War days, British boxing writers travelled to and from world title fights in America on transatlantic liners, and they spent weeks afterwards dining out on verbal descriptions of Joe Louis' left hooks, which could be seen only on cinema newsreels.

The last thing to enter my mind, even in fantasy, were thoughts of emulating C E Nash or any of his worthy successors. Becoming a big-time boxing writer was as far removed from my line of vision then, as men one day walking on the moon was from everyone else's. Due to what I now like to think of as respect, I called him Mr. Nash until the day he died. Though, on reflection, I probably addressed him that way because I didn't fancy a clip round the ear.

In the social climate of that time, I would not have had to step far out of line to get a clip. This was long before the parents if the 1960s became Doctor Spock fanatics and handed parental responsibility over to their anarchic children. I am not advocating a return to the old values, just recalling them. Those were the days when we snotty-nosed teenagers were seen and not heard. If I had ever dared confess to Mr. Nash that I wouldn't mind a job like his one day, I would probably have been run out of the building for ever for backchatting an elder and a superior.

My immediate superior, as I took my first, faltering steps up the Fleet Street ladder, was a gentleman called Alf Drury. He was a Dickensian figure who wore a waistcoat and a splendid watch chain and called all his messenger boys 'Jimmy'.

Looking back now over a span of 60 sometimes unbelievable, certainly unimagined years, it is chastening to recall that the messages I relayed as a 17-year-old were a million times more momentous for the population of Britain than the commentaries I would later send around the world from ringside.

For instance, I carried the communiqué from the Ministry of Information to the *Evening News* that the *Ark Royal* had been sunk with the loss of hundreds of British sailors. This was one of the most depressing news items the nation received during the early part of the war.

Even more depressing, on a personal level, was the morning I was carrying another piece of war news, only to run into the ruins of some of the lovely old lawyers' buildings in The Inner Temple, which was just up the road from the *News* office. I remember that the all clear had not yet sounded that morning when I cycled to work at 6am. It turned out that the Temple had 'copped' it that night, and I can still clearly see myself putting my bike on my shoulder and climbing over the smouldering rubble.

Sadly, that bike came to a sticky end, too, when a bus knocked me off it and buckled its wheels beyond repair during one of my errands from the City Office in Throgmorton Street back to Fleet Street. I abandoned the bike on the steps of St. Paul's Cathedral and legged it back on foot to breathlessly relate my little drama to Mr Drury. His reaction was, I was later to learn, a classic Fleet Street one: 'But you got the copy back to the office, Jimmy, and that's all that really matters, innit?'

The tragedy of the *Ark Royal*, the loss of that bike and the fear of the air raids were like so much water off a duck's back compared with the emotional upheaval I experienced on the death of my god-like grandfather a couple of years earlier.

Arthur Prince – the 'Prince' was actually on his birth certificate, although the family never found out why – Gutteridge, one of the last of the bare knuckled veterans, died on 28 August 1938. 'A grand old sort and a grand old second', the American *Ring* magazine recorded at the time.

A man of action, old Arthur died fittingly with his boots on. Fishing boots. The old chap passed peacefully away sitting on a stool on the banks of the River Kennett. He was on his 50th annual fishing holiday at the time, and the stool he died on was the one he had used as a second to such fabulous boxing names as 'Peerless' Jim Driscoll, Ted 'Kid' Lewis and the immortal 'Ghost with the hammer in his hand' – Jimmy Wilde.

Doctors told us that grandad died of a 'tired' heart. The people of Islington were not too tired to come out and say farewell to him. People lined the streets, the men doffing their caps, as the horse-drawn hearse bore him to Highgate Cemetery where he was to have the coffin of the legendary bare knuckle fighter, Tom Sayers, for company, as well as Sayers' pet dog and Karl Marx to keep an eye on them.

Old Arthur Prince Gutteridge had earned the respect of his local community and, for a proud cockney, there could have been no more prestigious epitaph.

The proudest moment of my life came when my ageing idol gave me the greatest compliment I could ever hope to receive. I was 11 years old at the time and boxing in one of a regular series of exhibition bouts against my cousin Jackie, at The St Bride's Institute where my uncle Jack was the chief instructor. Out of the blue, Grandad decided to be my second one evening. There was quite a big crowd of other young boxers and their parents watching, and I didn't know whether to freeze or burst with pride. His presence must have inspired me because at the end of the bout, he exclaimed: 'Well, I'll be blowed, you're not a bad little boxer, are you, me son? Where did you come by all those moves?'

Every time I reflect on that magic moment, which is often, I still chuckle at the memory of the surprise in Grandad's voice. I mean, it wasn't as if I was from a long line of concert pianists or brain surgeons, was it?

Anyway, from that moment on, my Mum's 'Tyrone Power' tag was banished from my mind and I was prepared to settle only for 'Ringwise Reggie' or some such slick appropriate pugilistic epithet.

Once again, destiny or coincidence, call it what you will, had other ideas. The St Bride's Institute was only a long left jab away from the Old Bell Tavern and my Fleet Street future.

Although I idolised Grandad for his boxing, my lasting

photographic memories of him are of running errands from the Caledonian Slaughter House where he added to his irregular boxing earnings by being a part-time slaughterman. I wheeled his barrow, which was just a rickety box on pram wheels, back to his home with a fresh supply of meat for his show dogs. The barrow was painted dark red to hide the dripping blood.

'Old Arthur', as he was known throughout the neighbourhood and the boxing business, did not retire from seconding until he was 71, and the fisticuffs fraternity held a benefit night for him at the famous old Blackfriars 'Ring'.

Grandad was once presented to the then Prince of Wales, later Edward VIII, for rescuing some people from a fire. He kept an old photograph of that presentation, but by far the proudest perch on his mantelpiece was reserved for photographs from his beloved National Sporting Club. Incidentally, with him on one of these photos is an RAF pilot who made headlines by shooting down a Zeppelin at Cuffley in Hertfordshire; Flight Lt. Robinson.

The National Sporting Club was the most authoritative and prestigious organisation in world boxing in its heyday. It was the equivalent of the British Boxing Board of Control, which was not formed until 1929.

Its members were descendants of the 'Fancy', the wealthy grandees of the 18th and 19th centuries who used to have their own 'champions' – much as owners have thoroughbred race-horses today. The grandees paid those ancient gladiators out of their betting winnings in the days when 'milling' – as the noble art was then known – was illegal.

Yet vast crowds would flock to the 'secret' rendezvous

deep in the English countryside to bet on, bellow for or berate their particular favourite, in much the same way as today's TV fans do.

In 1891, when bare knuckles were replaced by gloves and boxing was eventually legalised, Arthur became the first professional boxer to appear at the National Sporting Club's famous arena in Covent Garden. In practical terms, it meant that he was the first boxer to receive a pre-arranged purse from the Sporting Club.

This was the little piece of history that set him apart from other men and, in my young mind, made him the object of my undying admiration.

I had dreams of my own to pursue now. After winning the National Boys Scouts Championships, which was quite a big deal then, I was entered for the famous London Federation of Boys Clubs Champions. I was devastated when I failed to make the correct weight for my division and was ruled out on a technicality.

Soon after this disappointment, however, I was paid another compliment, which pleased me almost as much as Grandad's approval of my talents had done. Bill McGowran, the *Evening News* sports editor had come to see me box at a show run by the Canonbury Tower Club, which turned out a string of well-known names. As I was lighting the fire in the office next morning – yes, we actually had coal fires in our offices in those days – Mr McGowran tapped me on the shoulder and said: 'You should turn pro, young Gutteridge. You can go all the way.'

He also made me blush by adding that if he had a son of his own, he would have liked him to be like me. True to his word, it was Bill McGowran who wrote to me when I lost my leg later, saying that there would be some kind of a job waiting for me at the *Evening News* when I recovered.

What that job would eventually turn out to be could not have been further from my mind at this time. Boxing was in my blood. It came as naturally as breathing. But it almost became the cause of my never being able to breathe again one Saturday afternoon when I was boxing at the Walthamstow Avenue Football Ground – while I'm name-dropping like this, I might as well throw in the fact that I often trained in the gym at Highbury when the Arsenal stadium was closed down because a barrage balloon was on the pitch.

At the height of my battle with a boy whose name I cannot remember an air raid suddenly started and incendiary bombs dropped all around as first the audience, then the boxers, and lastly the seconds – still instinctively carrying their precious stools and buckets – legged it for cover into the bowels of the stadium.

That incident must have been Herr Hitler's way of warning me that there was more of the same to come from him, as far as I was concerned. The cheek of it! Especially, as my mum came from a line of Germans named Schmidt! Still, life is full of little ironies like that, don't you find?

There is another retrospective irony to consider. Or could it have been destiny again?

Working for a newspaper gave me the urge to start a little cuttings book of my own, featuring my own boxing exploits. When I tried to take it home, an eagle-eyed front hall porter spotted me leaving the premises with company property under my arm – i.e. an Associated Newspapers folder. I was duly apprehended and taken to the management, accused of stealing. Later, I was released of course and admonished.

Apart from feeling a bit resentful, I thought no more about the incident or the cuttings until several years later when, on my return home after recuperating from my amputation, Bill McGowran kept his promise and wrote to me saying that there was a job waiting at the *Evening News* sports room although just what that job would be he had no idea.

It was on reading this letter that the long-lost and sadly unfinished cuttings book popped back into my mind. For the first time, I began entertaining strictly private ideas that I might even try my hand at the writing game and start a big-time boxing cuttings book.

In between these coincidences, there was the little matter of a world war to attend to ...

CHAPTER FIVE

TO HELL AND BACK

'Boots-boots-boots-boots
movin' up and down again!'
RUDYARD KIPLING

When I was a baby, I was once told, I was so small and frail that my mother was afraid to bathe me and my aunt used to do the business for her by washing me in a flower vase.

Maybe that is why my dad never wanted me to box or to join the army. On the face of it, that makes my old man sound like one of the world's worst hypocrites. If there was a bigger boxing fanatic than him, I've yet to meet him and if there was a prouder Royal Artilleryman, I haven't encountered him, either.

But what Dick Gutteridge was really all about had much more to do with sentiment than hypocrisy. Whatever his reasons, there was no way my overprotective old dad was going to let his boy volunteer for the army. He never tired of telling me that I should wait for my calling-up papers. Yet, as he spoke, above his head on his bedroom wall hung a painting of a grief-stricken First World War horse artillery man on the battlefield, cradling his dead equine comrade's neck in his arms, with a caption entitled 'Goodbye old friend'.

In his own Army days, Dad had lavished so much

loving care on polishing his Royal Artillery cap badge that he insisted I wear it in my cap when I eventually joined the regiment myself.

When I was conscripted in the Autumn of 1942, however, it was as a foot soldier with The King's Royal Rifles. On the way to King's Cross Station, where I had to catch the train to York, I struck up a conversation with another recruit named Leslie Compton. We were destined to become firm friends in later life and he, too, had a leg amputated in his advancing years.

The difference between Leslie – who was, of course, big brother of the even more famous Dennis Compton – and me was that, before losing his leg, Leslie went on to fulfil his sporting ambitions in spades by becoming wicketkeeper for Middlesex and England and centre half for Arsenal and England. After having his amputation in the mid-1980s, Leslie went on to win a bowls competition, false leg and all, before he died just a few years ago.

Incidentally, dear old Leslie who was older than me, had his call-up deferred because he had volunteered to be a special policeman during the blitz when he had dug many a dead body out of the rubble.

The square bashing in the Royal Rifles was tough. Everything was done at the double Royal Marines' style, but I coped with it better than most because I was fit from the boxing training. What I most definitely was not, however, was worldly wise. I had never been outside London, except to Hastings for the wrestling, and this made me feel 15 rather than 18.

I felt much too shy to mention to either the officers or the other men in my barrack room that I was a boxer. I realised in those first few weeks in uniform that I did not have a violent nature and that the idea of preparing for war was actually quite shocking to me.

My first leave came as a massive relief. But going back to the regiment meant travelling even further from home this time because I was posted to Selkirk in Scotland. It was a very heavy winter and when my dad came to see me off at King's Cross, the pair of us were nearly in tears.

Until I laid my head on my kit bag, clutched my rifle to my chest and attempted to sleep on the corridor floor of that crowded train, I had never had a clue what misery felt like. I was the loneliest teenager in the world on that journey and yet there was so much human contact that there wasn't even room to turn over on to my side. I did not know what was worse – the puffing of the engine, the rattling of the wheels or the snoring. Anyone who has ever slept in a barrack room will know what I mean about the snoring.

Fortunately, though, I had gotten my wish and been transferred to the signals section of the Royal Artillery. So, there I was in the communications business again – funny old game this life, innit?

Bombardier Bill Anderson, a professional footballer in civvy street, was very protective towards me as was Stan Stainer, the man who was to drive the tank when I was wounded. With these older men looking out for me, it began to feel as if it was a home from home.

All this mollycoddling came to an abrupt halt one day when Sergeant Douggie Gardner, a tough-looking bald-headed man from Norwich, tapped me on the shoulder at pay parade and said: 'That's an unusual name you've got. Anything to do with the boxing family, by any chance?'

The moment that I confirmed that it was, he said: 'Right, Gunner Gutteridge, you'll be boxing for us.' That was it, no more questions asked, I was in the Regimental Boxing Squad of the 33rd Field Regiment of The Royal Artillery.

The only perk for boxing in wartime was a bit of extra grub to build us up. I expect the top brass had more serious combats to worry about in those days. How different it turned out to be in peacetime, though. Many years later, I chuckled when those great British heavyweights Henry Cooper and Joe Erskine were telling me about their cushy time as national servicemen in the 1950s.

They served together in the Royal Army Ordnance Corps. Welshman Joe recalled that the officer detailed boxers to go into A company, footballers into B company and cricketers into C company. At which point Erskine asked him: 'And where do the bloody soldiers go?'

This particular soldier had gone to a place called the Haining, a high and extremely cold region in the Scottish border country. Wealthy people lived in this very pretty location, but the army put a blot on their landscape by erecting a plethora of ugly Nissen huts for us soldier boys to live in.

The army also put a blot on my, as yet, undefeated boxing record. I remember losing on points to a couple of hustlers from other regiments and being convinced that I had won easily and that the verdicts had been for brawn over brains. This was the first time in my life that I had no Gutteridge in the corner to convince me that I was right and the referee was wrong. It still leaves a bad taste that my last couple of fights were lost on bum decisions. 'We wuz robbed' is hardly an original cry in the boxing trade, is it?

However, the boxing did considerably enhance my

popularity. So much so, that during 18 months of hard soldiering in Selkirk, I was transformed from being a shy youth into – and I cringe now to admit it – something approaching a Jack the Lad.

I certainly felt like Jack the Lad when General – later President – Eisenhower singled me out to speak to when he came to give us a pep talk shortly before D-Day. By then along with thousands of others, I had been transferred to southern England to prepare for the invasion.

Ike, who commanded the invasion force, came to inspect us and addressed us in a field near Rowlands Castle in Hampshire. To my amazement, as he came along the lines, he stopped in front of me and asked: 'How's the chow?'

I have never been so lost for words in my life. At that moment the odds against my ever becoming a commentator would have looked stingy at a million to one. I recovered my composure enough to try to work out what the hell he was talking about. I hadn't yet seen enough American war films to know that 'chow' was slang for food. I lunged in with: 'We're quite satisfied, sir.' As Ike moved, on all around me, the other squaddies began softly singing: 'Oh, you bleedin' liar'.

I tell you no lie when I say that no matter what words the five-star all-American general had chosen to inspire us that day, he could not have come even close to preparing us for the sheer hell of Normandy.

It was not until many years later when I read a book on the subject by Max Hastings that I learned that, apart from Stalingrad, Normandy had the highest casualty count of the entire Second World War.

Perish the thought of having to live with the responsibility of being a cornerman as Ike was, in a fight of that magnitude. Our own 'second' was a stiff upper lip Colonel straight from Sandhurst: 'If you see one of your comrades dead or wounded on the beach, you must ignore him and concentrate on getting the job done.' The Colonel finished his call to arms by advising us: 'Make sure you have a spare pair of boot laces with you at all times.' That bizarre instruction puzzles me as much as I write it down now as it did then.

I do not laugh at the memory of Normandy. Far from it. The Colonel was killed on the beach on the very first day of the Normandy Landings as he stood up in a Bren carrier. He was shouting a battle cry when a bullet went through him.

The Colonel was the first person I thought of when, nearly 20 years later, I was sharing a drink with a German sportswriter at the European Amateur Boxing Championships in Moscow in 1963. The German happened to mention that he fought at Normandy and my initial reaction was bitterness.

After a couple more drinks my attitude softened and I chided him that he was probably the so-and-so of a crafty infantryman who laid that Schu mine for me. 'No,' he replied, 'one of your artillery guns had already blown me up by then.' Whereupon he pulled up his trouser and we compared metal legs. What could we do but laugh together? Inwardly, we both cursed the waste of our lost comrades.

Yet the War still managed to offer me considerable compensation. In a very roundabout way, it gave me the courage to approach my future wife, Connie. Connie lived in the flat above ours and, naturally, she was known by our family as 'the girl upstairs'.

To my then shy eyes she was the best-looking girl in

our road by a street length. She had long auburn hair, which she sometimes cropped for what she assured me was the then fashionable page-boy bob. I fancied her from the first time I saw her, but in those pre-historic, naïve, innocent days when most boys knew as much about girls as they knew about the man in the moon, the prospect of chatting her up by myself was well and truly out of the question.

When I got to France, though, I dreamed up a perfect plan to get to Connie. The Normandy Campaign took place in high summer and our tanks threw up mini dust storms whenever they hit the road or the field. Some of the lads started taking to sending home for silk scarves to wear around their mouths like cowboys.

This gave me a marvellous opportunity to write home to Mum and, in ever such casual tones, mention that if 'the girl upstairs' had a silk scarf to spare she would be doing me a big favour by sending me one.

Two silk scarves arrrived by the next post, one orange, one green. I was wearing the orange one on the day I was wounded.

CHAPTER SIX
WHEN REGGIE COMES MARCHING HOME AGAIN

'Land of our birth, we pledge to thee
Our love and toil in the years to be.'
RUDYARD KIPLING

I read a potted history of Islington recently, which described my birthplace as 'a healthy hilltop which, in Elizabethan times, was known as Merry Islington'. It was said to contain dairy farms and was a welcome relief from the stench of the city in times of plague. Its attractions, apparently, included tea gardens and other amusements.

Well, the Islington I returned to in the autumn of 1944 had more traffic fumes than dairy farms; the tea gardens had become working mens' 'caffs' and my amusement was provided by wide boys, spivs, spielers, barrow boys, boxers, big bands and bobby soxers.

If I wanted to enjoy what the old place had to offer, I had to become mobile. So my first decision was to hump my flabby muscles and my false leg to the nearest gymnasium and get myself fit again.

A nimble body was also very useful when it came to ducking and diving from the doodle bugs and V2 rockets, with which Hitler in his death throes was still peppering us. Islington, like the rest of London and all the other British towns that had been badly bombed, was undergoing a massive mopping-up operation. Everywhere you went people seemed to be shovelling or sweeping up rubble.

Rationing was still very much with us, of course, and this continued right into the austere 1950s. All the street talk then, was not of drugs but of wheeling and dealing on the black market. There were coupons for food, clothes, petrol, the lot. Everyone was at it.

Even a well-known judge used to be a regular caller at boxing promoter Jack Solomon's office in Soho for a side of ham, half a dozen eggs or whatever other kind of tasty morsels Jack may have laid his manipulative hands on recently. Anything to make a change from spam and whales' meat.

The War had definitely turned in our favour by now so there was a lot of hope as well as weariness in the air. Boxers were beginning to come home again, too, and the pride and joy of the Islington fight fraternity then was Terry Allen, who went on to win the World Flyweight Championship.

He trained at Father Preedy's gym in Penton Street opposite Penton Street Drill Hall where I had my first-ever public bout. Father Preedy was a Roman Catholic priest who had a gym in the church grounds to keep the local kids off the street.

Terry's real surname was Govier and the story was that he changed his name to Allen to honour a dead pal in the navy. The word on the street was that he was once on the run from the services and that he got himself another identity card which belonged to a Mr.

Allen. I don't suppose the powers-that-be were too worried about that, however. They had far bigger problems to concern them. Certainly, dear old Terry won't mind me giving the game away now because he reported to the Great Time Keeper In The Sky years ago.

As for me, I began punching the big bag and doing some sparring at a gym in Great Portland Street, which happened to be situated near the BBC headquarters, and was run by a wrestler pal of my dad's named Mickey Wood.

During those late War years, one of the big variety hall acts featured an attractive red-haired, strong-armed, pin-up girl called Joan Rhodes. Her act, which even got her to the world famous London Palladium, was to tear telephone books in half and then take the mickey out of any macho men who were foolhardy enough to go up on the stage and try to emulate her.

One day, when TV was still very much in its infancy, a presenter called Joan Gilbert turned up to watch Joan Rhodes training at our gym. She intended to feature the strong woman on her show, *Joan Gilbert's Picture Page*.

When the lads told her there was a one-legged ex-soldier working out there she couldn't resist coming over to watch my little routine. At first she thought it was a leg-pull (if you will pardon the pun) because, as I obviously couldn't wear shorts and there was no such thing as tracksuits in those days, I had my trousers tucked into my socks and did not exactly look the part.

As soon as she was convinced I was the genuine article, though, she decided I would be a more topical subject for her show, and so it was that I upstaged a star. In January 1945 I made my first TV appearance doing my training routine at the BBC studios in Alexandra Palace.

Coincidentally, I was back at Alexandra Palace commentating for Sky TV as recently as 1997.

Workwise at that time, however, I still had to wait a few months for official clearance from the army before beginning work at the *Evening News* again. By now I was entertaining private dreams of maybe writing about boxing one day, so I decided to try my hand at it by getting some casual work on the *Boxing News,* which was and still is the fight game's bible in this country.

In order to get scraps of information for the *Boxing News* I became a regular at another gym. This was in Fitzroy Square and was run by an eccentric called Bill Klein, whose claim to fame was that his was the cleanest establishment in London. Bill would rush round the place with a feather duster flicking dust off the ropes, the ring posts and anything else that could possible gather dirt, but at the same time he would flick cigarette ash from the duster on to the unfortunate boxers. Bill must have lived in a dream-world because, in reality, the gym was in a dingy basement and it had the scruffiest tea bar in London. Hygiene did not seem to be a priority for Bill – just a pristine boxing ring.

Klein's was populated by some of the most colourful characters in London. Among the regulars at the tea bar were the Warren Street car traders who were so entertaining that they became a tourist attraction just after the War. They knew me because I was a member of the Gutteridge family and they had a whip round for me when I came home from the war which raised £12, a tidy sum in those days.

One of these gentlemen was a character by the name of Setty. He later became the subject of one of the biggest newspaper stories of the 1950s when he was murdered and his dismembered body was found floating in the sea.

Other headline characters included the fighters, of course. Many of them worked out at Klein's on a regular basis. There was Al Phillips 'the Aldgate tiger' and Dave Crowley, a brilliant boxer and a true gentleman. And there was the man who was to go on to become the famous manager, matchmaker and promoter – Mickey Duff.

Mickey had come to this country as a baby from Poland. He was the son of a Rabbi and he ran away from home to become a fairground boxer at the age of 15.

When he used Klein's he was an established professional, nicknamed 'the rasher' by my dad and uncle because, although he is now a portly man touching 70, he was sensationally skinny in those days. His slim build did not prevent him from being a very resilient fighter. He was a defensive spoiler and a very slippery opponent, who lost only three fights out of the 60-odd he fought during his career.

Of those 60 I saw at least 40. The one that, for obvious reasons, sticks in my mind most was when he was literally stoned by a section of the crowd. He was fighting in daylight on a Sunday, because of the threat of air raids, at the open-air Mile End Arena. Mickey won a tight points decision and stood there smiling when he was cascaded by what he, initially, mistook for nobbins but which he soon painfully discovered were real pebbles and bits of brick.

For the uninitiated reader, 'nobbins' are coins traditionally thrown into the ring by an appreciative audience for a particularly courageous performance. In this case, though, the boys at the back of the arena were picking up stones and bits of wood from the floor and pelting poor Mickey with them because they disagreed with the verdict.

Not even sticks and stones could break Mickey's bones, nor have names ever hurt him, either. For when he went on to becomeone of the big names in this country for many years, he must have been called every name his rivals and enemies could lay their tongues to.

Also on the scene in those days was Jarvis Astaire. He was already a manager way back then. He managed Billy Thompson of Hickleton Main who was trained by my dad and actually lived with us in Islington at one time. When Billy hit the big time, Jarvis sold him to Benny Huntman for £500, which was a big deal in those days.

The fight game did its best to stay alive during the War by roping in boxers when they were on leave and sometimes even when they were not. Most shows then were attended by Military Police waiting to, in their own sympathetic words, 'nick absent-minded fighters for going Absent Without Leave'.

Fortunately, the MPs were courteous or diplomatic enough to wait until the fight was over. Obviously, even the hardest-hearted among them did not fancy dealing with a potential riot from world-weary citizens who had been deprived of entertainment for too long.

Often, some of the top men were in this country between postings abroad and the temptations to cash in were obvious. A few shillings service pay did not compare with the few hundred pounds they could earn in the ring. Consequently the bills in those days often represented a kind of military 'Who's Who'. Household names had their ranks printed instead of the titles they held.

For instance, there was Pilot Officer Len Harvey, RAF Sergeant Freddie Mills, Sergeant Jack London, Sergeant

Instructor Larry Gains, Petty Officer Ben Duffy, Stocker Al Phillips, Royal Fusilier Harry Lazer, Irish Guards Sergeant Arthur Danahar, RAF Sergeant Harry Mizler, Sergeant Instructor Dave McLeave, etc, etc, etc.

By far the biggest fight in the war years took place in 1942 just before I went into the army. It was when Freddie Mills, arguably the most popular British boxer ever, took the heavyweight title from the then declining Len Harvey. My dad was in Harvey's corner and I was squatting a the end of the front row of ringsiders. It was Dad's habit to pass his boxer's dressing-gown down to me to look after it.

Len's dressing-gown was a regal deep maroon and I draped it lovingly over my knee because this gown belonged to one of the most respected men ever to lace on a pair of gloves.

Many years later, I went to visit Cornishman Len just before he died in his little house opposite Holloway Prison in London and that dressing-gown was still hanging on his bedroom door.

I persuaded Len's wife, who was nicknamed 'Blossom' to sell Len's Lonsdale belts to Mickey Duff's son, Gary, who keeps them for posterity, along with other items of boxing memorabilia at his home in America.

The mention of dressing-gowns reminds me of an astonishing little piece of social history. Throughout the 1930s and 1940s whenever the *Evening News* carried a photograph of a boxer, the art room would paint a vest over the man's torso because they refused to print pictures of nipples. I know this because, as a messenger, I had to take the pictures to the art room for doctoring.

In retrospect, one of the most remarkable facts to resurface from those distant days, was the number of fights boxers had and the frequency with which they fought.

Freddie Mills, for example, fought four times in the space of six months just after the War and three of those bouts were headline-making top of the bill contests.

Freddie, who was a close friend of the Gutteridge family, fought the American World light heavyweight Champion Gus Lesnevich, with his pal, Dad, in Lesnevich's corner just a few weeks before Dad died in 1946. There were no hard feelings from Freddie, incidentally. He knew it was just another day at the office for Dad.

There had been tremendous pre-fight anticipation for this bout. With so many of our fighting men home from the war and thirsting for thrills of a different kind, Haringey Arena could have been filled three times over.

Even though Freddie was stopped in the 10th round, he put on a courageous performance and the event lived up to expectations. So much so, that it has to go on my list of all-time great scraps.

The return bout, just four months later, was at the open-air White City Stadium in front of a much bigger audience and Freddie won on points over 15 rounds. Unbelievably, by today's standards anyway, he took on the much heavier, Bruce Woodcock just a month later and was outpointed himself.

That was in July 1946, yet less than a month later fearless Freddie was in action again. This time, thankfully, his opponent lasted less than a round. He was, incidentally, a Swedish Air Gunner by the name of John Nillson. Although what Sweden – with all due respect to my many Scandinavian friends – were doing with an air force at the time I never did find out.

Another British champion heavyweight, Jack London – father of the equally well-known Brian, who performed in the 1960s – was having his 141st contest, no less, when he lost his title on a sixth-round knock-out to Yorkshireman Woodcock at White Hart Lane, a month before the Japanese surrendered and ended the Second World War in 1945.

It took another 40-odd years to resurrect the Spurs' ground as a big fight venue. First, for Frank Bruno versus Joe Bugner and then the ill-fated, Chris Eubank–Michael Watson tragedy.

The main reason that modern big-time boxers fight so infrequently in comparison with old-timers is the taxman. The purses are so much bigger now that, if a modern fighter fought four times within half a tax year, he would finish up owing the taxman more than he earned.

As for dear old Freddie Mills, he went on to endear himself even more to his adoring British public after he lost his world light-heavyweight title to the classy American Joey Maxim in 1950.

At that time, some of the proceeds of most fights still went to the various charities. It was an old tradition in boxing, especially during the War years. The three fights I had myself, against my closest rival and close friend, Peter Lee, were all on behalf of what was then called the 'War effort'. They were held during 'Aid to Russia Week' 'Islington Spitfire Week' and 'Red Cross Week', respectively.

Freddie attended a similar charity concert on a Sunday afternoon, just a few days after the heartbreak of relinquishing his world title, during the course of which Maxim knocked out a couple of his teeth.

Mills still managed to entertain the audience at the concert by going up on stage and singing a popular ditty of the time call 'All I Want For Christmas Is My Two Front Teeth'. That took a lot of guts, even for a courageous ex-fairground boxing booth scuffler like Freddie.

Talking of teeth reminds me that when I saw the veteran Hollywood actor Gregory Peck on the Channel Four Racing Programme recently I was struck by his dazzling Hollywood smile, which he still has in his eighties. Racing nut, Gregory, is also a fight fan. I remember interviewing him for the *Evening News* at ringside after that Mills–Maxim fight.

Jack Solomons, the leading promoter in those days, did love to have celebrities at his shows. He even enticed the Duke of Edinburgh to attend one night, when there was a Belgian on the bill who was stinking the place out. During his fight I turned to Jack and said sarcastically: 'Where on earth did you get this Belgian from?' Solomons replied unashamedly: 'Belgium'. The Duke obviously tickled by Jack's dry sense of humour roared with laughter.

In some ways, though, the most laughable incident I was involved in during that colourful period concerned one of those war-time fights when one of the contestants must have been nabbed as he was going over the wall from the army.

A top middleweight called Paddy Roche was due to fight another top man, who shall be nameless, at the Caledonian Road Baths. Nearly all the shows during the War were held in daylight because of the danger of air raids. This one was set for a Sunday afternoon, and when I arrived the promoters were breaking their hearts because Paddy's opponent hadn't shown up and it began to look like they would have to give the punters their money back.

I came to their rescue by mentioning to my dad, who was a cornerman, that, on my way in I had spotted Dickie Johnson, a very good local middleweight, queuing up to get into the Gods for two-bob, which was the equivalent of a couple of pounds today.

The Master of Ceremonies promptly called up to Dickie that if he came downstairs the promoters would be happy to give him his entrance money back. When Dickie duly arrived they delighted him even more by informing him that he was now top of the bill to fight Roche and would be recompensed accordingly.

That little gem made all the national sports pages, but the budding Fleet Street journalist, namely yours truly, did not get a penny for it. I happened to mention it to a local freelance who promptly, like the good professional journalist he was, sold the story. He was a young man named Maurice Kinn who, unsurprisingly went on to make a name for himself as an entrepreneur.

Incidentally, my news sense then was no better than my instincts at the romancing game. I was still woefully slow when it came to getting off the mark with Connie and had made no further approaches since returning home.

CHAPTER SEVEN

THE TWINS

'The tumult and the shouting dies'
RUDYARD KIPLING

A very good friend of mine, that great American sportswriter Red Smith, once memorably wrote: 'Death is no big deal, the very least of us can manage that – living is the trick.'

Well, when it comes to low-key deaths, my dear old Dad's took the ticket. I shudder to think of the cold, lonely, impersonal way he died on the top deck of a number 38 bus. He suffered a heart attack on the journey from Victoria Station to our home in Islington. He had been in Brighton at the gym, where he trained. It was a Sunday evening – just another routine day in his seven-day working week.

Dad was only 48 years old when he died. His worldly wealth amounted to £30. So boxing really was the hardest game where he was concerned.

The only time in my life I have ever had cause to hate anybody in the fight game came a few weeks after Dad's funeral when a small-time boxing promoter by the name of Nat Yess wrote requesting me to send him £3, which he claimed Dad owed him.

Some years later when I was being by-lined in the *Evening News*, this same Mr Yess wrote to me again, saying: 'You give plenty of publicity to the big promoters.

Don't you ever feature the less fashionable men like me?' I wrote back: 'Dear Mr Yess, No!'

Uncle Jack died in 1952, four years after Dad with what, both metaphorically and literally, was a broken heart. The doctor said Jack's heart had actually broken in two, but his spirit had been broken by Dad's demise. He had no enthusiasm left for the pro game and, apart from doing the odd bit of schoolboy coaching, he went into retirement.

Like his father and brother before him Jack, too, died with his boots on. He collapsed and expired underneath the arches opposite Holloway Road Underground Station.

It pains me to say this, but in some ways it was a relief to Mum and me not to have a daily reminder of Dad. The worst thing we could have done was give Dad's clothes to Jack. Jack lived in the next street and every time he came round the corner in Dad's overcoat, it felt like having a knife stuck in our ribs.

Some genetic experts seem to reckon that twins are two halves of one personality. Well, maybe that is true where the Gutteridge twins were concerned. Broadly speaking Dad was the introvert and Uncle Jack was the extrovert.

Jack was the hard twin, the minder, so to speak. The only way you could tell the pair of them apart was from the scar on Jack's cheek that had been administered by a broken glass when he was attempting to stop a fracas in a pub.

I once saw his famed left hook in action myself when I was a kid and Jack felt the need to demonstrate it to a big-time German wrestler called Carl 'Reginsky'. My dad and my uncle were in the corners at the old Alcazar in Edmonton when, during the action 'Reginsky' deliberately kicked out from the canvas and hurt my dad. In the dressing-room later, Jack draped a small towel around his wrist and let 'Reginsky' have the hook on the point of his granite-like chin. There was no retaliation from the German or from any other wrestler – then or ever!

The twins truly were like peas in a pod among the boxing fraternity. It was not uncommon for a dazed fighter to return to the wrong corner. Some of the poor boxers must have thought they were seeing double when Dad was in one corner and Jack in the other.

They were both acknowledged internationally as supreme seconds in their own right, but put them in the same corner and, I am proud to say they were dynamite. I still have dog-eared yellow newspaper cuttings to prove it ...

The Star 16 December 1938: 'Had it not been for the skill of the Gutteridge twins in Eric Boon's corner, he would never have been able to carry on the fight let alone win it.'

Sporting Review 11 February 1939: 'The Gutteridge corner went through the card at the National Sporting Club. They sent out every winner and have done the same thing for three weeks running.'

The *Evening News* 12 July 1939: 'The brothers Dick and Jack Gutteridge had a big night at The White City when every winner came from their corner. This is not a record, the Gutteridge twins have done it before at the open-air show.'

Dad's obituary in *Boxing News* read more like an eulogy. It began: 'When George Charles 'Dick' Gutteridge was laid to rest at Highgate Cemetery, the fistic art lost one of its most respected personalities. Dick Gutteridge, one of the 'inseperable' twins, had spent his lifetime in the game and, as a trainer and a second, he had few equals. It was only natural that he should choose a career in boxing, as his famous father Arthur was both a boxer and then chief second at the old National Sporting Club from the day it opened until the day it closed. In fact, he was once described as 'the most widely known man in boxing.'

'For over a century the Gutteridge family had been in boxing, so it was not surprising that, even as a schoolboy Dick started as pageboy at the old National Sporting Club.

'As a young man, he was taught boxing by 'Peerless' Jim Driscoll and among the famous fighters he handled were Len Harvey, Maurice Strickland, Tommy Loughran, Eddie Maguire, Dave Crowley, Billy Thompson and Bobby Ramsey.

'But Dick did not always have a top-liner in his care – although he must have seconded every champion in his time – he worked just as hard for and gave the same attention to novices and four-round curtain raisers.

'Dick's shrewd judgement and his uncanny way of guessing what the other man would do next made the little roly-poly expert invaluable to the man he was seconding.

'He was a past master when it came to mending a cut eye. We remember how he drew blood from the eye of Eric Boon with his mouth and he repeated the process on Gus Lesnevich ...'

That Boon blood put Dad in hospital and earned him newspaper headlines as 'The Vampire'. It happened during Eric's championship fight with Dave Crowley. 'Boy' Boon, as this colourful character was known, sustained a lump on his eyelid that grew to the size of a large plum.

Dad nicked the cut open with his scissors and then drained the blood from the swelling with his mouth. So, instead of being blinded by the blood, Eric was able to go on and beat Crowley. Dave, a close family friend, moaned to me for years afterwards: 'If it hadn't been for your old man I would have won back my title that night.'

But Dad finished up in hospital with blood poisoning. They kept him in, of all places, 'The Temperance Hospital' for a few weeks. Perhaps they thought he was turning into a 'bloodaholic', especially when he went and pulled the same trick for Gus Lesnevich against another big buddy of his, Freddie Mills. As Freddie put it, at the time: 'who needs enemies when you've got friends like Dick Gutteridge?'

Scissors are the tool a second uses most, what with the reams of bandages needed for fighters hands. Scissors figure a few times in Dad's saga. Would you believe that he often gave a young boxer a quick short back and sides between rounds if his hair fell into his eyes blocking his vision? Can you imagine some of today's image-conscious youngsters standing for that?

Those were, indeed, the days of innocence.

However, there was nothing innocent in the intentions of one colourful rascal, an American manager named Bill Daly, who used Dad's scissors for a spot of GBH one night. Daly, who could have stepped straight out of the pages of a Damon Runyon book, was dubbed 'Honest Bill' by sportswriters across the pond, which was an obvious mickey-take. Anyway, he managed New Zealander Maurice Strickland when he clashed with the German, Walter Neusel, in London before the War. New Jersey-born Daly had been rumoured to have run with the mafia in his young days and boasted that Frank Sinatra's dad was one of his oldest buddies.

During the Strickland–Neusel fight Paul Damsky, the German's blond hard nut of a manager, protested to the referee about what he considered to be an infringement and then, to compound the 'insult' he walked across the ring between rounds and berated Strickland's cornerman, which included my dad.

After the fight, my dad was cutting off Strickland's hand bandages in the dressing-room. When Strickland went into the shower, Dad noticed that his scissors had disappeared. Seconds later, he heared a commotion and screams emerged from the German's dressing-room across the corridor.

It transpired that there had been a blood-letting. Damsky had been badly cut about the face and Neusel had scarpered out of the Empire Pool Wembley and into the London night.

Arthur Elvin, the Wembley supremo at the time who was later knighted, was understandably furious and ordered an immediate inquiry. By the time it came to Dad's turn to give evidence his scissors had mysteriously reappeared in his bag and he made the diplomatic suggestion that perhaps the door of one of the metal dressing-room lockers had been left open and had caused the injury.

Damsky declined to call the police, so the matter was dropped. That incident and Dad's explanation earned me a lifetime's protection from any American lowlife that I might run into. Even in his old age, when Daly thought someone had insulted me while I was on an assignment in the USA, he assured me that if I wished it, he would deal 'very severely' with the matter.

The Wembley incident occurred when I was still at school, but just to demonstrate what a small world boxing is, when I was wounded I was sent a cutting from the *New York Daily Mirror* recording that the son of Britain's most respected boxing trainer had lost a leg in Normandy. The article was written by the paper's well-known sports editor, Dan Parker, the man who had first satirically tagged Daly 'Honest Bill'.

Anyone of advanced years will inevitably have suffered their share of bereavement. I am sure they will agree with me that nature eventually compensates for the loss by coaxing your memory to retain the laughing images of the loved one rather than the sad times.

Personally, the one memory of the twins that makes me laugh out loud is of watching them attempt to teach Primo Carnera to box when I was still a kid. Carnera, you may recall, was the 'The Ambling Alp'. An Italian peasant of gargantuan size, but very limited brainpower. The twins were given the almost impossible job of smoothing the rough edges of Primo's primitive boxing style.

They could not speak a word of Italian and he could not speak English so they used a whistle to stop and start his antics in the gym. I still have a *Keystone Cops* image of these two identical, tubby little men in roll-neck sweaters whistling their brains out at a man-mountain in shorts and singlet as he stumbled through his paces.

You could have said it was like watching a couple of Jack Russels terrorising a Rottweiler except that poor old Primo was as passive as a pussycat.

One foreign heavyweight of that era who was far from passive was the legendary German, Max Schmeling. His considerable claim to fame was that he was the only man to stop the incomparable Joe Louis when Louis was in his prime.

In 1938 Dad took South African Ben Foord to Hamburg to meet Max in his 'own backyard. In those pre-apartheid days, Ford was the British and Empire heavyweight champion. He had been in with all the top men of his day and managed to go the distance with Schmelling. However, it was not the fight that stuck in Dad's memory. It was the souvenir he brought home with him. Obviously, travelling to Hamburg was akin to you or I venturing out into space as far as Dad was concerned back then. Apart from his First World War service in France, going to Canvey Island was travelling abroad for him.

Boxers, not even champions like Foord, rarely stayed in fancy hotels then, and Dad and Ben were billeted with a German family. Among the presents Dad received from his generous hosts was a table flag that just happened to be a swastika.

In his innocence, Dad put this in pride of place on our mantelpiece to show off to the neighbours that he was a well- travelled man. To be fair to the old man, though, although he was not much of a politician, he did have the nous to tell us: 'I'm not too happy with this Hitler geezer. He looks like a dodge pot to me.' That at least put him ahead of Neville Chamberlain in the 'sussing out stakes'. To think I would marry a Chamberlain later – none other than dear old Connie Chamberlain upstairs.

Anyway, to use a catchphrase of a famous war-time radio comedian called Rob Wilton, 'on the day war broke out' I'll never forget the panic in Dad's eyes as he rushed into the backyard to burn that German flag, shouting: 'They'll nick us for being bleedin' spies.' I got involved in a spot of flag filching myself some years later.

Now, not a lot of people know this – as Michael Caine would say – but it was our own inimitable Jack Solomons who started the ritual of national flags and national anthems for international fights just after the war.

The Mills-Lesnevich clash got the full Solomons treatment and Gus's patriotic manager, Joe Vella, was so knocked out by the crowd's reception to his ex-American naval hero fighter that he asked me whether I could persuade my dad to give him the American flag to take home.

Knowing what a mean old so-and-so Jack was, I knew I would have to roll the flag up and nick it while Jack wasn't looking, which I duly did. He carried on about the missing flag later and I had a guilty conscience for a while, but when, many years later, Lesnevich died in, of all places, a doctor's waiting-room, it put the whole episode and, for that matter, the whole of life, into perspective. As the aforementioned Ben Ford put a bullet through his own brain in 1943, I suppose this whole shooting match can be summed up as a case of *c'est la vie*.

Yet, although it was short and financially frugal, what a life Dad had! The gym Dad and Jack started in Britannia Row Islington in 1934 went on to become a virtual Hall of Fame, with almost every top fighter of that era sparring there.

Ironically, Britannia Row is off Essex Road, which has since become The Knightsbridge of Islington – at least as far as the restaurant prices are concerned – and is now, I am told, the haunt of well-known celebrity diners.

No one could ever be more famous than the little man who performed the opening ceremony all those years ago. He was none other than 'The Ghost With The

Hammer In His Hand', that immortal Welshman Jimmy Wilde. Jimmy was quoted in the papers the next day as saying: 'No men living today are better equipped to teach the noble art than the Gutteridge brothers – Dick and Jack.'

As epitaphs go, that will do for me!

CHAPTER EIGHT

MOURNING HAS BROKEN

'The cure for this ill is not to sit still.
Or frowst with a book by the fire:
But to take a large hoe and shovel also.
And dig till you gently perspire'
RUDYARD KIPLING

The last thing on my mind on that sultry summer's evening in August 1946 was tragedy, when two uncles from my mother's side of the family turned up to tell me that Dad had just died. I was in a jazz club in Oxford Street, where the music was encouraging me to try to pluck up the courage to ask Connie for a date.

Obviously, I had lost good mates in the War, but this was different. Much too different to even attempt to put into words. In War you half expect tragedy, but nothing could have prepared me for a shock such as this. In retrospect I can see that, instead of being struck dumb, I went manic. All I could think of was the black greyhound that I had first brought home that very morning and the bad luck it must have brought us. Something compelled me to rush home and get that dog out of the flat as soon as possible.

Its name was Tea Drinker.

At least that was his registered racing name. He was

more used to being called 'Stinker' and worse by the man who gave him to me. That man, Jack Harvey, was the leading trainer at Wembley and Tea Drinker was the disappointing son of a much admired Greyhound St Leger winner named Grosvenor Bob.

As in my case, great things had been expected of Tea Drinker, so I sympathised with him. Sadly, he had turned out to be what all owners dread – a 'fighter' and turned his head at final stages of his races, so snatching defeat from the jaws of victory on a regular basis.

I knew all this because it was my job to know it. Newspapers, as anyone who has worked for them knows, seem to prefer their reporters to be jack-of-all-trades rather than masters of one. So it came as no great surprise to me to learn that, when I did eventually return to the *Evening News*, they had decided to groom me as a boxing reporter by making me a dog tipster.

Fortunately, this was not as downbeat an appointment as it sounds because greyhound racing was enjoying a truly astonishing period of popularity. Crowds were so big that there were often 10–20,000 people at a dog meeting during the post-war boom years.

I was also being assigned to minor boxing shows and acted as a 'leg man' to Charlie Nash, the paper's celebrated boxing writer. I was even being asked to ghost-write football comments for those Arsenal soccer legends Jimmy Logie and Alex Forbes – both of whom happened to be dog-racing fanatics, which made it possible for me to kill two birds with one stone by listening to the footballers between races.

None of this was too convenient, though, when it came to the more basic requirement of attending evening classes in English and shorthand. I'm afraid further education just had to be abandoned – go on, say it if you must 'it shows'.

Still, this was the biggest selling evening newspaper in the world at that time so if they were not complaining I must have been doing something right.

Back to Tea Drinker and, more importantly, Dad. Jack Harvey had kidded me that if ever there was an appropriate man to take a fighter off his hands it was me.

That was how Tea Drinker came to be waiting at the foot of my bed for me on the night Dad died.

I had been intending to make him a surprise present for Dad, whose own pet, Trixie, had recently died.

When I rushed home on that fateful evening, apart from attempting to comfort my distraught Mum, all I could think of was how to get rid of Tea Drinker. For some totally illogical reason I seemed to be blaming him for what happened to Dad. I can only think now that it must have been the Good Lord's way of getting me to take my mind off what was happening to Mum and me.

My mum's brothers came around at the crack of dawn next morning to comfort her, so I wasted no time in taking Tea Drinker to Haringey Greyhound Stadium, which was just a couple of tube stops away at Manor House Station, in the hope of kennelling him there.

No sooner had we arrived at Manor House, then Tea Drinker slipped his lead and was off and running into the traffic. A one-legged handler had no chance of getting up those steps in time to catch him even if he wasn't the fastest dog on four legs. Miraculously, when I arrived at street level, I saw him across the road and I instinctively whistled. He came to me, ducking the cars and lorries. I wished he hadn't.

Even more miraculously, I grew to love him. I am sure

Dad would have loved him too. Haringey Stadium agreed to race him for me and he amazed us all by winning his first race at 4–1.

He never once turned his head in a race at Haringey and in the space of one week he pulled off a double at 525 and 700 yards. He died peacefully as the pet of a fellow greyhound reporter in 1965.

Meanwhile my career as a tipster was taking off. Showing the tipping game up for what it is – more luck than judgment – I managed to come second in the Southend naps table one year and my system was never to go near the track. I was so superstitious about this that whenever I took a trip to the seaside that summer I made sure I did not even look in the direction of the dog track just in case ...

I was also uncannily lucky at Walthamstow one evening when a spot of selecting did my reputation no end of good in American fight circles.

Joey Maxim came to fight Freddie Mills for the world light heavyweight title in London in 1950. Joey, who is, incidentally, on my personal list of all-time greats, was managed by Doc Kearns, who was the archetypal Runyonesque New Yorker. An ultra-colourful character, he once moaned to A J Leibling, author of boxing best-seller *The Sweet Science* that: 'Writers are always crabbing about fighters we got now, but look at the writers you got now. All they think about is getting home to their wife and children instead of lazing around saloons soaking up information. Like writers did in the old days.'

The only information Kearnes was intent on soaking up when he arrived at the Walthamstow dog track during that trip was which dogs were going to win the eight scheduled races.

He naturally went straight to the top by asking the owner Frances Chandler to advise him on this very important subject. My heart sank into my one boot when she designated me for the job. Trembling with tension, I came up with the mini-miracle of seven out of eight winners.

Every time I saw Kearns in America after that he showed me off to his cronies as if I was a London Mafia Don. 'This is the young man who has got the London gambling scene all sewn up,' he would boast as I blushed, knowing full well that if he had bought the *Evening News* that same evening he would have been privy to my selections for the purchase price of a penny.

Thankfully, however, full-time boxing writing was soon destined to outstrip my tipping career, although the dogs would come back to haunt me when I became a TV commentator some 20 years later.

I had already made my big-time debut as an assistant boxing reporter by the time I met Kearns when I was sent to Belfast to help cover the world flyweight championship between Irishman Rinty Monaghan and cockney Terry Allen on 30 September 1949. That was when I made the necessary discovery that there was more to fight reporting than merely presenting a pen portrait of the action to the readers, however graphic that might be.

The events that took place after that memorable fight were every bit as readable even if, as a greenhorn, I didn't have the courage to print some of them. For instance, I am ashamed to confess that I neglected to tell my paper or my readers about a post-fight street party where celebratory bonfires were lit. Hilariously, at the height of the shenanigans Monaghan leapt on to the top of the bonfire and tried to pull a sofa out of the flames. He was dragged away cursing and making the shamefaced confession that he had buried some money in that sofa before the fight and had not told his wife about it. It almost ruined his wonderful night watching those greenbacks going up in flames.

Just as funny was the post-mortem conducted by co-promoter Jack Solomons and myself, which was held at a nearby hotel in the wee small hours of the following morning with referee Sam Russel as the principal witness.

Sam, who was an habitual racegoer from the East End of London, had declared the 15-round thriller a draw – a verdict that ensured Rinty kept his title. There were no judges other than the referee in those days and drawn fights were extremely rare occurrences. Even more puzzling was the length of time it took Sam to reach his verdict and the menacing unrest this caused among the spectators.

Sam knew full well what his scorecard read after 14 rounds and it would have taken only a matter of seconds to tally up the last round and raise one of the boxer's hands.

When we asked dear old Sam about the reason for the delay, he explained: 'It took me quite a while to weigh up the odds. It all boiled down to family and friends. I reckoned that if I gave it to Terry, there would have been a riot and my missus, Rosa, would have had a heart attack, listening on her radio. Then, I thought to myself, on the other hand I go racing a lot with Terry and his mates and what are friends for? In the end I plumped for keeping everybody happy!' That bizarre explanation was never printed either, although in these more quote-conscious times, today's reporters would have killed for off-beat information like that.

Monaghan was famous for being the first fighting Irish tenor. His crowd-pleasing specialty was to grab the MC's mike after a title contest and win, lose or draw, give a rendition of 'When Irish Eyes Are Smiling.'

That song became Rinty's signature tune when he finally retired and went on to sing in working mens' clubs and appear in pantomime.

As for tiny Terry, he took hisidentity papers around the world and back when he became far and away the most widely travelled British boxer of his time. He appeared in title fights. In Honolulu twice and he also fought in Tokyo. The reason he had to travel far and wide for opponents, was because most of the 'little big men' of the boxing world were reared in The East.

But it was just a three-minute tube ride that took Terry from his Islington home to the Haringey Arena where he became the first London flyweight to win a world title in 37 years. That event sparked off a knees-up round our way to rival even the VE day celebrations, which had taken place a few years earlier.

I did not report the fight – Terry won a clear-cut 15 rounds points decision over Frenchman Honore Pratesi – but was sent to report on the party instead.

Adoring women admirers got Terry to autograph their ration books and even their pawn tickets as Chapel Market celebrated all night and into the next day. At one stage, Terry had to take refuge in a shop because he was in more physical danger from the backslappers than he had been in the ring.

The evening after the fight, however, Terry was back at his 'day job' as a tic tac at Harringay dog track – only a right hook away from where he had just made his little bit of history. Yes, that's how tough it was for the participants of 'The Hardest Game' in those days.

Four months later, Allen had to travel to Honolulu where he lost his title on a dubious points decision to Dado Marino. To add insult to injury, Dado was a grandfather and Terry could only forgive himself when he found out later that the child concerned was actually only a step-child from Marino's second marriage.

Mind you, Terry need not have been quite so hard on himself because Mother Nature was later to present the boxing world with such big-name pugilistic grandpappies as Larry Holmes and George Foreman.

Terry took a second shot at Marino in Honolulu, where he again lost on points and he eventually finished his world title attempts with a challenge to the next champion, Yoshio Shirai in Japan.

Another neighbour of mine during that colourful era was British lightweight champion, Billy Thompson. Such a close neighbour, in fact, that he slept in the same bedroom as me.

Where Billy was concerned my dad broke the habit of a lifetime by allowing this young Yorkshireman to live with us when he came to London to train for his fights.

In truth, Dad never had a prayer when it came to this decision. Billy was such a lovely, little-boy-lost kind of a character that he brought out my mum's maternal instincts. She took pity on young Billy, overruling the old man and insisting that this lad from Hickleton Main stayed with us rather than be let loose on London town.

Now, one of the reasons why my dad never liked his boxers to live with him was the extra responsiblity that this entailed. It was hard enough looking after them in the gym but watching out for a lively young buck's welfare 24 hours a day was something else! Especially if as was the case with Billy, they had trouble making the weight. Desperately thirsty fighters with weight problems have been known to take the lid off the lavatory cistern to get at the water.

Still, Billy enjoyed a long and colourful career as our lodger. Ironically, it was the weight that beat him when he eventually lost his British Empire title to Tommy McGovern at the Wandsworth Greyhound Stadium.

Billy had to be carried into and out of the ring that night. First, by my cousin Jackie Pallo because the grass was so dangerously wet and then after McGovern had knocked him out. Irony of ironies, it was McGovern – a market porter – who was responsible for me getting my first ever by-line when I was sent by the *Evening News* to London Airport to interview him when he turned pro in America and flew home later to defeat my best mate in 45 seconds.

Almost as bitter was the fact that Billy lost at a dog track when I had enjoyed one of the best weekends of my life with him up at his family's home when we went with a crowd of his mining mates to thePitman's Whippet Derby at Wombwell.

Dear old Billy is still alive and I understand he has resisted all offers to sell his Lonsdale belts. They would be worth a fortune to souvenir hunters today. Yet I remember when we carried those belts in a brown paper bag on the Underground from my flat to Haringey for one of his big fight nights there.

CHAPTER NINE
CONNIE

'When all the world is old lad,
And all the trees are brown;
And all the sport is stale, lad,
And all the wheels run down;
Creep home and take your place there,
The spent and maimed among;
God grant you find one face there,
You loved when all was young.'
RUDYARD KIPLING

I might not have been in the Tom Cruise class when it came to the courting caper, but being a Gutteridge had taught me something about tactics. One maneouvre I remember my dad teaching his boxers was: 'Always take advantage of confusion', meaning that when an opponent showed signs of being flustered, it was an appropriate time to move in for the big finish.

Well, having Billy Thompson stay with us gave me the chance to take advantage of the domestic confusion this caused in our crowded flat – especially when Billy's girlfriend came down from Yorkshire. Her visits were the perfect opportunity for me to move in on Connie, at last. Or, more correctly to move upstairs to her flat and casually ask her mum and dad to invite me in for a cup of tea.

The Chamberlain family were up on the fourth floor. We were on the third so it wasn't too far to drag my dodgy leg. In Islington's palmy days of yore, the big house we shared with two other families had faced a tennis court. But those genteel courts had long disappeared and been replaced by an ugly brick air-raid shelter. Burglaries in working-class London were unheard of then so our doors were never locked. Most of us never even had locks, or if we did, they were broken. A common sight was the key on a piece of string, hanging behind the letter box. So the lyrics of that old music hall song 'Come round any old time and make yourself at home' were literally true.

Connie tells me now that the scarves she sent me in Normandy were meant as an invitation for me to get to know her better, but she says I was 'too slow to catch a cold then' and that, what's more, I am still totally unromantic now.

Connie's mum, Ruby, was the hardest working woman I have ever met. Ruby had two charring jobs a day and also managed to find time to serve in a shoe shop. Connie's dad, Jack, had soldiered, in India. He was now a window cleaner, but spent more time inside the 'caffs' guzzling tea than outside cleaning their windows. Jack drank tea by the gallon, so I worked out that asking for a cup of tea was the best way to win his approval.

My job was taking me either to dog tracks or boxing halls, or both, on most evenings so our opportunities for cups of tea were limited and it was never just tea for two, anyway.

Connie was an assistant secretary at an antiques reproduction furniture works in a mews off Tottenham Court Road. She and the company secretary, Dot Davies, remained close friends from the early 1940s until Dot died, at the age of 89. So, as well as being a looker, my future missus was as loyal as they come.

She did not appear to be courting due to the time she spent at home in the evening. I knew this much because I got my old man to 'suss' out the situation for me. He said he heard Connie singing most nights, but had never yet heard her finish a song. Just to prove that old habits die hard, I can report that she still does the same thing now that she's in her seventies.

Our big moment came when I plucked up courage to ask her for a date. I'm ashamed to confess that the most romantic venue I could come up with in those unsophisticated days was a speedway meeting at Wembley Stadium. To think my mum used to call me 'Tyrone Power'.

I took the trouble to explain to Connie that, although I was a Haringey Tigers fan, I had taken a shine to Wembley because my dad had massaged and treated a few of their riders for injuries, as he had done for the Wembley Lions Ice Hockey Team. You can imagine how all this smooth talk went down with a girl who was a fan of popular music lyrics.

I am even more ashamed to say that I introduced her to the players afterwards as 'my landlady'. Honestly, that's how it was in those pre-women's liberation times for shy young chauvinists such as yours truly.

Connie never became either a speedway or a boxing fan. Thank God she didn't because we soon learned to argue about every other subject under the sun – we still do.

After a few more daring trips to cinemas and dance halls, we eventually got married on 26 September 1953. And – shades of *Forrest Gump* here – what an auspicious year for sports fans that was.

Legendary soccer veteran Sir Stanley Matthews won his long awaited first FA Cup Winners' medal. Ditto Sir

Gordon Richards and his first Derby, and England won back the Ashes from Australia after 20 years.

As she did not wish the wedding reception to degenerate into a 'boys only boxing pow wow' Connie gently barred all known members of the cauliflower ear syndrome. Freddie Mills turned up at the church with his little daughter, Susan, insisting that he was 'family' and that wild horses wouldn't keep him away. Even Connie, who is as game as a pebble, did not have the bottle to give the most popular pugilist in the country a hard time.

The biggest change for both us, of course, was that we would be moving away from home permanently. We went to live in High Barnet in Hertfordshire, which was relatively 'posh' middle-class compared with Islington. We laugh at it now, but Connie's big worry at the time was 'will the trolleybus ride be too far away from my mum?' Neither of us would have believed that we would still be in that same house, in the greenery of Barnet 44 years later – a house in which we raised two beautiful daughters and where our grandchildren visit us now. A house, incidentally, that cost less then than it does to have the roof repaired now. On the subject of money, by far the biggest extravagance I had so far ever indulged in was when I booked a room in The Dorchester Hotel for our wedding night. It must have cost at least two weeks wages. It felt as if we were staying in Buckingham Palace and I remember that we were far too nervous to call room service when we were thirsty in the middle of the night and that we finished up drinking the cold water from the champagne bucket.

It was a first for both of us, too, where the champagne was concerned.

When we came down to reception to settle the bill, however. I was both astonished and delighted to learn that Bill McGowran had paid in full. You wouldn't get too many sports editors making a gesture like that nowadays. That act of benevolent kindness said a lot about the changing times I have lived through. Our honeymoon – a week in Bognor Regis was par for the course then, too. We did not complain. That was the good life.

CHAPTER TEN

THE BIG TIME

'If you can dream – and not make
dreams your master'
RUDYARD KIPLING

My work, too, was very much the good life as far as I was concerned. My one big regret, of course, was that Dad was not around to watch me fulfilling the dreams he had for me. The main thing about dreams, though, which I was later to learn, is that fulfilling them is never enough. Sustaining them in an exciting, but also remorselessly repetitive occupation like sportswriting required one quality above all others – stamina. My stamina was still, as yet, untested. But the excitement and exhilaration I felt from being involved with boxing and boxers remains unabated.

The prime source of excitement on the workfront in the 1950s came when I was sent to cover my first world championship fight in America. It would be criminal negligence, from a patriotic boxing purist's point of view, to wave goodbye to the 1930s and 1940s without first paying tribute to two of the best pound-for-pound heavyweights these islands ever produced – Tommy Farr and Bruce Woodcock.

Modern fans of Henry Cooper, Joe Bugner, Frank Bruno and Lennox Lewis would dispute that judgment, of course. However, in the premise that distance lends enchantment I must plump for the heroes of my youth. Most British sports fans of pensionable age will include among their most memorable boyhood moments that crackling early morning radio commentary in 1937 when Tommy went the full distance with the immortal 'Brown Bomber' Joe Louis. In this over-exposed media age, you just can't buy memories like that. Able to conjure up our own images from this word picture of that historic fight we were all convinced that Tommy had been robbed, even though the judges had correctly scored a very close contest for Louis.

That near miss of Farr's made us yearn more than ever to find a heavyweight to topple the seemingly invincible Yanks. The War interrupted that sporting dream, of course, but with emergence of Woodcock a decade later that wish became a national obsession.

Welshman Tommy was still on the scene by then, punishing himself, as do nearly all top line fighters, way beyond his sell-by date. What a shelf life he had. From the humblest of professional beginnings when he earned three shillings and sixpence for his first fight and a pound note for knocking out the star of a fairground booth in Ystradgyniais, he became the first Briton to fight for the world heavyweight crown in 40 years. At that time, Tommy could make the truly incredible boast, for the big punching heavyweight division, that he had boxed more than 1,000 round and never taken a count.

When, as recently as 1996, British Boxing Board of Control Inspector, Bob Lockhurst, got around to researching Tommy's amazing career he counted more than 200 contests! For good measure, the old warhorse became a boxing writer after his eventual retirement from the ring and carried his pen to hundreds more battles before succumbing to cancer just 11 days before his 73rd birthday.

Woodcock, a Yorkshire railwayman in his youth, learned his boxing at the Doncaster railway sports club – Kevin Keegan would later be taught to use his fists there before discovering that his feet were of more use to English sport.

A natural stylist, Bruce graduated from the Amateur Boxing Association championships – where he scored four wins in one day at the Royal Albert Hall – and later became the first British heavyweight to win the European Crown.

Only two things, both of them admittedly insurmountable, prevented him from fulfilling our collective dreams for him. At 14 stones, he just was not heavy enough to compete with giants like the 15-stone American Joe Baksi who gave him a terrible hammering. He was badly mismanaged by Tom Hurst, a no-nonsense northerner who sported rolled-up sleeves and braces in his corner, but did not have a clue when it came to the cunning collar-and-tie art of matchmaking.

Sadly, then, the fights that brought Bruce his biggest headlines and therefore stick in the memory most were both controversial ones.

One of these was an out-and-out scandal. In my experience, fixes are much rarer that many cynical fans like to believe. However, when the *Daily Mirror* came up with the headline 'Oma Coma Aroma' for Woodcock's apology of a fight against America's Lee Oma, these words were, I am afraid, the colourful truth.

It was a comeback match for Woodcock after his beating by Baksi. However, Oma had been so blatantly handpicked for the job that he barely landed a blow.

Even the London fans were so disgusted that they kept yelling for Oma to lie down and get it over with, which he duly did in Round Four.

My uncle Jack was working in the American's corner and he was the first to the fallen Oma to remove his gumshield. When Oma opened his eyes, winked and then closed them again, Uncle Jack said he felt like giving the big shyster a whack himself.

Lee was such a ham actor that there were more laughs than jeers from the audience, but the whole sorry episode was very damaging to Woodcock's reputation. As for Oma he went on to feature alongside other American 'heavies' in the famous Marlon Brando film *On The Waterfront*.

Budd Schulberg, who wrote the script, told me years later that Lee, who was having alimony problems, failed to show up for the closing scenes and requested that his name be taken off the credits. Budd could only assume that it had not occurred to the big palooka that his face was there for his ex-wife and everyone else to see in all its cauliflower-eared glory in many of the earlier scenes.

Bruce was involved in another near-fiasco when another American, Lee Savold, was disqualified for a low blow against him. The American's manager, the aforementioned larger-than-life Bill Daly always said that he would have make Woodcock a fortune if he handled him on the American circuit.

On this inauspicious occasion, he was earning himself another Oscar by inviting the British Press into Savold's dressing-room afterwards and donning the foul-proof lower body protector himself.

Each of us was invitied by Daly to kick him in his protector-covered testicles to prove that Woodcock could not have been hurt by a low blow. We were happy to oblige. However, wily old Daly knew that it is easier for the brain to make the body become taut when it knows a kick is coming. It is another thing entirely when an unexpected blow shocks or shifts the protector.

In any case, the controversy was not about whether Woodcock was hurt or not. It was simply a case of Daly's man wantonly flouting the rules. Worse was to come when we were tipped off later that Daly had arranged the entire business in order to bring about a lucrative re-match between these transatlantic crowd- pullers.

I kept in regular touch with Bruce and his wife, Nora, until his death at 76 during Christmas week in 1997. Bruce was always something of an introvert during his career and he stayed that way. He did not make the papers again until he 'sorted out' some young hooligans who were robbing his allotment. A proud man, he reluctantly accepted some money from our Jack Solomon's Charity Trust to cover the hospital costs of his final illness. I know, because this modest gift was delivered by yours truly.

I can't talk about Farr and Woodcock without thinking of Don Cockell, too. Cockell came along after these two legitimate legends and was only a blown up light heavyweight.

Sadly, though, Don's main claim to a place in the memory came from the desperate ill-luck that cursed him all his life. He was a superbly talented British light heavyweight champion until glandular fever caused his body to permanently balloon up to two stones above his natural weight. No matter how hard he trained and sweated he could not rid himself of the surplus pounds.

Nine courageous rounds against undefeated Rocky

Marciano in San Francisco in 1955, in which 'The Rock' perpetrated every foul that had ever entered even his grisly imagination , earned Cockell a leading place in the folklore of 'great British losers'.

That tragedy with his weight meant that, to earn a living, he had to keep going in with the heavies who were all too big for him. After that Marciano epic, his career petered out to an ingnominious end when he was knocked out in two rounds by a giant Tongan named Kitione Lave at the Earls Court Arena a couple of years later.

All these years on, I have to report with shame that I was partly responsible for that result. Don had never seen Lave in action so he invited me into his dressing-room before the fight to 'mark his card'.

I still wince at the memory of it, but this is what I told him: 'He's got a very useful right hand, but he cocks it and shows it to you, before he lets it go. So you had better move inside it. Make sure you don't try pulling away from it or he'll probably connect.'

A textbook left hook from Lave put Don out for the count.

As he was making his way back to the dressing-room afterwards, Don stopped by the Press seats, glared at me and growled: 'You forgot something, didn't you? The left wasn't too bad either.'

For once in his life there was a happy postscript for Don. Next morning a national newspaper carried a leader (yes, a leader, on the leader page not the sports pages) complaining that Cockell had been grossly overweight and had not trained properly for the fight.

Cockell took the paper to court and, with a future Lord Chief Justice presiding, he produced the Cooper twins, Henry and George, as witnesses to the fact that he had sparred with the pair of them on a daily basis for many weeks in the preparation for the Lave fight

Battersea-born Don was awarded £7,500 damages, which was enough in those days for him not to have to go back to his boyhood job of blacksmith. With his luck, however, it was not long before he got cancer of the throat and had to have a voice box implanted. He wound up working as a maintenance man for the London Underground. Whenever I met him in those days I would wind him up by saying: 'I can insult you as much as I like now and you can't answer back.' He would simply give me a broad grin by way of reply and wave his big fist at my chin.

One amusing anecdote concerning Cockell was when he started to coach his half-brother at the boxing game. One day, in the gym, an Irish manager, Jimmy McAteer, who was no bigger than a featherweight even when wet through, was leaning on the ropes watching his own man go through his paces and dragging away on a full strength cigarette.

Disapproving Don told him to 'Put that fag out pronto'. The little fellow replied: 'Oh no, this is part of his learning process. He'll have to get used to fighting in smoky halls ...'

Not amused, Cockell repeated his 'no smoking' order. This time the gutsy little so-and-so said: 'If it was Rocky Marciano smoking, you wouldn't be telling him to put out his fag, would you?' Cockell laughed.

Don died at the age of 45. I read somewhere recently that scientists are now saying good and back luck is inbuilt into human genes. Poor old Don must have copped for a double dodgy set, bless him.

The American fight scene in the 1950s was

undoubtedly as colourful as the old game has ever been before or since. It was captured in inimitable style by that doyen of boxing writers, the late, great A J Leibling in his memorable book *The Sweet Science*. It was a period that was dominated by the immortal Marciano, of course.

Things were not exactly dull this side of the pond either, and one of the most satisfying moments of my career came when Terry Spinks won Britain a flyweight boxing gold medal at the Melbourne Olympics of 1956.

Spinks was only 18 years old when he beat the world's best amateurs. I am proud to reveal that had it not been for me and the late Walter Bartleman who wrote for another London evening paper, *The Star*, Terry might not even have been in our Olympic team.

He had been overlooked by the English boxing selectors and Wally and I had to launch a daily campaign to get him picked. He did us and the rest of the country proud. However, the British government of the day did not do him proud in return. Perhaps they were too busy with the unsuccessful Suez invasion at the time, but neither Terry nor swimmer Judy Grinham, fencer Gillian Sheene and steeplechaser Chris Brasher who also won gold were included in the Honours List. Brasher was honoured for his London Marathon organising nearly 40 years later.

Even though Terry is now 60 perhaps this book will persuade Islington boy Tony Blair to correct this oversight in the very near future. Dick McTaggart, who also won a gold (and best stylist award) was honoured many years later.

Grinham's family are still in touch with Spinks and still hoping to be honoured even now. Many people have pressed the various governments to do something about it, so it's over to you now, Mr. Blair. You will make a lot of people proud and happy if you say 'yes' Prime Minister.

It is not as though Terry has every done anything to be ashamed of – he has no criminal record, he was divorced a couple of times and he did once have an alcohol problem, but the booze is behind him now. Every day, Terry's cousin, Rosemary, drives him to see his father who is in his nineties and the two of them spend their days together in Terry's boyhood 'manor' West Ham.

Terry is not a well person. He has a damaged vertebrea and has difficulty walking. Recognition of his outstanding sporting achievement would brighten up the autumn of his life. He has a short-term memory loss, but he remembers everything from his youth, particularly when he was a stable lad for race horse trainer, Marcus Marsh. He also recalls his triumphant years, when he turned professional and went on to win the British featherweight title. After he quit, he became coach to the South Korean boxing team, and had a postage stamp tribute by the Dominican Republic. So he had an extraordinarily productive life until the alcohol and painful divorce cut him down.

Like Woodcock before him and a good many other fighters both before and since, Terry's name will be remembered most for a fight that ended in unhappy circumstances.

This was his epic British featherweight title tussle with Scotland's Bobby Neill, which ended with Bobby's life in grave danger and necessitated the loser having to undergo brain surgery.

They fought three times, Spinks won 2–1. His 14th

round knock-out for the title finished Neill. When Bobby got back to the dressing-room everything appeared to be OK, but suddenly vomited and this brought on a brain haemorrhage. I was on my way to the dressing-room when I saw an ambulance taking him away. The ambulance was involved in a minor accident in the Wembley car park, which did not help matters.

Bobby reached Wembley hospital in the nick of time to have a brain operation and luckily the medics chose the right spot – they were never sure in those days. Apparently the clot could have been on either side of his brain.

Even when he was recovering in hospital, with his head heavily bandaged, brave Bobby had an argument live on radio with Lady Summerskill, who was the scourge of boxing at the time. She was very compassionate and polite in her exchanges with Bobby, but she said his case proved once and for all that professional boxing was far too dangerous and should be banned.

Lady Summerskill eventually became Baroness Summerskill but this change in status did nothing to alter her attitudes towards boxing. She abhorred the sport, maintaining that it was not only dangerous but barbaric. She tried to get the game barred by campaigning for the abolition of boxing, both in and out of the Houses of Parliament all her life. I am not going into that controversial subject at this stage of my story except to add an ironic touch to Edith Summerskill's much publicised opposition.

Years after her radio clash with Bobby Neill, I found myself in a running public debate with her, during the course of which I asked her whether she was aware that her son was in the boxing team at his public school. She seemed genuinely surprised on two counts – first, that her son was, indeed, an amateur boxer and second, the fact that I knew about it. I was aware of this because Bill Williams, a referee I knew, happened to be the PE teacher at her son's school.

In the Commons, Dame Edith's arch opponent was Bessie Braddock, the fiery MP from Liverpool who was, if possible, even more pro boxing than I. These two ladies regularly supplied the newspapers with colourful copy recording their verbal clashes over the pros and cons of the fight game.

As for Bobby, he made a complete recovery, just as Rod Douglas was to do years later when he suffered a similar injury in a fight with Herol Graham. Bobby has always made jokes at his own expense since about his memory lapses, but he claims he had a bad memory even when he was boxing and before. Bobby is a clever fellow, and there are dozens of newspaper pictures of him in his bowler hat twirling his umbrella when he was 'something in the City'.

I'll never forget the explosive way Bobby first burst on to the boxing scene when he came down south from his native Edinburgh. He fought the great Dave Charnley when they were both amateurs. Everyone in the game knew that Charnley was going to be the best thing to happen to British boxing since Ted 'Kid' Lewis. As a kid Dave was with the prestigious Fitzroy Lodge Club. One night the York Hall, Bethnal Green, Fitzroy boxed against one of the leading Scottish clubs, Sparta of Edinburgh.

The matchmaker that night was a man named Ray Bartlett, who was later to go to America with Dave when he fought for the world championship. Ray thought that

Charnley's mismatch against this unknown Scots kid who came as a late substitute, was going to be too brutal to watch and he went to the back of the hall, averting his eyes from the massacre, which he expected to be over inside a minute.

I was at the back with him, talking shop, when I took a peek at the ring moments after the opening bell had sounded. 'Oh, blimey, Ray, he's on the floor already,' I reported. 'I knew I shouldn't have made that match. Let's hope he gets it over with quick before the kid gets badly hurt,' exclaimed Ray. 'Not too quickly,' I corrected: 'It's not Neill who's on the floor, its Charnley!' Dave went on to win, on points, but we knew then that Bobby was going to be tasty, too.

Obviously, that terrible injury he sustained against Spinks finished Neill's pro career, although he went on to become a successful manager. So successful that I found myself in trouble over it.

When Bobby left hospital and was recuperating he decided he wanted to stay in boxing and I was the one who helped and advised him. I marked his card about the up-and-coming fighters he should try to sign up.

After a while, I found myself being accused of being his sleeping partner, which I never was. He had pulled off a top drawer coup by signing three men, Frankie Taylor, Alan Rudkin and Johnny Pritchett.

Rudkin fought three times for world titles, Pritchett lost only one fight throughout his career by disqualification and Frankie was headlined whenever he fought before going on to become a successful sports journalist.

The next thing I knew was that Jack Solomons, the promoter, invited my Editor to lunch. A little agent called Bobby Diamond, who had himself been in the ring with the famous Frenchman Georges Carpentier, also attended that lunch and he blew in my ear that Solomons was putting the poison in for me.

Solomons was mixing it with my Editor, Reg Willis, because Bobby's boys were fighting on the then up-and-coming Mickey Duff's shows and not on his. Solomons said that I was managing these fighters and using Bobby Neill as a front man. Looking back, I realise I should not have been doing what I was, but it was in all innocence that I tipped Bobby off about the best amateurs around. The simple truth was that I admired his courage in fighting back from such a serious set back – I had personal knowledge of how that felt.

In fact, it had been a wonder that Bobby had ever been allowed to box at all. A daredevil kid, he had several motorbike accidents in his youth, had steel plates in both legs, and consequently was too stiff to move properly or he would have been an even better fighter than he was.

Reg Willis, to his credit, never questioned me about it, but it could have been a very awkward situation. Incidentally, I have always appreciated Reg as an Editor, if only because unlike some editors I've known he did not regard the sports side of the paper as the toy department.

He kindly took the trouble to prove this one day when, up to his neck in the Cuban Missile crisis, he called over to me from where he was sitting to say that he had noticed that some fairly obscure boxer had moved up a weight.

It was Reg Willis who gave the sports editor the OK to send me on my first trip to America.

CHAPTER ELEVEN
THE BIG APPLE

'I gloat! Hear me gloat!'
RUDYARD KIPLING

I did, indeed, gloat when I heard that I was New York-bound. To an unsophisticated, unwordly Brit such as I was then, a trip to the Big Apple really did represent an adventure on the road less travelled. We even had beds in the aeroplanes, above our seat, would you believe? Mind you, they cost as much as a night at The Savoy and I was far too excited to sleep, anyway. In those days, we got suited and booted in our Sunday best to meet the hand-picked beauties who were glamorous enough and lucky enough to be air hostesses. As we boarded, these handmaidens pinned a rose to our lapels and then fawned all over us throughout the long, noisy journey in one of those old-fashioned propellor planes.

As novelties went, it certainly was something to boast to the neighbours about. Secretly, I was almost as intimidated by New York as I had been by Normandy. It was still BC - before crack and cocaine – when I first went there, so there were fewer muggings and far fewer murders.

I had imagined those awe-inspiring skyscraper canyons to be only shadows on the cinema screen and that intimidating New York rudeness to be just poetic licence from the Hollywood scriptwriters.

Then I encountered my first New York cop and for, the first time in my life, the street-wise cockney turned, in one embarrassing moment, into an out-of-town hick. In my excitement, I had forgotten the American expression for the tube. When I enquired of a local cop how I got underground, he simply growled: 'Just drop dead, buddy,' and strolled off, twirling his nightstick.

It could only get better, I supposed. With butterflies as big as eagles clattering around in my stomach, there were no guarantees. Asking a greenhorn like me to send back instant, literate fight reports via cable from halfway round the world was a much more frightening prospect than even my first public appearance in a boxing ring.

When I was a kid, my mum regularly had her tea leaves read by a neighbour. One of the most persistent predictions from this old lady was that I would travel the world. It was an outrageously optimistic guess on her part. It always gave us a good giggle because practically the only working-class people who travelled very far in those days were train drivers.

I couldn't help casting my mind back to those days as I checked into my hotel and found myself giggling again in spite of my nervousness. I managed to summon up enough bravado to book into The Pennsylvania Hotel because, as a Glenn Miller fan, I had read that one of his most famous songs had been written there.

Thereafter, I stayed there on subsequent visits so that I could ask people to ring me back and when they asked for the number I would sing 'Pennsylvania Six Five Thousand'.

Boys will be boys, eh? I was in a man's world now,

and, as such, found myself all alone in New York. The main reason for my trip was to report on the big Sugar Ray Robinson-Carmen Basilio world middleweight title fight in Chicago along with the rest of Fleet Street's hand-picked finest.

The *Evening News*, bless 'em, had indulged my whim to make a personal pilgrimage to that Mecca of boxing Madison Square Garden, where I could cut my foreign correspondent's teeth on another tasty little title fight morsel.

The fabled Garden came as a slight disappointment. It had a narrow entrance, no bigger than a cinema's, which was tucked next door to a hat shop. But, once inside, the sweaty, perfumed magic of names like Joe Louis, Rocky Marciano and all the other great American prize fighters soon seeped into your veins and flooded your imagination.

The fight or – rather the aftermath of it – provided me with some off-beat copy with which to repay the sports editor for his generosity in sending me to cover it.

The contest was a final eliminator for a world welterweight championship challenge in which Virgil Akin knocked out Isaac Logart in six rounds. The colourful copy materialised the next day when the New York Boxing Commision held an inquiry into the fight. The manager in question was an interesting character who gloried in the name of Willie Ketchum and brought several big-name fighters to Britain in later years.

Willie acquired his name in Jack Dempsey's bar where the managers and trainers hung out at that time. Willie's real surname was Friedlander, but he changed it for a gag name that was to stick with him for life. When his cronies in the bar kept exhorting 'Go catch 'im, Willie,' every time he reported that he had spotted a bright new prospect.

Hence, Willie Ketchum – geddit? Thankfully, the paper did and when they rang Pennsylvania 65000 to praise me for my little contribution to that day's news, they rewarded me by saying that not only should I procceed to Chicago for Robinson-Basillo, but that I should go on to Los Angeles for Hogan Kid Bassey-Ricardo Moreno. While I was there I should look in on the Hollywood studios to see whether I could pick up any little showbiz gems! Needless to say, I checked that last piece of information out, assuming it was a mickey take. But they were serious, and this expanded my chest measurements by about six inches.

It also gave me a whole new perspective on old ladies who read tea leaves!

In Chicago, though, I knew I was going to be up against the big guns of Fleet Street boxing writers and there was no bigger piece of artillery in those days than the aforementioned George Whiting, who was my direct rival for the London *Evening Standard*.

I intend to describe George more fully in a future chapter, but suffice it to say for now that he was a wily old bird who liked nothing better than to beat the opposition.

So as I boarded the internal flight to Chicago I felt as though I was moving away from the devil and closer to the deep blue sea. The devil was, of course, the loneliness and anxiety I had felt on my first solitary bite at the Big Apple and the humiliation of the policeman advising me to drop dead in the snow. I would not keep on about that if I could have thought of a quick verbal retort to even the score, but, as I said, my customary cockney bravado went AWOL for a while.

The one thing that never got any easier throughout my career in newspapers was the fact that wherever you went in the world you had to hit the airport tarmac running because there was always a preview piece to be written and precious little time to – as Doc Kearns would say – 'soak up the information'.

Fortunately, thanks to my connections back home, when it came to getting the information I knew a man who did know. He was that most famous of trainers – Angelo Dundee, originally known as Angelo Moreno before he worked with Cassius Clay and the pair of them changed their names.

Angelo was looking after Basilio the American Italian, who was labelled the 'Onion Farmer from Syracuse' by the American headline writers. I phoned him at the hotel and he immediately invited me round to see them.

Now, pre- and post-fight Press conferences were unheard of in those days so you had to find your own way around. The news on this occasion was frank and fertile. I politely inquired of Basilio where he would be after the fight if I wanted to get some follow-up quotes and he promtly said: 'Well, I expect to be in hospital for three or four days to start with.'

My mouth fell open because I wasn't used to this kind of direct talk. I didn't know then that most American sportsmen, unlike some of their tight-lipped British cousins, are like manna from heaven for journalists.

Craving your indulgence, this is a good time to break off for a brief selected anecdote. In the 1970s that infamous American footballer, Joe Namath, took part in the first ever big sporting event to be played on an artificial surface.

After the match, he was asked by a journalist:

'Which do you prefer, Joe, grass or Astro Turf?' 'I don't know, man,' drawled Namath. 'I ain't smoked none of that astro turf yet!'

Anyway, back to Basilio. Carmen had very good reason to fear finishing up in hospital because he had fought Robinson once before. On that occasion, the great Sugar Ray had unashamedly shown that not only was he the most beautiful of boxers but that he could butt like a demented billy goat, too.

That was why Carmen explained to me: 'I know that son of a bitch is gonna have his head on my face the whole time. So I expect to get busted up.'

As it turned out, Basilio was proved right up to a point. For the first minute they butted each other rotten. Then suddenly, there seemed to be an unspoken armistice. Both men stood off for a moment and appeared to telepathically agree: 'If you stop, I'll stop' – like a couple of squabbling kids in a playground.

There was nothing remotely childish about the rest of this memorable fight, however. They went on to produce a spectacle to die for – talk about getting me off to a foreign flyer!

The *Evening News* splashed it on the front page underneath my name, and my old man must have been blushing as red as Karl Marx in that cemetery they were sharing in Highgate.

SUGAR CANES HIM was the headline that Editor Reg Willis came up with after Robinson was given a points decision after 15 truly pulsating rounds. I suspect Reg only became a fight fan because early morning world title fights from America were not only big news but in those pre-television days, they fell in evening paper edition times, meaning that we got the story before the dailies, which pleased the old boy no end, of course.

The sheer ferocity and skill shown by both men made most of what I had so far seen of British boxing look like kindergarten games by comparison.

Reporting the fight was the easy part, getting it back to London was a whole new ball game, however. I kid you not, when I say that some of the Western Union operators were still tapping away on morse code – carrier pigeons had thankfully passed into history by then.

I had to construct my sentences in a new-fangled language called cable-ese and then hand it, page by page, to a lady with long earrings who had been allocated to me by the management and trust her to cable the right message to London. As she trotted off with her earrings noisily dangling, I prayed every bit as hard for her to make a go of it as I did when old Tea Drinker was negotiating the first bend at Haringey dog track.

If this was nerve-racking, the next part of the exercise was worse – except that I didn't know that yet. You see, George Whiting was a merciless old nobbler. So much so, that when I naïvely asked him how we could get to the dressing-rooms, to listen to what the principals had to say and then file more copy, he said: 'Don't worry, son. I've got a local lad looking after that for us.' After George had had his wicked way with the quotes our runner brought, he passed the pieces of notepaper on which they were written on to me and I thanked him profusely.

It was not until the office called to tell me that Whiting's quotes were much more illuminating than mine that I suspected foul play. When I confronted him later. He simply said: 'Well, that's the normal practice, son. The one who organises the quotes coverage usually keeps back a few bits and bobs for himself.'

Worse was to come, though, when Whiting's little piece of gamesmanship ruined an imaginary scene that I had spent days rehearsing. Some of the other British elder statesmen among the sports writers covering the fight were recounting tales about the 'herograms' they regularly received by cable from their offices, heaping praise upon them and their efforts.

I was working out whether I should sound excited or laidback when I read my first triumphiant 'herogram' aloud to them. What I got from the office instead was a cable urging me to send some more follow up copy as soon as possible because there were nowhere near as many meaningful quotes in my piece as there was in the *Evening Standard*.

Still, I did not have to wait long for revenge. That came – or so I thought at the time – when George and I breezed into Hollywood after the British-based, Nigerian Hogan Kid Bassy had beaten Ricardo Moreno for the world Featherweight title.

I suggested that George 'hold my hand' as I made my first and what was to be my last foray into showbiz reporting. I was over my nervous anxiety by now and soon persuaded some publicity men to arrange for a quick chat with Kim Novak who was a very big star at the time. Now, dear old George didn't know Kim Novak from the Keystone Kops, so I thought he would be very grateful when I fed him a few quotes from that very quotable lady.

His day's work done, George went for a little wander around the various sets while I played my master stroke and pulled off a secret little interview with the up-and-coming British starlet, Joan Collins.

I couldn't live with this guilty secret for too long, however. Over a nightcap that evening I confessed that I had the Collins quotes, which, incidentally, left a disinterested George completely cold. All he said was: 'You're learning son.'

The next day I roared louder than the resident Metro Goldwyn Mayer lion when the office informed me that they were not using the Joan Collins piece because they had never heard of her.

All George said this time was: 'I told you that you were learning, son.' And that is when he told me about those 'wrong again, prick!' postcards that I mentioned earlier.

To think that boxers call their profession 'the hardest game'!

CHAPTER TWELVE
LITTLE BIG MEN

*'Our England is a garden
that is full of stately views'*
RUDYARD KIPLING

Meanwhile, back in this green and pleasant land, heavyweights began 'burstin' out all over'. For reasons known only to herself, Mother Nature chose to bless British boxing with a harvest of heavies, the likes of which we had never seen before or since.

All of a sudden, you couldn't get elbow room in promoter Jack Solomons' office. It seemed to be full of incredible hulks and their insatiable managers. They were not all stately, of course. In fact, compared with today's gargantuan specimens, they were pygmies, each weighing in at considerably less than the current 15, 16 and even 17 stone models.

Yet, they were a promoter's dream in that they provided inter-city rivalry and stirred up ancient tribal allegiances. Who needed foreign imports when we had Henry Cooper, Joe Erskine, Brian London, Dick Richardson, Jack Bodell and, a little later, Billy Walker, Johnny Prescott and Joe Bugner to entertain us with their domestic spats? Even by international standards, none of them was a pushover.

Sadly, it would consume far too much space to highlight even a fraction of the thrills they produced for fight fans in the late 1950s and early 1960s, but I will indulge myself with the odd anecdote or two.

Henry Cooper is a giant in our collective memory because he won three Lonsdale Belts outright and because he has proved such a genuinely popular figure since his fighting days. At that time, all of Henry's aforementioned rivals enjoyed just as much affectionate popularity as he did.

Amiable Welshman Joe Erskine fought Henry no less than five times professionally, losing three times and winning twice. The pair also met many times as amateurs when Joe came out on top.

Outside of the ropes, Joe never hurt anyone but himself. A self-confessed gambler and boozer, he died of cancer in 1990. In life, he was among the best-loved men I have ever encountered. On his retirement, he summed up his financial status this way: 'I spent thousands on gambling, a few more grand on buying a pub, a lot more having a good time – and I just squandered the rest.'

I well remember a few quid Joe did not squander. Towards the end of his career, he fought rising Midlands star, Johnny Prescott in Birmingham and I was surprised to see that the locals were betting 2-1 against Erskine. Knowing he was a gambler, I informed Joe of this fact shortly before the fight and he immediately said: 'Put a few quid on me and we'll settle up later.' Just as I was leaving his dressing-room, Joe had second thoughts and said: 'Half a mo, what time does the fight start?' 'Nine o'clock.' I replied. 'Oh, that's all right, then,' he said reassuringly, 'my gout doesn't start until ten!'

Believe it or not, dear old Joe had to have the sides of his boxing boots slit open to accommodate the swelling. He was such a natural, gout or no gout, that he mastered Prescott from memory. Johnny, incidentally, was to become a bookie and a nightclub owner in later life, but I bet he never misread the odds like that in his own business dealings.

Another very popular Welshman was Dick Richardson. After quitting the game, he became a 'minder' for celebrities, one of whom was comedian Freddie Starr. European champion, Dick gained notoriety for disqualifications for butting. So when he met the equally aggressive Brian London at Porthcawl on the South Wales coast, it was like letting two young raging bulls loose at each other.

It was one of those natural needle matches. Referee Andrew Smythe was forced to nag both men throughout. At one point, London, who was unquestionably the better boxer, dropped his hands and taunted the title holder. At the start of another round, he even went so far as to rush Richardson who was still seated in his corner.

The proceedings came to an abrupt and bloody halt when London's eye was so badly gashed in Round Eight that he had to retire on his stool.

I should have said 'should have come to an abrupt halt'. But this was only the beginning of the most outrageous fracas ever witnessed in a British ring.

Thankfully the crowd was not involved in the ensuing melee, but everyone else – with the possible exception of the master of ceremonies – did seem to be.

It began when London walked menacingly towards Richardson's corner and was met halfway by one of Richardson's trainers, Johnny Lewis.(For what it's worth, trainer Lewis's son, John Salthouse – mother's maiden name– was a leading actor in the television series *The Bill*.)

From the moment these two collided the ring was a

blur of frenzied action, as trainers, managers, seconds and even fathers rained punches on each other.

Brian's father was the one-time Brirtish heavyweight supreme, and even he landed flat on his back. I still chuckle at the memory of the caption beneath a photograph in one of the next morning's papers which read 'Ex-Champ Makes Comeback!'

The only one who couldn't get a piece of the notorious action was Dick Richardson himself, who was being pinned to his seat by a team of Welsh policemen who looked as if they had stepped straight from the front row of a rugby scrum.

If all this sounds like a disgraceful slur on the good name of boxing, which it undoubtedly was, I can only plead in clemency that there were no spectators flinging beer cans because so many of the men in the audience had already had their fill of throwing missiles – such as hand grenades – during the war. At the Seabank Hotel later, the London retinue sat at an adjoining table to mine and started to laugh about the whole sordid business. While I was the first to admit that there were some very funny cameos during the fracas, I thought it wise to advise them that the Welsh constabulary would not find it very amusing and would be arriving any minute to question them all. Knives and forks were hurriedly abandoned and they scarpered, just in time.

Both boxers were suspended and fined and, needless to say, were never permitted to fight each other again. London carried on boxing for seven more years. A non-drinker and non-smoker he looked after his money, sold his successful Blackpool nightclub and now spends much of his time in Florida where his second wife is 'teaching him to be sociable', she informed me recently.

Obviously, fighters come in all shapes, sizes and

styles. An unfortunate few can be effective but ungainly to the point of being downright ugly movers. One man who fell into this category was Jack Bodell.

I was once asked by my old friend, Bill Daly, to sum up Jack's style because Bill handled a Puerto Rican named Joe Roman who came over to fight Jack at the Nottingham Ice Rink. I say 'asked' but I should have said 'instructed'. For this is what Daly said to me: 'Your Dad always told me the truth, so I expect the same from you. What, exactly, is this guy, Bodell, all about?'

Now, at this stage, Daly did not know what a difficult question this was to answer. Jack had enjoyed his share of successes, including outclassing Billy Walker, He had also forgotten to duck against Henry Cooper but beat Joe Bugner. He was no pushover. His southpaw style confused his opponents and his footwork meant that he was continually treading on his opponents' toes. When top-notch Irish-American Jerry Quarry knocked him out in London and was asked afterwards whether he had found Bodell awkward, Quarry had replied: 'Well, he fell awkward.' So what was I to tell big bad Bill Daly except to warn him that, win, lose or draw, his boy would find it impossible to look good against our Jack. After several frustrating rounds, Bill left his corner came over to the Press seats, wagged a finger in my face and said: 'You're not an honourable man like your dad. You lied to me. This guy is even worse than you said.' I'm happy to record that, clumsy or not, Jack easily beat Roman on points. Yet Roman went on to fight George Foreman.

Writer George Whiting memorably, yet affectionately, described Jack as the 'Swadlincote Swineherd', Swadlincote being the name of the Midlands town where Jack ran a smallholding. Today, cheerful Jack is dabbling in property and doing rather well for himself with his wife Jean's guidance. At one time I and most of his friends thought he was trying to get out of Swadlincote bit by bit. You see, awkward old Jack had managed to chop off part of his finger in the fish shop he was running a the time and then part of his toe while mowing his lawn.

But that awkwardness gave Jack a vulnerable charm that few people, including Muhammed Ali, could resist. Ali once broke off a tour of Britain to officially open Jack's fish and chip shop. Some swineherd!

Some era, the 1960's was, too – in more ways than one. On the boxing front it was not only a boom time for British heavyweights, there were some headline names in the lighter division, too – none much bigger than Dave Charnley, Terry Downes, Howard Winstone, Alan Rudkin and Walter McGowan.

Sadly, it was a time of some very big boxing stories, too. None bigger than the suicides of Randolph Turpin and Freddie Mills, which I shall attempt to deal with later.

CHAPTER THIRTEEN
THE PRICE OF FISH

'You may talk 'o gin an' beer
When you're quartered safe out 'ere,
An' you're sent to penny-fights'
RUDYARD KIPLING

O f all the many grudge matches in boxing history none was as intense or unyielding as that beween the promoters Jack Solomons and Harry Levene.

These two old-fashioned Jewish caricatures hated each other so much that each refused to utter the other's name. When one or other of them found it absolutely unavoidable to mention his rival in conversation, he would refer to him as 'the other fella'.

They first fell out over the price of black market fish in the early post-war years. Fishmonger Jack supplied nightclub manager Harry with sea food.

The club, The Bagatelle, was a fashionable West End establishment that was later to boast Princess Margaret as a regular patron and featured showbiz greats such as Sophie Tucker and Johnny Ray in its cabaret.

The twist to this story was the role reversal involved. Flamboyant showman Jack, with his innate flair for publicity, should have been the club manager, and penny-pinching Harry the tradesman.

Their childlike lifelong feud lit up my own life with

its black humour and I remember both of them with nothing but fondness in my heart.

Harry had worked with my grandfather when he was a young manager and when I became a boxing writer he ruined my Sunday tea for years on end by ringing up to remind me that he and Grandad used to be the best of pals — before pitching a story at me just as I was about to tuck into the shrimps and winkles.

In his low growl, Harry could talk himself speechless in his younger days and I once referred to him in the paper as 'Harry The Hoarse Levene'. He took exception to this and wrote me a rude letter. But we soon made it up.

It was the same with Jack after he had taken my Editor to lunch and stirred it up for me over Bobby Neill. I went back too far with the pair of them to hold grudges – if only the same could have been said about them!

Harry was the best dressed man I ever met. He always looked as if he had stepped straight out of a mens' fashion magazine and Jack wasn't far behind him in the Beau Brummel stakes. I never saw either of them look remotely dishevelled, even in the wee small hours during the post-fight celebrations.

It was Solomons who was doing most of the celebrating during the 1940s and 1950s. He was undoubtedly the top dog then. And I use that 'top dog' cliché purposely, knowing it was one he would have approved of. For Jack was so passionate about greyhounds that he could not keep away from the dog tracks. He even staged all his big promotions on Tuesday evenings because that was the night with fewest dog meetings in London, when only Walthamstow and Romford raced. As he often said: 'I could never back a winner at either of those gaffes, anway.' He told me once that his wife never ever mentioned boxing, but that at bedtime during the winter months she always sarcastically remarked: 'I hope you tucked your little doggies into bed and gave them a kiss goodnight, we wouldn't want the little darlings to catch cold, would we?'

In my days as a youthful greyhound tipster, Jack treated me to dinner in the Haringey Stadium at many meetings and picked my brains. Before each race, I would mark his card with the traditional betting code of 'dot' and 'c' beside the names of two selected greyhounds. This stood for dot on the card and 'careful'. After the race, Jack would mark his card with a 'c' and a 'b' which meant either 'copped' or 'blew out.'

Although I am not Jewish, Jack and I became such a regular pairing at Haringey dogs that the restaurant waiters thought I was his son. In truth, I did regard him as a kind of uncle figure in those impressionable days of my youth. One evening, he decided to put this 'filial' loyalty to the test. Giving me my regular lift home, he suddenly stopped the car and said: 'I am going to tell you something I haven't spoken to anyone outside of the interested parties about yet.' He then paused for effect and said: 'I've made Randolph Turpin versus Sugar Ray Robinson for London.'

Now, this was as big as boxing in Britain ever got, before or since. Sugar Ray was as big a drawing card as there was worldwide back in 1952. He was universally recognised as the best pound for pound fighter ever and he was coming to fight over here. Little Reggie Gutteridge had the story all to himself. The only stipulation, and what a nerve-racking stipulation it was, was that I should sit on the news for three days until Jack had tied all the ends up.

In those less frantic times newspapermen, especially

specialists like sportswriters, were prepared to do this kind of thing and take the long-term view that if we broke a confidence we could never go back to the source again. I needed Jack Solomons' co-operation to make it as a boxing writer.

Turpin v Robinson, for the middleweight championship of the world, at Earls Court in 1951 was a fight that will live for ever in the memories of every British fight fan who saw it, heard it on the wireless or read about it in the newspaper.

It was a landmark event. Turpin had been offered by the street corner bookmakers and the unofficial layers inside the hall, at 33-1 to win on points. Yet he won on points and when, in the 13th round, the crowd eventually started believing this was possible, they did something I have never heard before or since. To a man, they lifted their voices for chorus after chorus of 'For He's A Jolly Good Fellow!'

As was his wont, Solomons had been a very shrewd fellow ; his spies had told him that Robinson had been living it up on a recent tour of Europe and that if he was ever going to come unstuck, now was the time. When Sugar reported for training at a gym above The Star and Garter pub in Windsor, Jack was reliably informed that judging by the size of his extravagant entourage Sugar was indeed sweet for the taking.

Sugar's personal staff included such luxuries as a valet, a barber and a golf pro. And there were 53 suitcases to house his extensive flashy wardrobe.

The tension at Earls Court that night was more tangible than I have ever known before or since. As each round ended, there was a collective sigh of relief that Sugar had not caught up with our man yet. It was too much for a relative of Solomons who collapsed and died during the contest.

The Duke of Fife, who became ABA President, told me that King George VI interrupted a function at Buckingham Palace to listen to the radio commentary and that when the verdict was announced, His Majesty threw his arms in the air and shouted to his guests; 'He's won it! He's won it!'

The biggest winner, though, turned out to be Solomons. He capitalised on this triumph by reigning as the seemingly, impregnable Czar of British boxing until the next decade. Those were happy times, indeed, for yours truly. Now established as a boxing correspondent in my own right, when I wasn't on the road reporting fights I was in Solomons' office, which was the hub of the domestic fight game at that time, doing a Doc Kearns and 'soaking up the information'.

Jack used to invite young boxers to come in and look at the pictures of famous fighters on the wall to inspire them. He had a paternal arm around each one in the pictures, of course.

My fondest memory of one of these little sessions is of the time he persuaded the Welsh welterweight Eddie Thomas to sing for us all. I can still see Eddie standing there now, in his miner's flat cloth cap, singing like an angel.

Eddie, who went on to manage great fighters like Howard Winstone, Ken Buchanan and Colin Jones once kidded me that the higher up the mountain you went in Wales, the higher the voice. The foothills were full of baritones, but higher up, nearer the peaks, you came across the tenors like him.

He, of course, scaled peaks of courage ouside the ring when he became the hero of Aberfan – one of Britain's worst-ever domestic disasters when a slag tip collapsed on a school killing scores of children. Eddie rescued many helpless mites with his own bare hands. He is no longer with us but his memory lingers on, especially in his home town where he was known as 'Mr. Merthyr' and where they are currently trying to raise £35,000 to builda statue in his honour.

On a more cheerful note, Solomons' Soho office was as lively a location as you could come by. It was a part of his gym, above a snooker hall and opposite the infamous nude theatre, The Windmill.

He would never eat alone, which meant I was taken to lunch a lot. This was always at Jack Isow's restaurant, a few doors up, where Jack had his name inscribed on a plush leather chair, as did his pal and partner in a bookmaking sideline business, the much-loved comedian Bud Flanagan.

Isow always got a big kick out of trading insults with his more famous customers and he had a ball with Archie Moore, that great American light heavyweight champion who was as cagey a boxer as any in history. Isow enjoyed his banter with Archie right up until the moment the boxer started spitting his steak out on to the plate.

The proprietor took great exception to this, so much so that the veins stuck out on his ample forehead and he clenched his fists as if he was prepared to do battle with this living legend. Moore placated him, however, by explaining that as he was weight watching, he was using a tip he had picked up from the Aborigines where you simply sucked the juicy goodness out of the meat and then discarded it.

The one thing the otherwise jolly Jack Solomons, sadly, never discarded was the mean-spirited side to his personality, which helped make him such a formidable businessman.

It was this unattractive trait that provided an

THE INSEPARABLE GUTTERIDGE TWINS

Seconds to many
Second to None!

AFTER THE ORIGINAL BY Roy Ullyett

SPARK '77

My uncle and father, the world famous seconds, the Gutteridge twins by the cartoon master, Roy Ullyett.

Top: A gathering of boxers competing at cards, then a £1000 novices competition at Empire Pool, Wembley, 1934. Dad keeps watch. I'm on the safe side of the ropes, aged 10.

Bottom: Len Harvey, who fought at eight weights, gets the kiss of success from Mrs 'Blossom' Harvey, after winning a heavyweight belt. Dad and Wally May keep a firm grip on it.

Inset: Me in my soldier's regalia, with boyhood pal George Sewell, now an actor.

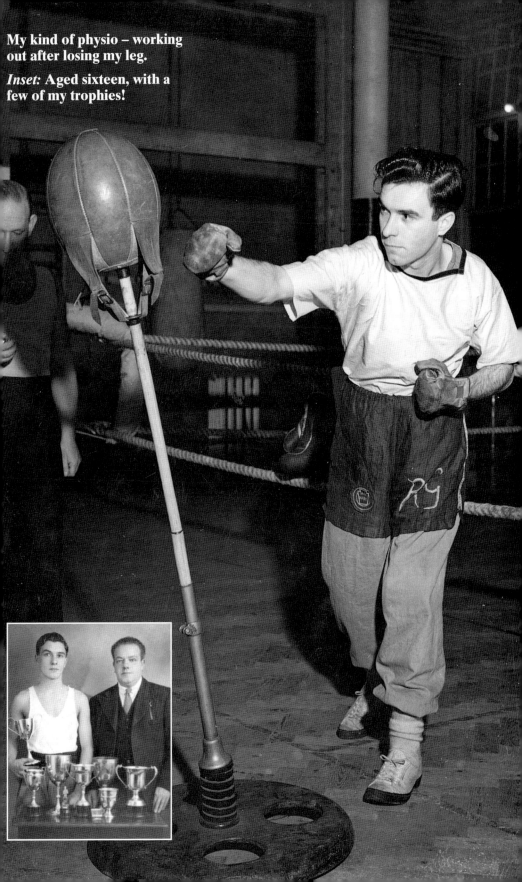

My kind of physio – working out after losing my leg.

Inset: **Aged sixteen, with a few of my trophies!**

Top: My first time facing a TV camera – 1945. Appearing on the *Joan Gilbert Picture Page*, Alexandra Palace. Seconds are Mickey Fox and Mickey Wood. I never knew anybody with a TV set.

Bottom: Among the old world champion rivals - Joe Louis, Jersey Joe Walcott and James J Braddock – Lewiston, Maine 1965.

Top: Not lost for words in the ring when Ali and Joe Bugner play act in Kuala Lumpur. Don King *(right)* keeps his distance.

Bottom: With the Main Man, Ali, Stateline, Nevada.

Henry Cooper's undercarriage collapsing, hit low by Italian Tomasoni.

Top: The roar of the crowd. The trials of ringside commentating, Darlington 1985.   © *John McDonald*

Inset: A typical pose from Ali!

Bottom: Sonny Liston takes a left to the eye. He lost this title to Clay in the seventh round.

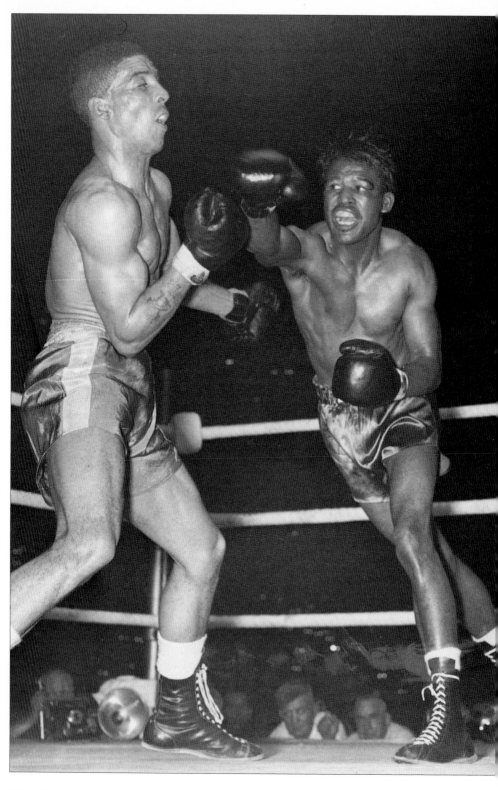

Randolph Turpin wins the World Championship against the master,
Sugar Ray Robinson.

overnight education for me on the ways of the materialistic world, however. I recall sitting on the sofa in his office one day when he was having a telephone conversation in which he appeared to be sympathising with the person on the other end of the line.

'You silly boy, you shouldn't have got yourself into trouble like that,' Jack was saying, then he added soothingly; 'Never mind, leave it to uncle Jack, I'll get you out of it.'

The moment he put the phone down, he burst out laughing and told me: 'He doesn't know it was me who got him into trouble in the first place.' This shocked me. This was one side of the fight game I had never yet encountered. But, like most things in life, you soon learn to live with it and I must confess I could not supress a grin myself whenever I heard Jack raise his voice on the phone and say in an incredulous way: 'How much?' Nine times out of ten, the other guy would take this as a warning and lower his sights. Then, after completing the deal, Jack would gloat: 'If only he knew it, I was surprised at how little he was asking for, not how much. I'd have paid him twice what he settled for.'

A born show-off Jack loved an audience but he was never loud or uncouth. He was in his element down in Wales once when rain was threatening one of his open-air shows – a world championship – and he hung a bucket out of the hotel window saying that if the water went over his chalk mark he would cancel.

As this little drama was enfolding close to our copy deadlines, I had to sit there for hours with the other evening paper men, watching the water drip into that bloody bucket before Jack decided he had enough fun for one day and eventually declared that the show must go on.

Little did he know it, but this was around the time when the first holes began appearing in Solomons' own bucket.

He did not find it funny when his supremacy was challenged and finally superseded by Levene in the 1960s. In later years, Jack, suffered a stroke from which he never fully recovered before his drawn-out death in 1979.

As with all empires, Jack's began crumpling both from without and within. The last really big event he staged was the first Henry Cooper/Cassius Clay non-title fight in London.

By the time Cooper fought Clay again it was under Harry Levene's banner at the Arsenal football ground in 1966. The greatest was now universally known as Muhammad Ali and Jack was known in his own circles as 'an also ran'.

Levene was the enemy without and fighters like Terry Downes and Billy Walker turned out to be the enemy within.

Harry was aided by the rising new stars of the promotional firmament, Jarvis Astaire and Mickey Duff, who were later to become powerful themselves.

TV helped to topple Solomons. He was dead against live shows because he did not want to 'kill the gates'. He allowed recorded programmes to be shown but not until 24 hours after the event. As younger and more forward-thinking men, Mickey and Jarvis persuaded Levene to embrace TV, especially pay at the door cinema closed circuit.

Levene, had managed most of the top men in his younger days but so far he had always been second best to Solomons in the promotion stakes. Solomons' strength was that he had the Haringey arena and some other venues sewn up. Appropriately, the Greyhound

Racing Association were his landlords at Haringey and White City, so if you had the hall, you had the show.

One of Levene's great claims to fame was that when he worked in New York as a newspaper circulation hustler he could count that great American writer Damon Runyon among his personal buddies. Poetically, then, it was that Runyonesque character, the aforementioned Willie Ketchum who also did a lot to break Solomons' stranglehold on the big London shows.

No top American champs could fight in this country at one time without Solomons' say so. He had a tie-up with the Madison Square Garden people who were known as the International Boxing Club.

Jack operated a bit like equity does today in showbiz and the Ministry of Employment does in soccer. If he said Americans couldn't work here, they didn't work here. That was until Ketchum turned up with world lightweight champion Jimmy Carter and put him on top of a Levene bill.

Willie said he didn't give a 'shit' about this club or its rules and regulations and that Carter was fighting for Levene whether Solomons liked it or not. If Solomons didn't like it, Willie said he should present his grievances to certain close friends of his back in Brooklyn.

The box office, at that time, still needed the big-name American fighters. The day was still a long way off when, in the words of our own 'Dark Destroyer' Nigel Benn the more indiscriminate British promoters imported 'Mexican road sweepers' as opponents.

Suddenly there were chinks in big Jack's armour and Levene exploited them further by luring that great crowd puller Terry Downes away from Solomons on the short-term basis of bigger purse money to meet lesser fighters.

The fighter who finally toppled the king was a young man who failed his army medical even though he was the gamest guy in the business. Blond bomber Billy Walker, the heavyweight who was the subject of more headlines than any other non-champion in history, was the definitive crowd-puller who put Levene on top for the next 20 years.

Yet, the way in which Billy got the chance to become a professional boxer in the first place, is to my mind the best as yet untold boxing anecdote.

Billy's manager was, of course, his older brother, George, who went on to make and lose millions as a city tycoon. George, an extremely tough light heavyweight who, incidentally fought on the Robinson–Turpin Earls Court bill, had a grudge against Solomons and was determined that Billy would not fight for him.

George had been involved in arguably the bloodiest fight ever seen in a British ring when he clashed with Dennis Powell in Liverpool. Both men were cut to shreds, but the referee eventually stopped the fight in favour of Powell.

As well as being sore from the road map that his face had become, George was also sore at Solomons on two counts. Jack had not bid for the fight and was paid a measley £500 and he had been forced to travel to Liverpool where, he reckoned, cockneys would get no favours.

So, although Solomons didn't know it then, George Walker was an accident waiting to happen for him. What an accident! As the head of Brent Walker he later dealt in the kind of sums that made all of Solomons wheeling and dealing look like small change by comparison.

Yet the cheekiest coup George ever pulled off was in

persuading the British Army that they had no need of his kid brother. He says himself that the main reason why it wasn't easy for him was because his old dad was a King and Country man of the old school. Fortunately, it never quite came to that. When Billy got his call-up papers for National Service, he was already being groomed for glory. He had good looks, abundant courage and, above all, a helluva knock out punch.

George could not bear to see all this money-spinning potential go to waste on square bashing. So, on the day of Billy's medical, George dressed him up to look like 'Lil Abner' the American halfwit hillbilly who was a popular comic-strip cartoon character of the day.

Billy wore his trousers halfway up his muscular legs, the jackets of his sleeves were halfway up his hairy arms, he carried *The Beano* and *The Dandy* comics under his arms, he drooled and dribbled from the mouth and had the ugliest minder imaginable in tow.

With George waiting outside, the minder who shall remain nameless except to say that he was the brother of a famous boxer, led Billy in and explained to the Army doctor. 'I'm sorry, guv'nor, but this kid's such a dozy git that if you upset him, he's liable to go berserk and smash the place up. He can't help it, he's highly strung.'

The minder then added ominously: 'I know you want to see him in private, but I'll wait just outside the door so that if he misbehaves, you can shout to me for help and I'll come in and spank him for you.'

Billy managed to answer the nervous medic's questions so spectacularly unsuccessfully that he was rated Grade Four and unfit for service. He still laughs at the memory and says he has no guilty conscience about it. 'If it had been wartime and there was an enemy to fight it would have been a totally different matter, but all my mates who had to go in the forces then said they spent two totally wasted years skiving.'

Young Walker went on to hit the headlines with the force of a juggernaut when the English amateur boxing team scored an unheard of 10–nil whitewash over the Americans, and Walker produced one of the most spectacular knock outs ever seen in the amateur ranks.

However, it was when Billy turned professional that Harry would take off like a rocket with him. Levene knew that George would never allow Billy to fight on a Solomons bill, but it was a question of if and when Billy turned pro.

The Walker brothers had informed him that they had first set their hearts on winning a gold medal at the forthcoming Commonwealth Games. In a never-to-be-forgotten BBC TV interview, Harry the toff sat in a high-backed chair in his Chantung gold and scarlet dressing-gown, with a Windsor knot in his tie. He stared straight at the cameras for what seemed like an eternity, then said: 'I've told that Billy Walker straight. I've said to him: "Gold medals? What do you want with gold medals, son? With the money I'm prepared to pay you, you can buy a sackful of medals."

Harry lived with a charming titled lady who told me later that when she arrived home from an evening out with friends that night, Harry couldn't wait to ask her: 'Did you see me on TV, my dear?' She then added: 'I said: "Yes, but I do not wish to discuss it."'

The money Harry was talking about was £9,000 for three six-rounders, which was a bargain and a half for the Walkers in those days. In fact, it was the beginning of the 'Hot Potato' restaurant partnership for the pair from which George launched his phenomenal business career.

The highlights of Billy's barnstorming boxing career,

were the series of fights he had against Johnny Prescott. Billy was the idol of London, Johnny the idol of Birmingham. They were both handsome, eligible young bachelors with a nice line in 1960s chat. They were often noted talking to each other during clinches. But they revealed that, unlike the macho hate talk that became fashionable later, they used to compare notes on how to 'pull the birds' and other good-natured youthful chatter.

Another great Levene crowd-puller was Terry Downes, who quit fighting for Solomons and switched over to Levene.

In the popularity stakes, Terry was way up there with the very best of British. It was a well-recorded fact that this London-born boy had served more than four years in the American marines.

He confided to me the heartwarming story of why he went Stateside in the first place. He was a teenager at the time and his beloved sister was working as a trapeze artist in the USA. She was involved in a bus collision that caused her to lose an arm. Immediately he heard this news, young Terry worked his passage on a merchant ship and went to comfort her.

After he quit boxing Terry opened a betting shopwith his old manager Sam Burns, who went on to become the managing director of William Hill. He also dabbled in property and made enough to send his three sons to the prestigious Haberdashers public school. He retained his cockney accent, continued to call his nose his hooter and talked through it so nasally that people assumed he was punch drunk. Nothing could have been further from the truth. 'I've always talked like this ever since me voice broke,' he once told me.

When he compiled his autobiography, ex-world middle-weight champion, Terry called the book *My*

Bleedin' Business and lending libraries refused to stock it because of what they said was a swear word in the title.

One thing that made Harry Levene swear was if he had to wait too long to find out if he had made a profit or a loss on one of his shows. Although he had a reputation for being mean, he insisted on paying everyone – managers, boxers, seconds, the lot – within 48 hours of the final bell of the evening. He even phoned everyone involved, begging them to come and collect their money.

Harry lasted the distance, delaying the Grim Reaper until his 91st year. He kept on coming to the line despite a fading memory that brought plenty of giggles from the more callous young pups at Press conferences. Having said that, it was difficult not to smile at Harry's amnesia at times. World champion Maurice Hope wasn't the first or the last boxer to recount this little tale. Maurice recalled how he said 'hello' to Harry one day only to be asked by the old boy: 'Do I know you, young man?' Maurice replied: 'You should do, I was top of your bill last night.'

My own favourite along these lines was when, shortly before the end of his life, I went to visit Harry. When his young Spanish maid had finished pouring our tea and had left the room, he confided in me that he was 'leaving her a few quid in his will to pay for her son's education'.

Thinking that he may have dropped his mean old guard at last, I took this as the perfect moment to try to sell him some boxing charity raffle tickets. Harry thought about it long and hard and finally said: 'On me, Reggie, you can't rely.'

On Jack, though, we could. When he died he left £80,000 in a trust fund for impoverished boxers. That was big bread then and it got even bigger with interest. I am the link between the Trust's executors and the ex-boxers associations. Whenever we help anyone, it has been my job to hand over the cash.

Sadly, the two biggest Solomons superstars, who were in most need of financial help in later life were Freddie Mills and Randolph Turpin. Both of them had died by their own hand by then. Maybe it was these tragedies that swayed old Jack to make such a generous exit himself.

CHAPTER FOURTEEN
REQUIEMS

'Though I've belted you an' flayed you,
By the livin' Gawd that made you,
You're a better man than I am ...'
RUDYARD KIPLING

At the funeral service of Randolph Turpin in 1966, the Reverend John Haselden said of him: 'He was a simple, naïve man, who needed friends to protect him from spongers. To our shame, he was let down.'

I could only murmur a guilty amen in response.

At the funeral service of Freddie Mills a year earlier, I could neither see nor hear the clergyman when he spoke because my eyes were blinded by tears and my ears were pounding with sorrow.

Like most other people who loved boxing, I felt an irrational personal responsibility for their terrible fates. I had basked in both men's reflected glory but was nowhere to be seen when they needed a shoulder to lean on.

Suicide has this kind of effect on you whether the victim was a professional acquaintance as Randy was or a close family friend such as Freddie.

A sportswriter pal of mine once said: 'If you can't write about boxing, you can't write about anything. It is a microcosm of life itself.' If that truly is the case then nothing could have epitomised the ephemeral and intrinsically empty nature of fame and fortune more than these two brief human existences.

A day after becoming world middleweight champion, Turpin waved proudly to the people of his native Leamington Spa from the mayor's car as RAF jets swooped overhead saluting him.

Ten years later, at the still young age of 38, he was driving a lorry through those same streets as a bankcrupt scrap metal dealer who was now resigned to handing himself over to the tender mercies of God.

His reign had been one of the shortest in boxing history when he was defeated in a rematch with Sugar Ray Robinson at the Polo Grounds, New York, in front of 61,370 spectators just 64 days after his initial triumph.

He had begun his boxing career in the traditional way by being a boy wonder in a fairground booth, fighting for nobbins. By the time he finished, the Inland Revenue had collected more than £40,000 and were pressing for another £15,922, which they claimed he still owed them.

Turpin's accounts, such as they were, were a pile of papers on a desk in a room over the transport café run by his second wife, Gwyneth, in Russell Street, Leamington. He seemed by then to be resigned to being fleeced by so-called friends, and a notice he had hung on the café wall said it all.

'That which seldom comes back to him who waits is the money he lends to his friends.'

His enemy, the taxman, sent him one last demand for £200 on 17th May 1966 – the day he killed himself.

When Gwyneth returned from her morning shopping trip, she found a note that began: 'I hope you will forgive me for this terrible thing ...'

Turpin had shot himself with a .22 revolver in the attic bedroom, injuring his beloved two-year-old daughter, Carmen, in the process. The first bullet lodged against Randolph's skull and was not fatal. He finished the dreadful deed by firing a second bullet into his heart.

Freddie Mills shot himself, too. This was confirmed to me by 'Nipper Read' the famous detective who is now, coincidentally, President of the British Boxing Board of Control.

Mills's body was found, slumped in a car, with a shotgun in his mouth in an alley beside the Chinese restaurant in Charing Cross Road that he owned in partnership with a Chinese actor named Andy Ho. In our courting days, Connie and I had shared a table there with Freddie and friends once a week every week.

There was speculation, almost on a daily basis, in the media for months afterwards that he might have been murdered, either by London protection racketeers or a Triad gang. It transpired that, like Turpin, he was in extreme financial difficulties,

All this time later, as death takes its toll of more and more old friends and relations the 'whys and wherefores' of Freddie's demise become less personal and less painful. But the memory of that jutting jaw, the missing front teeth and those mischievous eyes remain as vivid as ever.

I also lost my dear old mother in the 1960s. She died of cancer in the London Hospital where I was born. I would need to be a poet to say a suitable requiem for my mum – what boy wouldn't?

So I'll restrict myself to this short prosaic postscript that, be assured, is as long as eternity itself on fond memories.

CHAPTER FIFTEEN
LEGACIES

'Teach us delight in simple things,
And mirth that has no bitter springs.'
RUDYARD KIPLING

Sadly, like Dad and Uncle Jack, Mum also died before her time, at the age of 61. She lived long enough to experience the joy of having grandchildren – my daughters Sue and Sally were six and three when Mum passed away.

Having to live with nothing but boxing, wrestling, dog racing and football chatter all her married life, she was delighted to be able to indulge herself in some girl talk, at last, with Connie and the babies.

As for me, and more importantly for my artificial leg, it meant that there was no need for me to make excuses that I was unable to get down on my knees and nag them to keep their chins tucked in behind the left lead or teach them to hook off the jab, as I imagined I would have had to if they had been boys.

I decided that the best way for them to get used to the fact that their old man had a wooden leg was to laugh about it, especially as I invariably took it off indoors and they were always having to shift it around like a piece of furniture when they were helping their mother with the housework.

In fact, they both became quite attached to it. Never

more so than when we were on holiday and the leg became a status symbol to go with the bucket and spade.

The girls' favourite beach game, when they were toddlers, was to bury the artificial limb in the sand with the false foot sticking up and then to submerge me far enough away for them to tell any passer-by who was interested that I was a 'daddy longlegs'.

There was one incident, when they were still children that did shock them a bit and embarrassed them even more. That was when the bloody thing fell off in the street and Connie had to shove it in her shopping bag.

It was not just any old street, either, it was on a main drag in Gibraltar. I had splashed out to take us all on a cruise aboard the *Canberra*. We were all indulging in some sightseeing ashore when I heard this tearing noise coming from inside my trousers. The flesh coloured gauze surrounding the wood, or more accurately, the hard cork had ripped as the lower leg came away from its moorings and the foot fell off into the roadway.

It was the one and only time this type of accident ever happened to me, so we were all a bit flustered. I had to hop to the nearest wall and perch on it while we tried to cover up our collective embarrassment. Connie popped the offending leg in the bag she had been hoping to fill with souvenirs.

Some people who had been on the ship with us were close behind when this mishap occurred. One of them, a woman, who had previously had no idea that I was handicapped, asked me whether she should send for a doctor. I replied: 'Not really, thank you, my dear, but I could do with a carpenter, just as long as it's not Harry.' By this time the girls were bent double with laughter and this kind woman was able to take them off our hands while Connie and I retreated back to the ship in a cab. As I hopped up the gangway, the Master at Arms gave us an old-fashioned bemused look, as he hadn't noticed a one-legged passenger until now.

As for the girls they experienced the satisfying thrill of learning to swim in the pool on that ship so the last thing on their minds at that exciting time for them was old daddy longlegs.

Outside of the family, I decided the best way to cope with one leg was to tell as few people as possible about it, so that it did not become a souce of boring conversation.

I've resolved to indulge myself just a little on these pages in the knowledge that after 58 years of living with it I've paid my dues and am entitled to cash in at last.

As I'm told by my most ferocious critic – her indoors – this is the only story that still makes her grin. I'll begin these few shaggy leg stories with the one about Sonny Liston.

I'll have more to say about Charles 'Sonny' Liston as a boxer and a man later, but suffice it to say, that anyone who can remember him will surely agree with me that, as monsters go, he made even made Mike Tyson look like a choirboy.

Against all the odds and certainly against my better nature, Sonny and I became genuine buddy boys. He was, if you can be persuaded to believe this, a bully with a soft centre. He possessed that precious gift of sometimes being able to laugh at himself, although you had to be very careful when choosing your moment.

I usually pick my friends on the 'what-you-see-is-what-you-get' basis, as is most definitely the case with a gentleman like Henry Cooper. But, if you had the time, opportunity and patience to look for it, there was a rough charm beneath that well-rehearsed Liston scowl. So much so that I felt the need to go and pay my respects at Sonny's Las Vegas grave when he met his untimely and mysterious end.

His was the introduction from hell. He was attired in, of all things, a kilt. He was in Scotland on a tour of Britain at the time. Sonny told anyone who would listen that his Scottish hosts had only put the sporran on him to cover up his lunch box and so prevent the local ladies getting killed in the rush to take a closer look at him.

Instead of shaking hands with me at that, our first social meeting, he flicked his enormous fingers at my unmentionables and as I bent double with pain, he drawled: 'Take a bow'. Then he gave out a great belly laugh. When I had recovered my composure enough to tell him that I did not think it was funny and that I would have to go to the mens' room to inspect the swelling that was already growing, he just grinned again and said: 'Mention my name and they'll give you the best seat.'

Our jobs meant that we were destined to see a lot of each other. My chance for revenge came one night in a hotel bar when we were resting between engagements and were both, to coin a well-worn cockney phrase, slightly Brahms and Liszt.

Milking his bogeyman image for all it was worth, Sonny suddenly said to me: 'Why is it that you white guys think black guys look like gorillas?' 'Come on,' I protested, 'I've never said anything like that in my life.' I did not realise he was setting me up for another of his favourite party tricks. And for winning a bet which, as a notorious gambling man, he was very partial to, of course.

'Bullshit, man,' rasped Sonny, 'You're just like all the other white guys, you think us blacks are just big hairy apes. Well, I'm issuing you a challenge here and now – I'll bet you any money you like that you've got more hairs on your goddam leg than I have. So, come on, put your money on the table and roll up your trousers.'

For the sake of my health, I went easy on him and only bet a tenner. Then I slowly rolled up my left trouser leg and exposed the hairless imitation in all its temporary glory.

Sonny called me, among other things 'a cork-legged limey son-of-a-bitch' but laughed heartily and paid up.

Between that meeting and our next he had other more pressing matters on his mind, such as a possible upcoming fight with Cassius Clay, for instance. By the time we came into contact again, he had forgotten that earlier betting skirmish.

On this occasion and in this particular hotel bar we happened to be drinking together again and I was addressing him as 'Charles' in a phony upper-crust English accent, as I always did, when Sonny suddenly said: 'You Brits are a bunch of faggots. All you got is horizontal heavyweights.'

Game for another life, I got lippy and said: 'Your tough guy act is so much bullshit. As old as I am I could show you what a real tough guy looks like. I've got $50 that says I'm tougher than you.'

Astonished, intrigued and decidedly forgetful Sonny pulled out his $50 and covered mine, saying: 'What you gonna do little guy – arm wrestle me?'

His mouth dropped open when I rolled up my trouser, took an ice pick out of the drinks bucket and began plunging it into what he thought was my bare leg

It was only after ten 'stabs' that he suddenly remembered who I was. He was so taken with me this time that every time I saw him subsequently he would beg me for an encore so that he could win some easy money from 'some other sucker'. Poor old Sonny never lived long enough to enjoy many more party tricks, his own or anyone else's.

These fun and games backfired on me, too. I had to go back to Roehampton Limb Fitting Centre to have the leg repaired. It looked as though a woodpecker had been at it.

The leg legacy that affords me most pride, however, came when I applied for life insurance in middle age and was sent by the insurance company to be examined by Dr Adrian Whiteson in upper Wimpole Street. By coincidence, Adrian is chief medical officer for the British Boxing Board of Control, which means he and I have been friends for years.

He was astonished to discover that I was one leg short of a full set and, like so many other people who knew me well professionally, he had no inkling of my handicap.

I still thank my lucky stars that I was not wounded at Waterloo under Wellington. From my layman's knowledge of history it is more than probable that I would have had to go around begging for alms for the rest of my life.

This luxurious jet set lifestyle of mine still has its niggling disadvantages for the disabled. Nothing was more irritating than when I asked a British airline if I could have one of those seats with leg room near the exit. They refused on the grounds that disabled people could not be allowed to sit there in case they obstructed other passengers in the event of an emergency exit. Pardon me for living!

That little grouse apart, I have managed to turn the handicap into a reason to have a giggle or two. By the time I went to commentate on a fight in France quite recently my missing leg had been revealed by Mohammed Ali's doctor, Ferdie Pachecon in his autobiography, *Fight Doctor*.

Armed with this information, a French journalist

working for the local paper had worked out that my leg had gone missing very near the venue for this particular fight. This resourceful young Frenchman suddenly tapped me on the shoulder at ringside and inquired: 'Monsieur Gutteridge, I believe you lost your leg near here.'

I could not resist this smart ass reply: 'Why, have you found it, my son?' I'm slightly ashamed of that lack of courtesy, but sometimes I can't resist the clown that is in me.

On another occasion, I was changing planes at Singapore airport, where I was bound for Alan Rudkins' world bantamweight title fight in Tokyo. There was a five-hour stop-over involved and I found myself sleeping on a bench opposite legless war hero Douglas Bader.

When it came to going through the security gate, I happened to be the next one behind Bader in the queue. As the inevitable bleep sounded the security man recognised Douglas and promptly saluted him. When I went through immediately afterwards and when he could find no metal in my pockets, he scratched his head and started examining the machine for a possible fault. It was only when I rolled up my trouser leg that the guard permitted himself a bewildered smile, which turned to a grin when I told him: 'English is vellee funny people!'

The lack of a leg provided a laugh or two in my younger days when on trips to sunny climes where other newspaper lads would goad me into hopping out of whatever ocean we just happened to be lucky enough to be in at the time and clearing the beach by shouting 'sharks!'

I still grin, too, at the young car salesman who was attempting to sell me my first car. He pointed out that as the vehicle in question was an automatic: 'You won't have a clue what to do with your left leg.' I told him to take a refresher course in his selling techniques.

One of the funniest automobile stories I have heard concerned my old pal, Henry Cooper, in the days before the phrase 'road rage' was invented.

Henry, his twin George and their old manager, Jim Wicks, were involved in a contretemps over rights of way in a dark country lane one night. The driver of the other car came over to them shaking his fist and shaping up to fight whoever was inside what he considered was the offending vehicle.

Imagine his astonishment when the twins and old Jim all got out of the car to confront him. The other guy recognised them but they so appreciated his cheek and his courage when, in backing down, he said: 'It's only because there's three of you,' that they couldn't stop laughing.

This brings me very conveniently to an unashamedly chauvinistic chapter on 'our Enery'.

CHAPTER SIXTEEN

OUR BLEEDIN' 'ENERY

'O Motherland, we pledge to thee
Head, heart, and hand through the years to be!'
RUDYARD KIPLING

That line of Kipling's could have been written as a tribute to Henry Cooper. If there was no Henry Cooper, the British boxing public would have had to invent him. He was everything you could wish for in a warrior to represent your nation with dignity and honour.

His head contained an intelligent, tactical brain, which he used in the ring like a radar scanner to spot possible openings in his opponents' defences. His heart was as big as as St Paul's Cathedral and his left hand truly was the hammer it was cracked up to be.

But he was a bleeder. And he was liable to be cut at the most inconvenient moments, as he was in his unforgettable first fight against Cassius Clay when 'the greatest' came within seconds of humiliating defeat before his own extraordinary career had even got properly started.

Appropriately enough for such a patriotic man, 'our 'Enery' as he became affectionately known to so many millions of his countrymen, was born in Westminster Hospital. Just like my own dad, he had a twin brother to keep him company. In their youthful amateur days, George was reckoned to be the more promising prospect of the two, but he kept damaging his hands so badly that he was forced to quit the pro-game early.

Another tenuous link between Henry's family and my own was that our grandfathers fought each other in the old bare knuckle era. The nearest their descendants ever come to blows, however, is in our regular tussles on the golf course.

Henry holds a unique record in British boxing history, which can never be surpassed or even equalled. He is the holder of three Lonsdale belts at the same weight and a recent rule change means that he is the only man who will ever have such a distinction.

Boxing belts, as trophies, go back nearly 200 years. The first one was presented by King George III to Tom Cribb after he had beaten black American, Tom Molineux, on Copthall Common in 1810.

The first Lonsdale belt belonged to Freddie Welsh and was presented by the 5th Earl of Lonsdale after Welsh had beaten Johnny Summers at the National Sporting Club for the British lightweight title in 1909. The original belts were highly decorative and ornamental. Until the 1940s, when the war made the cost of the belts prohibitive, they were made from nine carat gold. They had solid gold links at the buckle and elaborate floral emblems of the rose of England, the shamrock of Ireland, the thistle of Scotland and the daffodil of Wales.

The Americans soon fell under the spell of our belts and, in 1910, the black population there contributed nickels and dimes in their millions so that the legendary Jack Johnson, the first black world heavyweight champion, could be presented with an all-American belt studded with 200 diamonds and worth more than $25,000 at that time.

In this country, Lonsdale belts were awarded to any

boxer who fought successfully for the British title three times at the same weight. Cooper was the only man to win three of them. In 1987, the rules were changed to insist that the belt could only be won outright more than once by a boxer who fought at different weights. So far, that has not happened and it is extremely unlikely that it ever will.

One dark little secret of Henry's which can now be revealed is that he, too, suffered from that most unlikely ailment for an athlete – gout! He still has to pop a daily pill to keep this painful condition at bay.

I say he, too, because the odds on both Henry and his most frequent opponent, Joe Erskine, being plagued this way must have been millions to one. Unless, of course, they laced the bromide when they were putting it in the tea at Blackdown Barracks where both men did their national service army square bashing. For the younger generation, bromide was a mysterious potion that everyone swore went into the tea to keep the young squaddies' minds off sex!

Speaking of which, and to copy the in-chat of today that refers to sexy football, there surely has never been a sexier boxer than the young Cassius Clay when he came to London to do battle with our national hero.

Giving us a taste of the flamboyant personality that was to bewitch the universe over the next couple of decades, Clay came into the ring at Wembley wearing a splendid crown.

He had found it at the London Palladium earlier in the day when after the weigh-in there he had indulged that boyish curiosity of his by exploring backstage and coming upon a pantomime crown that he 'borrowed' so that he could make a regal entrance for the fight.

It was not the pantomime crown or even a pantomime

slipper that caused so much mayhem. It was, of course, Clay's glove, which mysteriously split, necessitating a delay and giving him controversial precious extra seconds in which to recover from the effects of Henry's hammer, which had floored and so nearly finished him.

That split glove, incidentally, finished up on display in Albert Dimes's Soho betting shop the next morning. Albert, a colourful underworld character, was a pal of Henry's manager, Jim Wicks. I can only wonder where it is now and if – like Geoff Hurst's equally famous hat-trick World Cup final football – it will ever turn up again?

In boxing circles, over a few drinks, the arguments about that glove still occasionaly rage all of 35 years later. Some cynics speculate that Clay's trainer, Angelo Dundee, deliberately split the glove with scissors or a razor to give the then 21-year-old Cassius time to recover from a spectacular knock down.

I beg to differ, and I have witnesses to back up my judgement. Tufts of hair were seen coming out of Clay's glove during the third round. The then British Boxing Board of Control secretary, Teddy Waltham, and his Chief Inspector Andy Cunningham, who were sitting alongside me, began debating as to where they could quickly come by a replacement. Cunningham actually left the ringside to go to the dressing-rooms for a new glove, which dispels the belief that Dundee had deliberately cut the already damaged one.

It was just five seconds from the end of the fourth when Henry nailed his man with that inimitable trademark left hook of his. When the count reached four the bell, which was barely audible in the roar of the crowd, brought a compulsory and, from Cooper's point of view, a fateful end to the round.

Had that punch landed earlier it was long odds-on

that Cooper, a deadly finisher, might have put an end to the proceedings and, of course, with it engineered a change in boxing history.

In later years Clay-turned-Ali confessed he would have 'hung on, OK.' He later proved bravely capable of recovering from knock downs.

Whether or not it would have been a welcome change for Henry is another matter because the winner was due to meet the aforementioned fearsome Sonny Liston next.

Anyway, the rumpus between rounds was unprecedented with Dundee, having worsened the tear with his thumb, shouting to anyone and everyone that the glove needed changing. The official ruling was that the replacement would have to take place after the next round, but Dundee had already poached a considerable delay for his man. Enough for Olympic gold medalist Clay to clear his head and realise that he had grossly underestimated our man. Henry still insists the delay was minutes. It was more likely some 40 seconds over time.

In less than 90 seconds of the fifth he had cut Cooper's face to ribbons, forcing the referee to stop the contest.

When he had finished cursing his luck old Jim Wicks, privately admitted that the whole affair – Henry's marvellous performance and his controversial defeat – was a mixed blessing. It meant that he could press for a return with Clay and duck Liston. 'I don't want my fella fighting that mahogany wardrobe' was the way wordsmith Wicks put it to his cronies.

Clay paid Henry the ultimate compliment when he declined to wear the crown after the fight, as he had previously intended to do. He also honoured Henry with a return match with his title at stake in London, which he also won on cuts in six rounds.

Amazingly, this fight was not screened on BBC until months

later. An appeal by the Postmaster General, A. Wedgewood Benn for live coverage was refused by Viewsport's closed circuit chief, Jarvis Astaire. I did the 'pay' commentary.

Many years later, by which time he had become the most famous man on the planet as Muhammad Ali, I was with them both when Ali held a door open for Henry to enter the room first as a calculated mark of respect for our much-loved man.

The saddest aspect of Henry's career was not so much the controversial way it ended – in a points defeat by rising star Joe Bugner in 1971 – but the long, bitter aftermath of that memorable contest.

After 15 intriguing rounds, a by now 37-year-old Cooper lost his treasured British heavyweight crown to the much younger challenger, but not the precious belts that are his for life.

The referee, that much respected official Harry Gibbs, gave the verdict to Bugner by the minimum margin of a mere quarter of a point. The reason why the decimal system of scoring was abandoned in January 1988, had much to do with this particlar fight, which the majority of observers reckoned was just too close to call.

In the dressing-room afterwards, Henry took the bitter disappointment in his usual gracious way by limiting his retirement announcement to one simple statement to the Press: 'Well, gentlemen, that's me lot.'

In his autobiography Henry criticised Gibbs over the verdict to such an extent that Harry took out a libel suit against him and won it. Gibbs declined the offer of damages, stressing that he did not want any money, but that he did place a high value on his honour and integrity and needed it upheld.

Bitterness was an emotion that was entirely out of character for Henry, who was the very epitome of that old-fashioned archetypal English sportsman so universally idealised many years ago as being gracious in both victory and defeat.

Thankfully, some years later, I was instrumental in reconciling my two mates. The three of us were attending a packed charity show at the Hilton Hotel. The atmosphere was still frosty between the pair when suddenly the Master of Ceremonies asked whether Henry and Harry would get up and give us a public handshake. On my persuasion, they climbed up into the ring and shook hands. They were cheered to the rafters and the ring was pelted with greenback paper nobbins for the grateful charity concerned.

Henry, as it transpired, turned out to be one of the last of the genuinely humble sportsmen like that earlier generation of famous footballers who travelled to the match by trolleybus.

Even though I had tipped Bugner to win, Henry's lovely Italian wife, Albina, was still generous enough to make us boxing scribes bacon and eggs when we called at his suburban house in Wembley the next morning for our follow-up stories.

Homespun scenes like that just could not happen in this TV-dominated age of the monster free-for-all press conferences.

Unless you have been in exile for 25 year or more, you will know, of course, that when Henry retired, he stayed retired. He also began a requited love affair with the British public that shows no signs of waning with time.

And Bugner? Well, for starters, he was never forgiven by many British fight fans for deposing their 'Enery and remained mysteriously largely unloved throughout an on-off ringlife that has spanned more than 25 years and is still continuing by virtue of the fact that he recently won the Australian heavyweight championship as a grandad in a farcical fight with fellow veteran, James 'Bonecrusher'Smith.

From a personal point of view, no other boxer has ever embarrassed me half as much as Bugner did. More than 30 years ago, he cost me £40 in cold blood when I used him to show off what I thought were my skills as a talent spotter.

I told my independent TV contacts that there was a young blond Adonis who would be a TV natural and urged them to sign him up without delay.

As I did not want to be beholden to the promoters, I personally bought three ringside tickets, intending to claim for them later, at the Anglo–American Sporting Club for Bill Ward, an executive producer, Graham Turner, head of outside broadcasting for Thames Television and John Bromley, who was later to become my boss.

You can imagine how their eyes lit up when they saw this Hungarian refugee with the looks and the physique to send ratings through the roof, but what does jolly Joe do? He goes and gets himself stopped in the second round by a young man named Paul Brown, who later became a Birmingham bus driver. Naturally, I never had the nerve to ask for my money back.

The TV men never stopped pulling my good leg for years afterwards but when, some 20 years later, he pulled an audience of 18 million for his fight with Frank Bruno at the Spurs football ground, I thought it was time to put in my belated expenses claim.

I felt I had earned it by then and, whatever else anyone says about this enigmatic giant discovery of mine, they cannot say he did not earn his money.

Joe had boxed 502 rounds before losing to Frank Bruno which is a vast amount for a modern heavyweight. And he still hasn't stopped.

CHAPTER SEVENTEEN
ROGUES' GALLERY

'Forgiveness free of evil done,
And love to all men 'neath the sun'
RUDYARD KIPLING

For me, an irresistible footnote to the Henry Cooper chapter is what his old rogue of a manager, Jim Wicks, had Henry get up to at the weigh-in of that first Cassius Clay fight.

Wicks, who always used the royal 'we' when referring to Cooper had observed 'we don't want to go into the fight looking too light or it will give Clay a big psychological advantage.'

For the intimidating truth was that even at the tender age of 21, Clay was more than a stone and a half heavier than our man, who barely touched 13 stones.

Now, as a die-hard punter at both horses and dogs, Jim was an expert on handicaps and racing weights. So what does he do? He slips lead plates into the soles of Henry's boots for the weigh-in to bring him up to 13 stones 3-and-a-half pounds. Wily Wicks obviously relieved Henry of the lead in time for the action.

I had the opposite problem. I was now carrying top weight by taking on three jobs at once – writing for the *News* and commentating for closed-circuit TV and for ITVs *World of Sport*.

Our sport was changing fast with the introduction of closed-circuit live TV in 1964 and ITV's brand new coverage a year later.

On reflection, I realise that it was not financial greed that spurred me on – none of the jobs paid all that well. However, having come so close to losing my life in the War, I wanted to live every minute to the full now, even the 'unforgiving' ones. And there were to be plenty of those.

The first came on my very first freelance assignment for ITV when I was sent to London Airport to interview incoming American middleweight Rubin 'Hurricane' Carter who was due to fight our own Harry Scott, 'The Bootle Bulldog'. Lovely, colourful names they had in those days, didn't they?

Colourful, too, was the language I used into the microphone, fortunately not on air, when we learned that Carter was not on the plane. A cluster of airport taxi drivers were mickey-taking this 'luvvy' TV crew – TV still being something of a novelty then – when my full frontal flow of four letter words shut them up. This, after all, was something the cabbies understood, identified with and respected. On the basis that it takes one to know one, they realised I was one of their own and soon became our minders, hustling away any intruders.

It is the same with me and rogues. I try hard not to be one, myself, but in my Islington boyhood I got to know and even identify with many a loveable rogue. Maybe that is why I love boxing so much, it reminds me of home. Perhaps I am spiritually connected to the fight game.

Had I been a public schoolboy, no doubt I would have become a rugby writer glorifying such sometimes smug virtues as 'play up school and play the game'. If so, though, I would also have found myself in the embarrassing position of having to explain away such unsavoury incidents as ear-biting in the front row at international matches.

If that last paragraph is a case of me getting my

retaliation in first, then so be it. It is simply an attempt to explain my affinity to the sporting sinners as well as the saints. If nothing else, the rogues make readable copy and screenplays about them put bums on cinema seats, even if some of the old B-movies of crooked fights and gangsters owe more to the imagination than to any known facts.

Anyway, this is my excuse for writing now about Carter and the other characters featured in this next chapter.

Rubin 'Hurricane' Carter sported a shaven head decades before they became fashionable à la Eric Cantona. He also favoured a goatee beard and had been blessed with a body of chiselled muscles that made him look like a sawn-off heavyweight. As frightening figures go, he was in the Sonny Liston and Mike Tyson class.

No official reason was ever given for the 'Hurricane's' non-arrival the day he stood me up, but he did eventually turn up in this country to fight Scott twice.

He trained in Freddie Hill's gym near London's Kings Cross and stayed at the Cumberland Hotel, Marble Arch, where it was reported by a house detective that he had stashed a gun in his room. No charges were brought against him in this country, but soon after he got back home he became the central character in one of America's longest ever criminal controversies.

Carter was wrongly convicted of a triple murder and it took him 20 years to prove his innocence. His story was carefully researched and broadcast by the BBC World Service as recently as 1993.

By the time of this broadcast, he had become a broken hero and had been adopted by a Canadian family, who believed in his innocence, and befriended by a lawyer, who worked for ten years with no fees to eventually free him.

These good people felt obliged to assist Rubin because they considered he was a victim of blatant racism when he was charged with shooting a white barman and two white customers in a New Jersey saloon killing.

Now in his sixties, Rubin was, indeed 'blowing a hurricane' at the time of his wrongful arrest and conviction, having had 40 fights and risen to number one contender for the world middleweight crown. A devastating puncher, he was the only man ever to put the great Emile Griffiths on the canvas in that great fighter's career.

Lou Duva, one of the wisest of the old American fight judges, says of him: 'He would have been a multi-millionaire if he had fought in modern times. The man could finish anybody with one punch and that includes latter-day champs like Marvin Hagler, Tommy Hearns and Sugar Ray Leonard.'

Instead, after a six-week trial, Rubin and his alleged accomplice were given three life sentences each and only managed to escape with their lives when the all-white jury recommended mercy. Carter said later: 'If there had been the slightest suspicion in their minds that we had committed the crimes, they would have fried us like bacon rind.'

As it was, inadequate hospital treatment in prison resulted in Rubin losing an eye and the man who was convicted with him having his fingers and toes amputated.

Their conviction had rested on the evidence of three witnesses who were, themselves, already on charges of robbery.

Like so many other fighting men from the wrong side of the tracks, Carter had fallen foul of the law earlier in his life and had served four years for assault before he took up boxing.

ROGUES' GALLERY

He has always maintained that his real crime was being an active and well-publicised political supporter of Martin Luther King's freedom fight and, as such, he had been interviewed by newspapers many times on that subject. He had also been one of the central characters in a 'freedom march' fracas, which had gained national notoriety as the 'Harlem Fruit Riot.'

In prison, Carter managed to write an autobiography entitled *The Sixteenth Round* which took several years to come to fruition. Bob Dylan wrote a song about it, Muhammad Ali organised marches on the two mens behalf, and they were released on bail in 1976.

Incredibly, another trumped up charge was brought against them and the triple life sentences were re-imposed. It was not until November 1985 that the 'Hurricane' finally got out of jail for good. Even then, the prosecution had already been to the appeal court 15 times in the two years since Carter had won his own appeal hearing in a Federal Court where the judge had no previous contacts with the prosecution and had not been poisoned with prejudice against Rubin.

The 'Hurricane' was a winner at last, then. But it was a hollow victory. He and his fellow victim of such gross injustice were never compensated and nobody in official circles ever apologised. The case was eventually stricken from the records but no one was ever prosecuted for the murders.

Sonny 'Stoneface' Liston was a very different kind of rogue to Rubin 'Hurricane' Carter. Charles, as he was named by his cotton-picking mammy and pappy when he arrived as the 24th of their 25 children down in Arkansas, insisted he was born in 1932. But as there was no official birth certificate and he could not read or write, anyway, that had to be taken on trust by the

165

boxing authorities. So, as trusting Sonny was not always a wise policy, it is safe to assume that he was already well into middle age when he was so sensationally deposed of his world heavyweight title by young 25–1 shot Cassius Clay in Miami in February 1964.

Impartial to freedom marching himself, old 'Stoneface's' turn-ons were drink, gambling, prostitutes, pranks, gangsters and, some say, drugs. So sensational was Clay's completely unexpected victory over this seemingly unbeatable 'monster,' that when Liston quit on his stool at the end of the sixth round, the cry of 'fix' resonated around the world for years and grew in volume when, after changing his name next morning to Muhammad Ali, the new champ also won the rematch this time with a so-called 'phantom' punch that landed or didn't land, according to your point of view, on Liston's chin after only one minute 52 seconds of the first round, without referee Jersey Joe Wallcott counting, it all ended in chaos and suspicions.

As there was no exceptional betting recorded on Ali in either fight, my own conclusions are that, first, it was the bottle and the years that had caught up with my old mate and that it was a decent punch that toppled him the next time. Not enough power, maybe, to have kept a properly conditioned heavyweight down. Liston got up, punches were exchanged, but he hadn't beaten the clock.

What did catch up with him, not many years later, however, was death itself. In the best traditions of the incorrigible rogue, his demise was a hotly disputed verdict, too. Some reports said he committed suicide, others that he had taken an accidental drug overdose and yet more insisted he was the victim of an underworld hit. Such a distinguished journalist as Ian

Woodridge of the *Daily Mail* even reported that he had been decapitated.

Harold Conrad, an American writer who was very close to Liston summed up his pal's life this way: 'Even though Sonny won the greatest title in sport, he was still searching for an identity. He died on the day he was born.'

Ironically, this man who told me he had been a target for police harrassment all his life, was given a police escort for his Las Vegas funeral in January 1971. As the cortege passed along the entire length of the famous 'Strip' casino workers and patrons bowed their heads. Paradoxically, when I went to Paradise Gardens to pay my respects at his grave, his headstone was simply engraved with the words 'A Man'.

The headstones there are laid flat because of low-flying planes at the adjoining airport. As they roared above us, I swear I heard my old bully boy pal cursing them for disturbing his sleep.

Although he was not as famous as either Carter or Liston, another black American, Jeff Simms, has an equally sinister story to tell. He was the number ten heavyweight contender when I encountered him. He was sparring with our own up-and-coming young Frank Bruno in the famous Grossinger's training camp in the Catskill Mountains.

Bruno put him on the floor and I heard Simms growl: 'That chain gang done slowed me up more'n I figured.' Curiosity naturally compelled me to challenge that last remark and out tumbled a young life story that was too far-fetched even for a film script.

Simms had also been one of a family of umpteen cotton picking children down in the deep south when he was imprisoned in his teens. He explained: 'Some dude stole my coat and shot me two times. Later, when I went to get my coat back, I shot him two times and wound up on the chain gang.'

Now, this is where the story takes its most bizarre turn. For those first two bullets are still embedded in Simms – one in his head and one in his body – along with three more that he received in a subsequent shooting.

This took place after Simms' release and probationary rehabilitation. He took up the story again. 'A reverend looked after some of us boxers and put me to living with another upand coming heavyweight.

'Well, it wasn't long before we got round to arguing. One night we argued about who should empty the trash cans and this flatmate dude shot me three times.

'I was helpless on the floor, when I heard that son-of-a-bitch reloadin'. I figured that he was good and mad, so I dived through the window and broke my leg on the pavement.' Simms tells his remarkable story in a matter-of-fact way and is not in the least bit bothered whether you believe it or not – except that, upon request, he is willing to show you the five holes where the bullets entered.

Mind you, Simms may have been the only boxer to fight with bullets inside him, but he was not the first to carry bullet wounds into the ring. One such man was Cleveland 'Big Cat' Williams, who earned the distinction, if that is the right word, of being on the wrong end of Muhammad Ali's best ever ring performance.

Ali was making the seventh defence of his title against Williams in Houston, Texas, in 1966. Black, supremely athletic Williams, also had Seminole Indian blood in him and he still carried the bullet wounds that had been inflicted by a Houston white police patrolman, named Dale Witten, some years earlier.

In search of a preview story, I phoned the local nick

and discovered that Witten was, at that precise moment, driving his patrol car around town.

Presumably intrigued by my British accent, the local constabulary could not have been more helpful and within minutes officer Witten was in my hotel room with Williams and me, brandishing the coloured photographs of the facial wounds he received at the hands of Williams when he had picked him up for being drunk and disorderly.

The cop went on to tell me that he had shot the 'Big Cat' in self-defence as the two men were wrestling in the patrol car. When I asked them whether they would shake hands and forgive and forget, they both agreed, albeit a little nervously.

It was soon smiles all round and Williams handed Witten two tickets for the fight and a pennant emblazoned 'Big Cat'. When the boxer's wife, Irene, asked the policeman whether he would root for her man tonight, the cop replied: 'I sure will, mam. I sure, will.'

Cleveland lost in three, but the exclusive picture of little old me sandwiched between happy cop and clouter made more than 100 newspapers in the USA and, of course, the *Evening News* back home.

Another amusing rogues story, which is right up there with the best or the worst of them, also involves a British boxer, Kirkland Laing, 'the whistling welterweight'. That epithet was given to him by his manager, Terry Lawless, who would tear his hair out when Laing, an immensely talented but uncommitted performer, got bored and whistled while he was in the middle of a fight.

Well, one night, Kirkland amazed everyone on both sides of the Atlantic by out-pointing the formidable Roberto Duran in America. Mickey Duff, who was managing Laing by then, says that a black American guy jumped into the ring afterwards and kept pumping his hand in congratulations and repeating: 'Where did you find him? Where did you find him?'

Mickey goes on to explain: 'It was only later that I discovered the fella had slipped the gold ring off my finger – I had no idea he was working.'

Talking of which, my work takes me on a regular basis to Pentonville, Wandsworth and Chelmsford prisons, where at the request of a prisoners' charity I show films and give lectures to the prisoners in their leisure time.

On one occasion an old lag stod up and asked me: 'What boxer was here in Pentonville before the War and is still here?'

I replied: 'You could not be more out of luck over this than you undoubtedly were on the day you got nicked. It just so happens that my old man trained him. He was Canadian Del Fontaine, who shot his girlfriend and her mother and was hanged and buried here.'

My personal favourite among the many loveable rogue stories that boxing has thrown up over the years took place in my own backyard, however. It concerns that colourful old Cockney heavyweight, Fred 'Nosher' Powell.

Out of condition at the time, he was once summoned as an 11th hour substitute in a title fight. Nosher was soon down on one knee and taking the full count. His purse money was withheld and he was ordered to appear before the British Boxing Board of Control. 'That man did not hurt you, Powell,' observed the chairman. 'No, but he wasn't 'arf bleedin' going to, your Honour,' said Nosher.

CHAPTER EIGHTEEN
TALKING WITH CROWDS

'If you can talk with crowds
and keep your virtue,'
RUDYARD KIPLING

The crowd I walked and talked with on the night of the first of the Muhammad Ali-Joe Frazier trilogy was unlike any other I encountered in 60 years around boxing. It was Ali's second coming, his championship comeback. Many of the fans entering Madison Square Garden, New York, on the evening of 8 March 1971 appeared to be as high on hope and fervour as a Billy Graham convert. But as this was a big fight and not a religious rally, they were not all virtuous. Oh dear, no. I can still see the sharks at work. As the hip legions of fur-coated, bejewelled men and women excitedly approached the arena, these dudes shouted: 'Show your tickets, first! Show your tickets here.' When the less worldy wise among the patrons did so, the hustlers just grabbed those precious pieces of paper and ran.

Such was the celebrity status of this historic sporting occasion that Frank Sinatra took pictures for a magazine and an astronaut hero could get no closer than the fifth row.

There was hostility in the electrified air, too. Political and racial hatred was being spouted as some white spectators exhorted Frazier to: 'Kill the son-of-a-bitch, shut that lip up once and for all.' It was almost four

171

years to the day since Ali's last title defence and he was the challenger this time.

During those years he had earned the displeasure of a considerable number of American people by declining their Government's invitation for him to join the Armed Forces and serve in Vietnam.

At that time, Ali had said, more than somewhat sarcastically: 'Those Vietcong never called me nigger.' He had consistently refused to retract that statement. Not that all the black Americans present were out-and-out Ali fans, either. Frazier was a brother and an undefeated champ. For many of them, then, this was a case of 'The King is dead – long live the King.'

As the closed-circuit commentator, it was impossible for me to convey this unique atmosphere to the early morning live viewers at cinemas up and down Britain. This really was one of those times when you had to be there. So I concentrated on the boxing instead and that, too, turned out to be as good as it gets.

If ever two fighters were made for each other, these two were. Their contrasting styles blended into the perfect spectacle to suit all tastes, an enthralling mix of the aesthetic, scientific and downright brutal. Ali lost on points and even survived a knock down near the end. But no one, not even the most volatile of his detractors, ever questioned his courage or his sheer nobility again. It was in this, his first major defeat, that Ali truly earned his epithet 'The Greatest'.

Some readers might feel that it is obscene for me to glorify a contest which resulted in both combatants being taken to hospital where, incidentally, the x-rays of Ali's jaw were stolen as souvenirs.

In mitigation, I have settled for this snippet from an anonymous American writer: 'We give maximum expression to our blood lust in the mass spectator sport of boxing. Some of us are Roman enough to admit our love and need of the sport. Others pretend to look the other way. But when a heavyweight championship fight rolls around, the world takes a moral holiday and we are all tuned in.' So, say hello to Reggie the Roman!

Ali and Frazier met twice more with Muhammad winning both times. In all, they contested 41 supercharged rounds and I have to say, hand on heart, that theirs were the three fights that will live longest in my memory.

Indeed, for me, the long-haired, kipper-tied, flared-trousered, flamboyant 1970s turned out to be the decade that surpassed all others as far as boxing was concerned.

The heavyweights were the undisputed crowd-pleasers of this era and everyone, from TV companies to tinpot dictators, vied for a slice of the action, creating a kind of carousel that propelled me to some of the most unlikely venues in the world.

Although America was still the headquarters and I was always very happy to report for duty there, some of the other unlikely locations during this magical period read like a one-legged hithchiker's guide to the galaxy. Manila, Jamaica, Jakarta, Zaire, São Paulo, Sun City, Kuala Lumpur and Tokyo all became almost just another day at this crazy office of mine.

If boxing was becoming a universal pantomime in which TV presented the world and his wife with the opportunity of choosing their own heroes and villains, the principal boys provided a very impressive cast list with the likes of Ali, Frazier, George Foreman, Larry Holmes, Leon Spinks, Jerry Quarry, Gerry Cooney and Ken Norton.

It was Norton who was unwittingly and indirectly

involved in both my brushes with death on 'active' boxing service. And it was Norton who consistently gave Ali most trouble in the ring. Although he lost twice to Muhammad on points, Norton succeeded in breaking Ali's jaw in their first fight and reducing 'the Greatest' to a state of total exhaustion in the second. This handsome marine-cum-boxer-cum-film star could have been a mythical pale horse rider, for all I know.

That third contest was staged in the old Yankee Stadium baseball field in New York in September 1976. For what was probably the one and only time in history the Brooklyn police force was on strike and all hell broke loose as a result.

The signs were ominous when it was announced that the media would be transported through Harlem in a locked vehicle and that no one was to leave it *en route* under any circumstances.

With only a skeleton security service on duty, muggings were taking place inside and outside the famous old venue. After the fight, a nightmare engulfed media personnel when the tunnel housing the dressing-rooms became a mass of trapped heaving humanity. We were lifted off our collective feet, gasping for air and most of us were convinced we were going to suffocate or, at the very least, have our ribs broken.

A disaster was only averted when a posse of huge black men appeared at one end of the corridor hoisting a woman aloft above their heads and shouting, 'Make way for Ali's Ma!' Although I am not quite old enough to have been present at the parting of the Red Sea, this little miracle was a dead ringer for that Old Testament one, I promise you.

I won't attempt to describe how they managed it because I just don't know, but somehow this regal party cut a swathe through what appeared to be an impenetrable crowd right into the great man's dressing-room where, we were reliably informed by those who were still trapped inside it for many hours, his exhausted prostate body was comforted by his mother.

As often happens on hairy occasions like this, the proceedings had begun with a touch of black humour. Would you believe, the Press toilets were bang in the middle of that no-go corridor? Suspecting that this might create a problem, I suggested to my neighbour, the BBC commentator, Harry Carpenter: 'I think we might have to pee under the ring.'

A New York accent growled back: 'Oh no, you don't buddy!' It came, I discovered, from one of a couple of TV technicians whose job it was to keep some wires in place beneath the ring throughout the duration of the fight.

My second close call via Mr Norton came after he was knocked out by Gerry Cooney in New York.

I was lumbered with the job of getting a tape of a TV recording on to the flight back to London. I was quite thrilled when a helicopter conveyed me and the tape from the top of the Pan Am building in Manhattan to Kennedy Airport. However, I was later horrified to learn that the helicopter that took off after mine, crashed into the street causing death and mayhem. The Pan Am pad was never used again.

So, even though I never turned out to be the ring tiger I aspired to in my youth, I have certainly been a lucky old pussy cat when it comes to using up my quota of lives.

CHAPTER NINETEEN
WALKING WITH KINGS

'Or walk with Kings – nor lose
the common touch'
RUDYARD KIPLING

You would think that a boxing contest that was covered by some of America's leading modern literary figures and was the subject of an award-winning film, first shown nearly 25 years after the event it portrays took place, would deserve the hysterical hype that claims it is – in the words of that most abused of all sporting epithets – 'The Fight Of The Century'.

Well, quite frankly, the 'Rumble In the Jungle' as it also became known, did not deserve it. As an exhibition of the 'sweet science' it failed even to rate in this 'commoner's' top ten.

'The Greatest' himself, however, would hotly dispute my verdict. After knocking out George Foreman in the 8th round in Kinshasa, Zaire, on 30 October 1974, to regain the world heavyweight championship, he said: 'This was a real scientific fight, a real thinkin' fight. For me it was, anyway. Everythin' I did had a purpose.'

But I think Foreman was nearer the mark when he told me years later: 'Ali didn't beat me, I beat myself. I punched myself out.'

No matter, as an atmospheric event, this epic was out on its own in the history of the prize-fighting ring. The leading players, the venue, and the shock climax made it almost as unforgettable as those Ali-Frazier sagas. The almost superhuman way in which Ali absorbed Foreman's powerful but ponderous blows convinced some fans that he could, indeed, walk on water.

Millions of words have already been expended on describing this unique occasion, so I do not propose to add my two penn'orth. But I would like to mention the disquiet I feel over the way it was depicted in the recent film *When We Were Kings*.

The American brothers who were responsible for this box office hit turned it into a hymn of praise for black America while, in my opinion, somewhat patronising their African cousins and totally disregarding some white 'faces' who had something to do with staging the event in the first place.

The most glaring omission in this respect concerned the two men who put up the letters of credit, promoters Hank Schwarz of New York Video Techniques and Londoner John Daly of Hemdale Leisure Corporation. The now departed despot President Mobutu had site rights but did not attend on the night for fear of being bumped off.

Don King, heavily featured in the film, was only the matchmaker. Schwarz and Daly were the promoters, a fact which could not have escaped the film makers' attention since both mens' names figured prominently in the posters and programmes in Kinshasa. There was no sight on screen either, of Ali's indispensable white trainer, Angelo Dundee.

The film, which is reported to have taken 23 years to edit, had a crew of 100 who spent 55 days in what was once the old Belgian Congo because of a postponement when Foreman suffered a cut eye in training.

Sugar Ray Robinson and I. For me, Sugar Ray has always been the best
pound-for-pound champion.   © Derek Rowe

The 'Ambling Alp', Primo Canera, 19st, towers over the Twins when training in London. He was world champion from 1933-34.

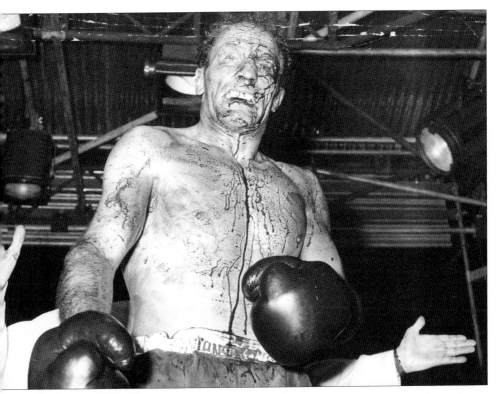

Top: The bloody end. Henry Cooper takes a battering in his second fight with Muhammad Ali.

Bottom: Presenting Sugar Ray Leonard with a memento in London. Our 'Enery approves.

Top: The football icons, left to right, John Charles, Nat Lofthouse, Sir Tom Finney with Henry Cooper and me, 1998.

© Sam Teare

Bottom: What a team! Me and Jim Watt.

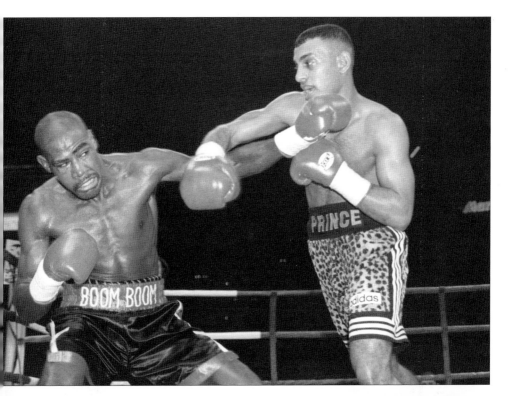

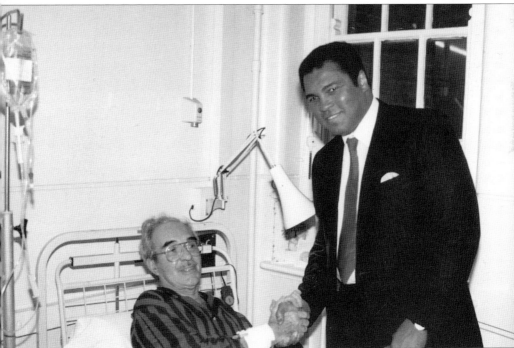

Top: Naseem Hamed shows might is right, defeating Tom Johnson to win a second world title.
                                                                                    © *Sam Teare*

Bottom: Trying to beat the final count – Ali's surprise visit to Hammersmith Hospital was the perfect tonic. Dr Swirsky was my winning second.

Waiting to receive my OBE at Buckingham Palace. My daughter Sally-Anne stands left, with my wife Connie and daughter Susan.

Top: Justin Fortune crumples under Lennox's onslaught, Dublin 1995.

Bottom: All smiles receiving my OBE.

A special moment; receiving an award for 'Excellence in Boxing Journalism' in New York.

© Jerry Munson

They painted a canvas that was as much to do with a musical carnival of brothers as it was a world boxing title fight. The invading American musicians and their motley crew of companions had a very limited understanding of or rapport with either the language or the culture of the French-speaking Zaireois.

I feel some sympathy for one of the musicians I became pals with. I must confess that this guy had me completely fooled. When I saw him accompanying Foreman on the heavy bag with his frenzied bongo drum beating, I thought he was, at the very least, one of those Leopard men who used to cause mayhem in those parts a few years earlier. He was done up in the most elaborate tropical gear you could imagine, complete with gaudy head dress. Thinking that he would make a great subject for an interview, I tentatively approached him and said in stupid, slow, pigeon English: 'What is your name and where are you from?' He looked down at me and drawled: 'I'm Black Mack from LA. And I'm working the lounge at The Inter-Continental Hotel.

But it was Foreman's manager, Dick Sadler, who best summed up the whole circus when he looked at a group of these imported crew one day and remarked to me: 'I can't wait to get away from my African brothers and home to my American mother.'

My special pal throughout this special trip, however, was an old Cockney sparring partner of mine, a throwback of an old pro who fought for many years out of Blackfriars. He was, Tom Daly, father of the young promotional entrepeneur John who is still currently producing big buck award winning films for Hemdale in Los Angeles.

I was so close to Tom that I broke a rule of a lifetime and secured an interview for boxing nut John when he was a teenager with a view to his becoming my tea boy at the *Evening News*. He failed to turn up and I gave his old man a right coating over it. Tom had the last laugh, though, when he sat beside me, as his son's guest of honour, in a ringside seat in deepest Africa all those years later.

John Daly also came to the rescue of many of the British journalists, whose proprietors were reluctant to fund a second trip after the initial postponement, by underwriting their travel costs.

As the then chairman of the British Boxing Writers Association, I was nominated to do this deal with Mobutu's media chieftan, a gentleman by the name of Tshimpumpu, who wore a large fur hat in temperatures that would have done justice to a greenhouse.

When it came to organising things, Tshimpumpu turned out to be one of the world's slowest administrators and I had to doorstep him practically day and night to get the appropriate air tickets to England.

Talking of briefs, this was the performance above all others that paid for Ali's ticket to ride to immortality. Approaching 39 years of age and after a prolific number of fights, he was universally tipped to be not just defeated but destroyed by the ferocious Foreman, who had recently smashed Joe Frazier to the canvas six times inside two rounds.

Like many of my Press pals, I had let my head overrule my heart and tipped Foreman to win, too. If there had been the faintest doubt in my mind this was expelled by the pre-fight quote Foreman gave me. Due to TV programming demands in America the bout was due to start in the wee small hours. When I asked Foreman whether this bothered him, he simply gave an evil grin and said: 'When I was a kid in Houston, Texas, I won all my fights in the early hours of the morning.' Then, as if I needed any more convincing he added that Houston had the highest crime rate in the USA. How strange then that this mean, impolite sinisterly handsome man of very few words has metamorphosed into the fat jolly grandfather who was still boxing, commentating and, miraculously, bible punching when this book went to press.

I became convinced, way back then, that a miracle of a different kind was about to happen when, just before the first bell, I was on the receiving end of an extraordinary verbal reprimand from Ali himself. He leaned over the top rope, wagged his finger at me and said: 'I hear you been telling the people in England that I'm gonna lose – shame on you. This nigger can't whip my arse!' I knew then that I had tipped a loser, but I felt like shouting for joy because, just like the entire population of Zaire, I loved 'The Greatest' too.

As for big George, he presented me with the silver microphone, which the American Boxing Writers Association awarded me for 'Excellence in Broadcasting Journalism' 20 years after Zaire. He told me then that his one big regret about those early years was that 'I wish I had been nicer to people'.

He also surprisingly revealed to me on another occasion that he sometimes felt genuine physical fear before a fight. Straightfaced, he swore: 'I was so afraid when Joe Frazier and I were psyching each other out eyeball to eyeball in the ring before our fight, that I was hoping he would not drop his eyes in case he saw my knees knocking.' Good on you, George.

Floyd Patterson, too, who happened to have the fastest hands of any heavyweight champ including Ali, told me when we were commentating together in South

Africa that he had felt fear in his first disastrous fight with the Swede Ingemar Johannson back in the 1960s. 'I had overtrained,' he said: 'And suddenly knew I couldn't do justice to myself and froze.'

Nice guy Floyd was so sincerely patriotic that, for weeks afterwards, he donned a beard and false moustache whenever he went out to 'disguise my shame for letting down my country'. You couldn't make it up, could you? Bless 'em!

CHAPTER TWENTY

PAL ALI

'If you can dream – and not make
dreams your master'
RUDYARD KIPLING

The last time I met Muhammad Ali, a year ago, we hugged, then he grinned and whispered in my ear: 'We can't keep doing this in public – they'll all think we're a couple of fairies.'

Those words and the irony in them brought tears to my eyes. For if there was one person on God's green earth who could have made me believe in fairies, and leprechauns or Father Christmas, even, it was this man among men – this fearless, fragile man child.

Tragically, his body had been vanquished by his own surreal dreams of – if not out-and-out divinity – then indestructibility, but those dreams will never master the free spirit in him.

What compelling dreams they were! The most accurate description of this extraordinary man comes from that doyen of sportswriters, Hugh McIlvanney: 'At the heart of the hypnotic appeal which his personality has for so many of us is an irrational suspicion that here is a man capable of willing his own outrageous image of himself into reality' wrote Hugh at the time when 'The Greatest' was in his prime.

None of us were to know then, of course, the horrible

consequences of his manic invitations to mighty men such as George Foreman and Larry Holmes to punch either his or their own lights out, as George did but Larry didn't. The stark conclusion of these fearless acts of folly inevitably proved that he was not invincible, but they sure as hell earned him immortality.

In 1989 when I was lying critically ill in a Hammersmith Hospital with septicaemia and pneumonia, Ali came and sat on my bed, took my hand in his and said a prayer for my recovery. My mind sped through the emotional gearbox from surprise to gratitude, humility and then downright terror. I thought: 'Blimey! If he's come all this way to pay his last respects, I must be on my way out any minute.'

In truth, my old pal and rival Harry Carpenter had just driven Ali from the BBC TV centre to visit me. He had been there taking part in a show and, as Frank Bruno's sidekick Harry, tells it, he kept asking: 'Where's Reggie?'

We go back a long way, Pal Ali, and me. And it's been a journey in which he's had me laughing, crying, holding my breath, saying my prayers and cursing the fates for him: but mostly laughing.

As a broadcaster, Ali ruined me for everyone else. He was like a highly trained Alsatian. Providing he took a shine to you, he would do anything for you. Sometimes he did things you did not particularly want him to do, just to feed his insatiable appetite for mischief and, of course, to keep you on your toes.

None of his antics with me were quite as bizarre as the time he got bored in the middle of a fight and requested me to interview him between rounds. Although, as I shall illustrate, there were plenty of other incidents that came close.

He got bored in this particular fight because it took place in Jakarta and Ali did not know many people there on a personal level. 'The Greatest' was not the only vain fighter I have met, in fact, they are all vain, to a man.

Just like every other performer, there is a longing to be universally loved deep inside everyone of them. Although, I must confess, that while punching people on the nose is a sure way to get yourself noticed, it is hardly an appropriate way of showing peace and goodwill to all men.

As he matured from an uncertain braggart into a philosophical adult, however, Ali had a need not, just for public acclaim, but for one-to-one communion.

The reasons he seemed to take me to his bosom may sound shallow, but for him they were valid. First he liked me because I was British and the British Boxing Board were the last official body to strip him of his title when he refused to fight in Vietnam.

Second, he liked my British manners. Saying 'please' and 'thank you', unlike so many of his American compatriots, were important gestures of respect as far as he was concerned.

Perhaps more significantly – and I blush to say this – he just found me a nice, cuddly little geezer.

In Jakarta, in 1973, he was fighting a man called Rudi Lubbers and he was toying with him. Now, this happened to be an important occasion for me as a commentator, because it was the first satelite show, sporting or otherwise, to come out of Jakarta to the Western world.

Between rounds, he suddenly leaned over the rope and said: 'Get up here, Reggie'. Flabbergasted, I told the people back in the *World Of Sport* studio in London about the little bit of history to which Ali was about to treat them. Talking to sportsmen before and after events was by now old hat, admittedly. Chatting them up in the middle of a match, however, was unheard of.

But, wouldn't you know it? The director, David Scott, with a news sense second to none, says in my ear, in the most matter-of-fact tones imaginable: 'You'll have to hold on, old boy. We've got an interview with a winning jockey at Catterick after this race. So yours will have to wait.'

When I called back to Ali that I'd talk to him later, he was, understandably, not best pleased. Luckily, after the next round he still had not put his man away yet and he shrugged off his sulks long enough to yell into the microphone while he was sitting on his stool. This is what he told millions of viewers in Britain: 'I want to apologise to all my friends in Great Britain for not putting this bum away yet. Years ago, I would have finished him off by now. But I'm getting old and tired, so you'll just have to excuse me, please, folks.'

Gloriously, and tragically, he was to go on fighting for another eight years.

After this fight, though, my old guv'nor, Head of Sport John Bromley, was so flushed with success at the unexpected coup that he asked me to follow it up with a highly unlikely piece. In the 1970s soccer panels were an all-the-rage novelty on TV here and there was one due on screen immediately after the big fight.

If memory serves, it comprised Malcolm Allison, Paddy Crerand, Derek Dougan and Brian Clough. The star of the show was Cloughie, of course, and 'Brommers' asked me whether I could get Ali to gee Cloughie up for the viewers' entertainment.

Now, old Big 'Ead may not be too flattered to hear this right now, but Ali did not know him from Adam. So, in the middle of the usual after-fight *mêlée* in the ring, I said to Ali: 'We've got a white guy in football back home who pops off a lot. Just shut him up for me, will you.' 'Pop off' is an American expression for talking too much. I added that the man's name was Brian Clough, not for a moment expecting that Ali would remember it. Good as gold, he looked straight at our camera and said: 'I hear there's a man in England who's worse than me for poppin' off.' Then he pauses and puts his gloved hand to his chin, as if he is deep in thought. At this point, I was going to yell 'cut' and prompt him.

Suddenly, he resumes speaking: 'Brian Clough – I hear you talk a lot. Well, Clough, that's enough. There's only one man in the world who's allowed to pop off and that's me. So, do you hear me, Brian Clough, that is enough.'

When the two men eventually met in America, Ali was shocked at how small Brian was. He had expected him to look like one of those American grid iron giants.

For sheer broadcasting excellence, though, Ali surpassed himself during the build-up to that first fight with Joe Frazier. There was so much adulation surrounding him that he could not get out of the hotel during the day. The only privacy he got was on his early morning run. One day I got a message to him that I needed him. Incidentally, with one exception, he never demanded or even requested payment from my TV company. Ali got word back to me that I would have to come round very early in the morning after the road running.

When I got to his room I was confronted with a floor full of snoring sparring partners and Ali was lying prostrate on the bed with a sheet pulled over him, apparently well and truly in the land of Nod.

The interview was to go out live in London and the guys in the studio were biting their nails when I reported that Ali appeared to be fast asleep.

All of a sudden, he pulled the sheet away from his face and sat up in bed. I mouthed the words *World Of Sport* at him, and I knew he was in the starting blocks. That esteemed award-winning journalist, Ian Wooldridge of the *Daily Mail*, did the telephone interview and after Ian had wished him a 'good morning' and asked after his wellbeing, Ali was off and running: 'Is this *World of Sport* in Britain?' He asked. When Ian informed him that it was Ali continued: 'Well, *World of Sport* – and with this second piece of free advertising he gave me a knowing wink – then continued: 'Yours is the best show in all of Britain, but I'm getting irritated with you, *World of Sport* 'cos you're making me nervous before the big fight.' Then he gave them a five-minute monologue and I had to make frantic signals for him to wind up.

He signed off with: 'I've got to go now, but I'm goin' to shock and amaze you against Frazier.' Then he imitated the hit records of the time, which faded out repetitively and slowly: 'The satellite's leavin', the satellite's leavin' and then, in a whisper, 'the satellite's leavin'.

With that, he handed the telephone back to me, pulled the sheet back over his head and I tiptoed my way out through the hulking prostrate bodies.

Ironically, the only time Ali ever asked me for money was when I lost him to the opposition – the BBC. He was in this country and in his prime at a time when TV companies were sometimes spending millions on a single show. He wanted a paltry £1,000 to be interviewed as a personality and not just a sportsman for an hour.

The programme controller at Thames TV at the time was a nice man named Brian Tesler. I suggested that a big name interviewer like David Frost or Eamon Andrews could do the job. Brian said he would very much like to, but that Jeremy Isaacs was doing a series in Bangladesh that was going to take up all his time and manpower.

So Ali went to the BBC instead and gave what Michael Parkinson or 'Parky' still says was his most entertaining interview ever.

During a second Parkinson-Ali interview 'The Greatest' memorably lost his temper. The main reason for that, I can now reveal, is that that some boxing people over here who should have known better wound Ali up beforehand by telling him that Michael was anti-boxing, mainly because he frequently ridiculed Joe Bugner.

Whenever I've been on the wrong end of Ali's temper, he has always been playacting, although he can make the act look frighteningly real, as he did once when we were sitting beside a swimming-pool in Las Vegas.

I had a bottle of beer under my deck chair and Ali asked for a swig. Just as he was taking it, he saw his manager, the black Muslim Herbert Muhammad, approaching us. Ali used his famous fast hands to such effect that within seconds he had thrust the bottle into my hand and and was screaming at me: 'Put that bottle down! I don't like people drinking near me. You should know better!' He was bursting to laugh as he said it; but just like a naughty schoolboy, he was afraid of the headmaster.

Unsurprisingly, Herbert Muhammad and the rest of his Muslim cronies eventually disappeared into the sunset.

Yet, in my opinion, Ali was the most devout one among them. He was the most generous-spirited man I've ever known. He was constantly giving unsolicited and unpublicised financial gifts to poor kids in the street and he had an unerring eye for spotting and helping people who were really in need.

The one thing that Ali would not put up with at any

price, though, was anyone who tried to take advantage of his generous nature by attempting to take the mickey out of him.

On another visit to this country, I warned him against appearing on a TV show with Freddie Starr because of that comedian's penchant for taking the mickey. Sure enough, this was confirmed for him soon after when he was taking a bow at a Joe Bugner fight when Freddie Starr, who was in the audience, stood up and began baiting him. When the thunderclouds started appearing in Ali's eyes, Mickey Duff tried to placate him by telling him that this man was the famous comedian. Ali simply fixed Freddie with an imperious stare and shouted back: 'They tell me you're famous. Well, I've never seen or heard of you, so sit down. This is my show.' Freddie sat down sheepishly, but this little story had a happy ending when the two men became pals later – strictly on Ali's terms, though.

Maybe, he couldn't take to Freddie at first because he fancied himself as a bit of a comedian, too. He wasn't half bad, either. He once gave me a wrist watch with a picture of himself on it. The next time he saw me, he asked: 'Have you still got the watch?'

When I replied that, of course, I still had it. He cracked: 'Well, all those niggers are smarter than you, they sold it.'

For me, that was vintage Ali. His sense of humour outside the ring was as impeccable as his sense of timing inside it.

The only way I can even attempt to come to terms with the suffering he has endured since his fabulous career took him a fight or two too far and Parkinson's disease compounded that error, is to find scant consolation in a lyric from a Don Maclean song about Van Gogh, which goes: 'This world was never meant for one as beautiful as you ...'

CHAPTER TWENTY-ONE
BOOMING BRITAIN

'When you've shouted Rule Britannia,
When you've sung God save the Queen'
RUDYARD KIPLING

Boxing was booming back in Blighty, too. Our fighters won as many as five world titles in the 1970s and that was before those honours were devalued by the proliferation of new boxing boards, councils and organisations and when world championship belts started getting tossed around like confetti. One even finished up in a London dustbin, dumped there by American heavyweight Riddick Bowe in a publicity stunt.

They were a fascinating ethnic mix, this fabulous five – Ken Buchanan hailed from Edinburgh, Jim Watt was a Glasgwegian, John Conteh was a coffee-coloured Scouse, John Stracey, a Cockney and Maurice Hope was born in Antigua. But the patriotic songs of praise that they inspired in bar rooms up and down the country sounded as British as 'Roll Out The Barrel'.

Buchanan was a carpenter with a chip on his shoulder, but what a winning chip it turned out to be. He never got over the hostility he encountered as a sensitive, introverted schoolboy on an Edinburgh council estate. That dispiriting experience motivated his will to win to such an extent that I rate him right up there with the late Ted Kid Lewis as Britain's best ever overseas boxer.

I can still see Kenny sitting in his corner in San Juan, Puerto Rico, in 1970 with an umbrella shielding his lily-white body from the blazing sun. He blasted out a 15-round points win in a bloody battle with Ismael Laguna to claim the world lightweight crown. Even then, though, nearly 30 years ago, there were squabbles between the governing bodies. The British Boxing Board of Control, who favoured the World Boxing Council, refused to sanction Buchanan's World Boxing Association's version of the title. So, Kenny, who always reckoned that the world and its dog was against him, had to go and do it all over again against Laguna a year later at Madison Square Garden before he was universally recognised as a genuine world champion.

And what a champion! He won five out of six fights at the legendary Garden and was revered by the American afficianados as much as he was in his own country. Incidentally, I pulled off a coup by obtaining the taped recording of that first title triumph for ITV for a paltry £1,000 by conning local TV executives that they were right in believing that our man had absolutely no chance.

Sadly this old world, which Buchanan so mysteriously mistrusted even into middle age, eventually had its wicked way with him and he ran into financial and health problems. As recently as 1996 he failed to turn up at a celebration dinner at Madison Square Garden, which had been arranged especially to honour him and some other outstanding ex-world champions. The last time we contacted each other he assured me that his life had improved and that he was taking it a day at a time even though he was right back to where he started – as a carpenter.

Another who is taking life a day at a time these days, is John Conteh, who happens to be a highly articulate colleague of mine on the after-dinner speaking circuit. As well as being one of the most talented fighters these islands ever produced, John was among, the most handsome and – not always for the right reasons – the most newsworthy. His drinking and drug escapades filled more newspaper column inches than the rest of his ring contemporaries put together, but I will discuss this in greater detail later.

For now, though, I prefer to remember the way this man had us all basking in his reflected glory when, at the age of 23, he outpointed Jorge Ahumada of Argentina over 15 gruelling rounds at Wembley to bring the world light heavyweight championship back to these shores – 25 years after my old pal Freddie Mills had last held it on our behalf.

John H Stracey, who was as Cockney as jellied eels, pulled off one of the biggest surprises ever when he dethroned that great Mexican Jose Napoles on his home territory. Napoles had footwork and moves that set me drooling, but Stracey's shrewd manager, Terry Lawless, was also a master of timing and he detected the rapid rate at which veteran Napoles was declining when he took his man to South America on their mission impossible.

After being put down soon after the start, Stracey stopped the seemingly unstoppable world welterweight champion in six rounds. That was in 1976 and, while we are talking about yesteryear that current TV heart throb, the supremely talented presenter, Desmond Lynam, did the round-by-round radio commentary on that one.

John H 'emigrated' up north after he quit the game and is now domiciled in the Wirral in Cheshire. He earns a good living as a singer and comedian on the northern nightclub circuit.

Maurice Hope and Jim Watt were both crowned in 1979. Maurice won the world light middleweight title against Italian Rocky Mattioli in the unlikely setting of a tent on a beach in San Remo. The reason for this was that TV was pulling the shots by now and the venue and the live gate money became almost insignificant when it came to the TV ratings war.

When Maurice's pretty girlfriend, Pat, fainted at the ringside from the tension of it all, I was nearly killed in the rush of British Pressmen anxious to give her the kiss of life. Only two Pressmen were present when Maurice married Pat a couple of years later in Las Vegas. Colin Hart of the *Sun* and Peter Moss of the *Daily Mail* acted as witnesses for the ceremony, which was held only hours after Maurice eventually lost the title to the new kid on the light middleweight block, Wilfred Benitez.

Maurice, who was once a close neighbour of mine, has now retired to Antigua where his teenage son was tragically killed in a car accident while on a visit to his father.

Jim Watt was to experience a similar horror when he, too, lost a son in a road accident. The pair were stablemates under Terry Lawless' management, as was Stracey and flyweight Charlie Magri who was also to go on to a world title triumph in 1983.

To coin an irresistible cliché, Jim really did belong to Glasgow the night he defeated Colombian Alfredo Pitalua in his native city in April 1979. He went on to make four successful defences of the world lightweight title, which was then a record for a British boxer.

Jim was to become my TV commentating partner for many years and ours is a friendship that I shall enlarge upon later. The most entertaining tribute he has ever been paid for his fabulous defensive skills came from a veteran New York critic, Barney Nagler, who was sitting next to the pair of us at a fight between two Americans in the USA and failed to recognise Jim. Upon hearing our conversation, Nagler started a verbal exchange with Watt that went like this: Barney: 'Are you a Brit?' Jim: 'Aye.' Barney: 'May I enquire what you are doing here?' Jim: 'Commentating.' Barney: 'Have you boxed yourself, by any chance?' Jim: 'Well, as a matter of fact I was a world champion.' Whereupon, Barney stared long and hard at Jim's handsome, unmarked face and retorted: 'Jeez! You must have been boring.'

But believe me boring was the last thing Jim was, as a fighter or as a man. The entire domestic boxing scene was anything but boring during this colourful decade. How could it be with characters like the Finnegan brothers, Chris and Kevin, and Chris's arch rival, gypsy Johnny Frankham, around? Olympic gold medalist Chris and his even more stylish brother were renowned not so much for their superb boxing skills as for their courage and endurance in the ring and in the pub.

When it came to Guinness either of them could have drunk it for Ireland. When Chris was forced to retire with a detached retina, nurses at Moorfield Eye Hospital swore he tore the stitches open when he was reaching for a crate of Guinness from under the bed. When Kevin won the European middleweight championship in Paris, one of my Press pals, Peter Batt wrote: 'The arm that launched a thousand pints of Guinness was raised in triumph last night ...'

The pair of them are still raising their arms and everyone else's spirits with their humour and *bonhomie*. Eccentric Kevin was, at the last time of sighting, an artist and a beach bum somewhere in the Mediterranean and Chris is, appropriately enough, a publican. Sadly, however, Chris's wife, Cheryl, died young. What a character she was. At an infamous Royal Albert Hall punch-up between the rival fans of Finnegan and Frankham, Cheryl was in there throwing hooks and curses that curdled the blood of most of the macho combatants.

The fascinating aspect of those kind of ringside bust-ups was that, in those days, they were more comical than frightening. Maybe it was because our generations were brought up on harmless Hollywood cowboy bar room brawls and not the psycopathic fare that is served up to youngsters today. All I know is that the kind of partisan brawls that occasionally erupted then were actually fun to watch and I still don't feel the need to apologise for them now.

Newspapers had a more cavalier approach to violence in those seemingly more innocent times, too. The Finnegan–Frankham shindig occurred on the eve of the Derby. Out on Epsom Downs next morning word got around that hostilities were about to be resumed as a preliminary to the big race.

The two chief protagonists were pictured in the papers shaping up to each other, but it turned into a cross between a jig and a knees-up between the rival supporters and not a blow was struck in anger.

Both Chris and Johnny laughed the whole affair off as a piece of harmless horseplay and declared that 'win or lose they would all have some booze'. I would hate to think that I am indulging in the whimsy common to all old men when I say that in those days everyone, in and out of the game, seemed to be more game for a laugh. Certainly boxing itself became a lot more soulless and far more calculating with the advent of the materialistic 1980s.

If I inadvertently give you the impression that a

bunch of comedians were running the show at this time then I could not be more misleading.

For those who had succeeded, those Czar-like characters Solomons and Levene were anything but a joke. They were more hard-headed.

If a young man wanted to throw punches for a living it would be an advantage to his career if he had the backing and the blessing, experience and skills of one or all of Messrs Jarvis Astaire, Mickey Duff, Mike Barrett and Terry Lawless. No one proved this more spectacularly or more painfully than the hot-headed John Conteh, who tried to go it more or less alone, with the help of his unqualified brother, and finished up beaten and near broke.

One of this formidable foursome was Jarvis Astaire, a wealthy businessman and boxing afficianado, who had been involved with fighters since the immediate post-war years as a part-time manager. 'Jolly' Jack Solomons had always been jealous of any possible rival, and so became aware of the threat Astaire could some day mount against his own supremacy and began calling him wrongly and vindictively 'Mr X' which was just the kind of label this shrewd old publicist hoped the tabloid newspaper headline writers would lap up.

This ruse rebounded on Jack in more ways than one. First, it lent Astaire an air of mystique, which he was not seeking; that gave the impression that the man was more influential than he actually was at that time. Second, when Solomons began to refer to Astaire, clearly wrongly and with improper motives, as 'Mr X and his syndicate' this campaign attracted the attention of the influential American *Ring* magazine and they printed a long article about Jarvis.

The magazine soon printed an abject apology – the only

time this esteemed publication had ever used the entire page of the inside cover on a single item. Solomons, himself, quickly and rightly became discredited by the affair.

Much later, a British newspaper acquired and published a copy of an agreement, signed in 1979. This document was described by Tom Pendry, the then Labour Shadow Minister for Sport and an ex-Oxford boxer as 'an oligopoly'. Whatever that meant. It was the kind of posh word that guaranteed an immediate Boxing Board of Control enquiry. After a six-hour meeting it came up with the verdict that the agreement did not contravene the law of the land or the Board's own regulations.

The Board added the following unsolicited testimonial: 'Far from being against the interests of boxing, it is considered that, without this group's active participation, boxing in this country would not be in the healthy state it is now.'

I must say that I agreed with the Board on that issue. Far be it for me, a fighter's man first, last and foremost to yap like an establishment poodle, but someone has to run the show whatever that show happens to be and, for me, this was a case of 'better the devil you know'.

Most boxing promoters, with the odd glaring exception, deserve no less of a bad press than film producers.

To his credit, Mike Barrett published a complete breakdown of Charlie Magri's earnings, which also showed promotional losses.

I enjoyed working friendships with all four men, but I never felt any sense of ambivalence towards the boxers, as a result. I did not see it as running with the hare and hunting with the hounds. The simple reason was this, although it pains me to say it, in 99 cases out of 100 disgruntled boxers were their own financial worst enemy. Those who went broke invariably took bad advice from family, friends and hangers-on. The fighters are not treated in a way that some people seem to want to think. managers, matchmakers and promoters – some retired boxers – work long and hard for their money, too. Their job is no picnic – one of those old trade unionists would have had a nervous breakdown looking at the hours some of these men put in.

Currently there are some 65 licenced promoters in the UK, only a handful consistantly make it pay. Without TV backing it's a risky gamble.

I have known Jarvis Astaire and Mickey Duff for most of their lives. The great financial advantages they had over their colourful predecessors was the growth of live televised boxing and sponsorship, which was unheard of in Jack Solomons, and Harry Levene's times.

Mickey, as I may have mentioned earlier, was as steeped in boxing as any man I've ever met, including my grandfather, father and uncle. He was a matchmaker at 19 and would love to have made matches for Solomons if he had been given his head. When he was a younger man, he had every boxing telephone number off by heart. Apart from his love of casino gambling, which he has confessed has won and lost him fortunes in his time, he has never had any other interests outside of boxing. You could describe him as obsessive. He talked about nothing else and when it came to talking he was definitely the undisputed 'word champion'.

Conversely, Jarvis tried to keep his name out of the boxing business as much as he could. He says it took up only 10 per cent of his financial interests, but represented 90 per cent of his reputation. And says that all will be revealed in an autobiography *Encounters*.

He's into property development and the entertainment

business now and was Dustin Hoffman's manager. By the 1990s he had become deputy chairman of Wembley Stadium and Arena complex. He is also very proud of his charity work with the London Federation of Boys Clubs (now of younger people) and as former chief barker of the Variety Club of Great Britain and fund-raiser for The Royal Free Hospital.

Mike Barrett was a man cast in the same mould of those Beau Brummels, Solomons and Levene. He was always immaculately groomed and seldom appeared at one of his own or anyone else's promotions dressed in anything other than his dinner suit and bow tie.

He owned wharves and warehouses and is married to a professional singer Rosemary Carr, who is still making records. His was a fresh face. He was always optimistic, enthusiastic and articulate. Apart from his dress sense, he was as unlike the old boxing stereotypes as you could possibly meet. Mike eventually wound down from promotions.

Unlike the other three, Terry Lawless was involved in the gymnasium on a daily basis with his large stable of boxers, who were no doubt the best collection under any one man's guidance in British boxing history. In addition to his four world champions that I have already mentioned, he was also responsible for world champs Frank Bruno and Lloyd Honeyghan in the earlier stages of their careers.

A superb tactician and teacher, he was a caring, sharing, emotionally involved manager. So much so that he was regarded by the cynics in the game as an old mother hen with a boxing brood. If he had not teamed up with the men of power and influence, his boxers would have had to 'sing for their supper' somewhere else and that somewhere else wouldn't have made his boxers so successful – until the emergence of Frank Warren anyway. But that is another story.

CHAPTER TWENTY-TWO

FORGIVE US OUR PRESS PASSES

'The water comes out of my eyes, yet
I laugh when it falls – why?'
RUDYARD KIPLING

When Muhammad Ali fought Larry Holmes in Las Vegas on 2 October 1980, they billed it as the 'Last Hurrah'. Ironically, this turned out to be the case for both the greatest and yours truly, but that fateful night gave neither of us anything to cheer about.

Ali, as the whole world now knows, was to be mercilessly beaten by his former sparring partner – a beating that must have taken a terrible toll on his deteriorating physical condition.

As for me? I was made redundant by the *Evening News,* which suddenly folded and merged with the *Evening Standard* after 99 years of publication. I still don't know whether to laugh or cry about that all these years on. I was bitterly angry about losing my job after more than 40 years, but although I didn't know it at the time, this was to be the prelude to my full-time TV career.

I was in what I can only describe as a disused gold mine at the time I heard the dreadful news of the demise of my paper. It was 3am and the tail end of a heavy night when Patrick Collins, who was our sports columnist then and my colleague at this big fight, joined a group of us at our hotel bar and told me that he had just been informed over the telephone from London that our paper was to close in just over three weeks. Meanwhile, if we wanted our redundancy money we were expected to 'soldier on'.

At that precise moment we happened to be 'square bashing' at the Aladdin on the Vegas strip. This hotel, where we were billeted, had had its gambling licence temporarily revoked and the bar we were standing at faced the roulette, dice and card tables, which had all been covered with ghostly dust sheets. The whole place had an empty, eerie end-of-the-world feel about it, which just about summed up my mood.

Until that cruel moment the *News* had always had a benevolent family feel about it. Our office was the friendliest in Fleet Street. They never paid us as much as their rivals paid their staffs, but there were more long-serving 'lifers' like me there than there were on any other national paper. The bitterest pill to swallow was – that old codgers or not – we still outsold the *Standard*.

The sad truth was that the immediacy of TV news had put paid to the huge London evening newspaper market. In its heyday the *News* had sold more than two million copies a day, but when it followed the *Star* into oblivion, it was scratching around at the half million mark.

Mind you, there was not much room for sympathy for the demise of 99-year-old in my thoughts at that time, however much affection I had for it. The even sadder truth I had to face up to was how to scratch out a living in my mid-fifties. True, I had done a bit of freelance commentating, but not enough to earn my keep.

I can't speak for the rest of the poor sods in the ever-growing army of modern middle-aged redundancy victims, but the thought of having nowhere to go and nothing to leave the house for in the mornings terrified me.

Now, I appreciate that you might find it very difficult to sympathise with someone who had the exciting kind of work for which many men would gladly have donated their left legs. If this is starting to sound like I am getting the old violin out, then so be it. Not that all my memories of work were of the wine and roses variety, however. I have to confess that, except on one occasion which I shall relate later, I always found journalism to be more stressful than commentating.

In the blink of an eye, I can still recapture that feeling of dread as I sat in a lonely hotel room with nothing but virgin sheets of paper in front of me, which often looked as cold and forbidding as an ice-bound river or as daunting as a desert.

I am not the first man to observe that fighters and writers seem to have a rapport that you seldom encounter in other sports. This may have something to do with the loneliness and discipline of the two pursuits. They both offer wonderfully wide avenues of self-expression, but also require the responsibility of regular training and the relentless need to come to the line and deliver time after time.

The kind of deadlines faced by us hacks were the stuff of nightmares. For shows in this country, the daily paper boys had to give blow-by-blow telephone accounts of several fights on the same bill, with the crowd screaming in their ears and, as often as not, a bored copy taker at the other end of the line sighing, 'Is there much more of this stuff, old boy?'

Theirs was a race to meet the different edition times of the various districts the fighters hailed from. They would have to top all of that with considered, carefully written accounts after each fight. Very often, they were still on fight three while fight five was enfolding in front of them. No wonder so many readers used to wonder smugly whether the reporters were at the ringside or the bar at those moments of truth.

I used to help them out by braving the crush of the dressing-rooms to get them the necessary post-mortem quotes from the participants and they would return the favour when I was up against a fiece deadline on the other side of the Atlantic.

Either side of the world, my copy had to be in the office by 7am Greenwich Mean Time come rain, shine, earthquake, or dodgy telephone or cable connections. Whenever I faltered, dear old Desmond Hackett of the *Daily Express* would whisper in my ear: 'Give them the Lord's Prayer, give them hieroglyphics, but be sure to give them something my old commander.'

Sometimes, I used to think he wasn't joking, either. During those frantic years when I doubled this work with the closed-circuit and TV coverage, I often did not know whether I was on my typewriter, my telephone, my microphone, my elbow or my arse. The only part of my anatomy I could ever be sure I was not on was the place where five of my toes used to be.

At the mere mention of the late Desmond Hackett, the memories come flooding back of those old Press comrades concocting a heady, nostalgic brew that is every bit as potent as the last of the summer wine. What a colourful, irreplaceable bunch of characters they were, that old gang of mine, every one of whom I was honoured to serve with on what, in my misguided youth, I had imagined to be the wrong side of the ropes.

How could I ever forget those old-timers, my own contemporaries, like Hackett, the late Peter Wilson, the late George Whiting, the late Wally Bartleman, the late JL Manning, and that venerable but still very much alive trio of OBEs, – Frank Butler, Alan Hoby and Harry Carpenter. I spent almost as much of my life travelling the world with these guys than I did back home with my wife and family. Few men could withstand grouchy George Whiting's withering stare on the rare occasions he decided to 'psyche' someone out. I'll never forget the hangdog expression on the face of an unfortunate American hotel porter who found himself on the wrong end of that Whiting frown one morning long ago.

Old George had a club foot and the only footwear he found comfortable were his well-worn cricket boots. Suitably disguised with black shoe polish, they accompanied him around the world. In those crime-free days, hotel residents left their shoes outside their rooms to be cleaned overnight. On the occasion when he was staying at the Edison Hotel, off Broadway, in New York, George awoke to find nothing but carpet staring up at him from the spot where his boots should have been.

The climax to this tale was spectacularly dramatic when the porter literally snatched those decrepit old boots from the burning mouth of the incinerator down in the hotel boiler room to where he had so sensibly consigned them.

Another little tale, which I think takes some topping, concerns one of the many aeroplane journeys Hackett and Peter Wilson took together. This one was on an internal flight across the USA back in the 1950s. As seasoned drinkers, they were considerably put out by the fact that, in those days, it was illegal to consume more than two alcoholic beverages on any domestic flight in the USA.

Making full use of the imagination that regularly

entertained four million *Daily Express* readers, Hackett persuaded Wilson that it would be a good idea to buy a toy fire engine for his then schoolboy son Julian's birthday. Whether Julian, who went on to become famous as the BBC horse racing presenter ever received it, I know not. But I do recall Hackett making the proviso that his esteemed colleague should be sure to purchase the toy rubber hose pipe that fitted into the engine's water tank.

Clutching the toy engine to his bosom, Wilson boarded the aircraft with his usual aplomb and, as an old Harrovian who carried a sword stick wherever he went, that aplomb was considerable by American standards. To complete the picture of two eccentric English toffs, Hackett was wearing his trademark brown bowler hat.

The two permissible drinks were polished off before the stewardess had time to say welcome aboard, but no matter, because the fire engine's tank contained not water but a quart of rye whiskey.

That bewildered stewardess and her cabin crew colleagues spent the flight frantically trying to figure out how these, by now, 'goddam limeys' were managing to get thoroughly sloshed on water in paper cups from the cooler at the rear of the plane to which they made frequent trips on increasingly unsteady legs.

It was only when one of this peerless pair of reprobates slurped too loudly on the hosepipe that their wicked secret was uncovered and they were handed over to law enforcement officers when they disembarked.

I never did discover what they said to obtain their freedom so swiftly, but would like to bet that it had something to with Desmond's off-quoted advice to 'never let the the facts interfere with a good story'.

Wilson much preferred the luxury of travelling around the USA on the splendid Pullman trains. Genuine frowns of anguish would crease his forehead whenever he told people about the indignity of travelling across dry States back in the early 1950s. The moment the train crossed the border into a dry state, a big black porter would come into the berth and confiscate his whiskey. 'It would not have been so bad if he had taken it away with him and out of my sight. But he would lock it in the cabinet and I would have to endure the agony of watching that seductive booze dance in front of my eyes for hundreds of miles until we hit civilisation again,' Peter would lament.

Another classic Wilson train cameo took place when he opened a window in the dining car and the ensuing gust of wind blew the playing cards off an adjoining table. The occupants of that table just happened to be big-shot mobsters and the game was at a vital stage with a big pot waiting to be won. Confronted by a furious verbal onslaught from some of the most dangerous men in the USA, Peter was forced to draw his sword from his stick and prepare to defend himself. The gangsters loved him for it and quit their game to yarn and drink with him for the rest of the journey.

For sheer visual black comedy, though, Wally Bartleman's misfortune on the morning after the Foreman-Frazier fight in Jamaica took some beating. Wally had been a tank major during the War and a shell blast had inflicted some facial damage and affected his eyesight.

Foreman had arranged an informal press conference poolside, and Wally's bedroom door just happened to overlook the pool in question. Late, he came striding across towards us fully clothed, notebook and pen in hand and walked straight into the pool. Apparently, in the glare of the sun, he had mistaken the pool for a patio. That old reprobate, Bill Daly, stood there open-mouthed and cracked: 'Jeez, I've seen fighters take dives, but this my very first news-paperman.'

Old Wally was tough as old boots and would probably have given Bill a right hander if he had not been too busy diving back into the pool in a forlorn attempt to retrieve his glasses from the bottom.

I suppose I should round off a chapter like this by throwing in another little anecdote of my own. This one concerns the last ever boxing show to be staged at Shoreditch Town Hall in the heart of London's East End. It was on 29 January 1975 and, when a bomb alert was announced from the ring, it was typical of this tough Cockney audience to remain seated and for one wag to sum up the collective reaction perfectly by shouting: 'As long as it's not in the bar we don't give a toss.'

The regular patrons there were nearly all straight out of 'Minder'. These included Jimmy the Jibber, who never paid to get in, Sailor the Doorman, who could roll with the punches if the going ever got really rough, Dick the Meter Reader, who claimed he could read the scorecard by the wiggle of the referee's pencil and always placed his bets accordingly. And there was the resident second Legs Cain and referee Harry Paudling who announced his own retirement from the ring at the grand old age of 66 with all the regal airs of a deposed monarch. It was a hall full of memories for me, like the time when world middleweight champions Terry Downes and Dick Tiger fought each other there for the paltry sums of £125 and £80 respectively. When asked who his next opponent would be, defeated Terry came out with one of his customary quips when he growled: 'The berk who made that match with Tiger'. This one was early in their careers and would have cost the promoters the proverbial bomb a few years later. Come to think of it, those two great Scottish world lightweight champions Ken Buchanan and Jim Watt once clashed on a club show for peanuts. How much would a modern promoter have paid for that one now, I wonder?

To digress yet again, which is an old man's privilege anyway, a brief potted history of Dick Tiger's life reads like the synopsis for a screenplay. Dick, a Nigerian, lived in Liverpool and favoured a distinguished way of dressing. When he went to fight Ruben 'Hurricane' Carter in the USA, he strolled around Broadway looking resplendent in an Anthony Eden hat and a Homburg overcoat. When a whipper snapper of a yankee reporter in a snap-brimmed hat had the gall to ask him whether he spoke English, he replied: 'Much better than you do, my good man.'

After winning world titles at two different weights, middle and light heavy, he became a captain in the rebel army of Nigeria during the terrible civil war there. He died from liver cancer in 1971 four years before the finale night I was attending.

Coming to the point of this yarn at last, I'd better switch straight to the *Evening News* headline of my piece in the following day's first edition. It read: GOODBYE TO SHOREDITCH AND TO MY WIFE'S CAR.

My own motor was off the road at the time and I had borrowed Connie's. Shoreditch being Shoreditch it got nicked. My mate Shaw Taylor was fronting *Police Five* at the time on ITV. This show was similar to *Crimewatch* today. When I told Shaw my tale of woe he just laughed and I thought he had forgotten it. But, for a leg-pull, he waited for *Junior Police Five* and told his young audience: 'My pal Reg Gutteridge has upset his wife by losing her car. 'Then he gave a description and the licence plate number of my missus' old banger and our phone number.

Within hours I received a phone call that went: 'Reggie, you don't know me, but my kid reckons the motor that's been stuck outside our house these past weeks belongs to you. If so, do us a favour and come and collect it. It's such a bleedin' eyesore, even for Shoreditch.'

Hollywood could not cast them, a larger than life duo known to the rest of their press mates as Butch and the Sundance. They were Hugh McIlvanney, wordsmith *par excellence* and Peter Batt, who wrote for more newspapers than Tommy Docherty had soccer clubs. Both were sports writer award winners. Their accents differed so much, as you would expect of a Scot and a Cockney, that it was a wonder they ever understood each other. The body language said it all though. They had done it all on the sporting beat – cursed more sports editors than anyone and they usually had photo finishes when it came to meeting their deadlines.

But their work was pure pro – to the envy of all of us.

Whenever Mac and Batt walked in, it was time to send for the sheriff. At the Montreal Olympics in 1976 they shared a room at the Meridien Hotel, where Friday night was variety night. McIlvanney was about to go down what he called the 'tunnel' to produce his masterly Sunday paper article. He would pace the room, swearing and sweating until the words flowed as only he could make them flow. Batt was then the columnist for my paper, his latest move in a career that ended with little in the way of pay offs or pensions pay off or a pension.

Hughie would bundle his cockney mate out into the corridor to stop him talking and interfering with the flow. 'Batty' would come knocking on my bedroom door, worn out by the day's 'slog' and carrying his mattress over his shoulder. Then he would lie down on his mattress on the floor at the foot of my bed like a pet pussy cat.

After growling a few rambling words he would finish with an imitation trumpet blast, through his fingers, of the last post.

CHAPTER TWENTY-THREE
TV TIMES

'If you can lose and start again at your beginnings,
And never breathe a word about your loss.'
RUDYARD KIPLING

Taking my cue from Kipling, I did not scream the place down when the *Evening News* eventually printed its definitive final edition on 31 October 1980. I was asked to describe my feelings about it on the evening bulletin of ITN's news.

I restricted my comments to the here and now, explaining that I had been due to cover Jim Watt's world lightweight title defence against Sean O'Grady of Oklahoma the following night, but that I was going greyhound racing instead, to present a winning owner with a trophy.

As it is, was and ever will be for all of us, however, the past and the future turned out to be entwined in that particular moment. I was going back to the dogs, where it had all begun for me on the dear old *News*. Jim Watt would later become my partner at the microphone and my pal for the next two decades.

The only glint of gold in the financial handshake I received from the *News* was the retirement watch with which I was presented. As I recorded earlier, that was nicked inside the next fortnight, anyway.

Fortunately, just as it was nearly 40 years earlier on

the battlefield, the 7th Cavalry was preparing to come to my rescue again. This time, in the shape of John Bromley, Head of ITV Sport, who called a Press conference the very next day to announce that he was moving me up from part-time to full-time commentator, but still on a freelance basis.

A former sports journalist, himself, 'Brommers' is a real diamond of a man both as a guv'nor and a friend.

It is at this point in my story that I suddenly realise, in retrospect, why I used that flowery sentence a couple of paragraphs back about the present, past and future merging into one moment – it was nothing less than a cunning old codger's cop out.

I knew I was going to have to start talking about my TV experiences and I am afraid that, chronologically, they are something of a timeless blur.

I crave your indulgence, then, if I am forced to present this mental video as it comes – sometimes on the 'play' button, then on the 'fast forward' and 'rewind' knobs and wherever my memories take me.

Objectively, I am happy to say that it is not too difficult to begin at the beginning. Subjectively, however, I am forced to fling fragments around as if this book was a cutting-room floor.

The first ever live televised boxing match on commercial TV went out on the first night that independent TV began broadcasting in 1955. It was obviously a black-and-white job, but as far as Len Harvey was concerned it was a complete blank. Len had been booked to do the inter-round summaries but could not get on the screen because of the adverts. Digressing again, for a moment, old Len fared no worse than those popular British middleweights Tony Sibson and Alan Minter did nearly 30 years later when they were suddenly blacked out because of a dispute over advertising on Minter's shorts. Millions of TV viewers were permanently deprived of one of the most spectacular knockouts ever when 'Sibbo' rearranged Alan's handsome features with a fearsome left hook.

But back to that first fight. It was between Terry Murphy of Canning Town and his fellow East Ender, Lew Lazar. Terry's son, Glenn, is now an actor on the hit TV show *London's Burning* and Lew later became an East End cab driver and publican. It was staged at dear old Shoreditch Town Hall and was a cracking fight. The only trouble from a purist's point of view was that people had never seen commercials before and they caused as much interest and comment as the boxing. Still, it says a lot about the crowd-pulling power of this sport of ours that the TV chiefs chose to screen it peak-time on opening night, doesn't it?

I can't remember my first televised fight commentary, but I can certainly recall the worst. There were four of them, in fact. All at more or less the same time and all taking place thousand of miles apart. I had read about those Indian gurus who could simultaneously manifest themselves in different caves hundreds of miles away from each other. I have also observed only recently that Murray Walker confession in a newspaper that he sometimes commentated on Grand Prix races from back in the studio via voice-overs.

On this particular night my experience in Maryland USA in March 1980 was absolutely ridiculous. I still shiver and break out in a sweat when I think about it.

My body was at ringside for Sugar Ray Leonard versus our own Dave 'Boy' Green. My mind, though, was flitting from Maryland to Las Vegas for Larry Holmes v Leroy Jones, to Knoxville for Eddie Gregory v Marvin

Johnson and on to I know not where for Mike Weaver v John Tate. All I do recall about that one is that I had to endure 14 rounds and two minutes fifteen seconds of the fifteenth before Weaver flattened Tate with a copy book knock out.

By the time man mountain Tate landed flat on his back I was almost a stretcher case myself. This was the last leg of my mouthing marathon during which the pictures from the other three fights were played back to the ringside monitor in Maryland. My screen was blank between rounds at the other venues because of the advertising and I was having to rely on the studio technicians telephoning me with the relevant visual images. As for my commentary, this was drowned by the noise of the Maryland crowd during the preliminary bouts on the Leonard-Green bill and I had to peer at the relevant live action though a towel covering my ears because I could barely hear the telephoned instructions through my earphones.

For the record, Leonard knocked out Green in round four, Holmes stopped Jones in the 8th and Gregory finished off Johnson in the 11th. My own record read: just about standing after completing four rounds in the flesh and 34 rounds 'dubbed', but floored by a nervous breakdown when I had to send a 1,000-word report to the *Evening News* as soon as I got back to the hotel.

Another nerve-racking experience occurred 18 months after this one, but on this occasion, I no longer had the writing job to worry me, too. That time, I was to achieve a mini-triumph. It was on an oppressively hot night in Las Vegas where the dry desert air tends to turn the throat husky.

The fight itself was one for the list of all-time greats. It was when Sugar Ray Leonard stopped Tommy 'Hit

Man' Hearns in the 14th round after being on the wrong end of what was looking increasingly like a merciless mugging until his trainer, Angelo Dundee, barked out the message 'six minutes to win'. Sugar suddenly turned into a dancing dervish before our eyes. It was not my eyes that were causing me problems, though, it was my rusty vocal chords.

Engineers receiving ITVs coverage back in London had been complaining from early in the fight that my voice was barely 'telephone quality'. Producer Lewis Williams, at ringside for his first big one in America, was reluctant to interrupt my excited flow. Then, horror of horrors, as soon as the action was over he was given the message that the entire commentary had to be done again because of the poor sound.

Time was running out, the ring lights had been doused and the ring was being dismantled before I managed to find a spare monitor in a caravan in the car park. As the pictures were to be transmitted direct, there was no chance of a pause for thought or a correction. The tape was rolled without captions or round numbers. The fight had attracted a huge live audience back home, so my nerves were being stretched to their limits once more. It was at moments like those that I wished I had been able to pursue my boyhood dreams of making boxing history instead of recording it.

It was with great relief, then, when I heard next day that at the executives conference, Michael Grade, the then controller of London Weekend TV had said: 'Great show. Reg was in top form.' John Bromley told me he enjoyed telling his boss later that it was a dubbed commentary. I felt good about fooling a fellow professional like Michael.

When it comes to professionalism, the golden survival rule for TV commentating is the same as in the boxing ring – think on your feet and always expect the unexpected.

Nothing could have been more unexpected from my point of view than when *World of Sport* decided that I was the man to describe the fad of watching madmen on motorbikes who, perversely, chose to do for a living what most people dread doing – miss the last bus.

'Evil' Kneivel and Eddie Kidd would deliberately hurl themselves and their machines over the tops of God knows how many buses to provide onlookers with thrills and themselves with a very lucrative living.

As for me? I'd never ridden on a motorbike in my life, not even on the pillion, but the trick was not to let the viewers know that. So on my first stab at this job I sent a message to Kneivel, a flash full-of-himself American who was holed up in a caravan dressing-room like the hero of some Hollywood B cowboy movie, enquiring as to whether he would use just one bike for his performance.

He was considerate enough to send word back that he would use one bike to get the crowd excited by a load of revving and roaring and then he would do the business on the second. This invaluable titbit of information enabled me to sound like a trained mechanic, as I explained the vagaries of motorbike engines and predicted the exact moment when 'Evil' would take off. He crashed on landing.

Unlike the TV wrestlers, of which my cousin Jackie Pallo was one, these motorbike maniacs did not know the script in advance and poor Eddie Kidd is still paralysed from a stunt that went horribly wrong for him.

Wouldn't you just know it, but I also found myself back at the dogs again doing greyhound racing commentaries on winter Saturdays when the rest of the sport fixtures were wiped out.

It was at a dog meeting at Wembley Stadium where I foolishly incurred the wrath of half the Scottish nation. At least that's how it seemed from the number of rude letters I received for remarks I made about the Scottish fans who had torn down the goalposts and trampled that stadium's hallowed turf after a match against England.

It happened like this: a plastic carpet had been laid to prevent the dogs making a mess on their way from the kennels to the starting stalls. As the runners were parading along it, I stupidly blurted out: 'It's a pity they couldn't have done the same for those Scottish supporters.' Oops! And to think that some of my best friends are Scots! Honest! Just ask Jim Watt.

On a more bizarre note, I was doing my doggie stint up in the press box at Haringey dog track and, after I'd finished that, I had to do a voiceover commentary from a monitor there on Ali's last ever fight, which was against Trevor Berbick in Bermuda while the tannoy at the track blared out all the necessary information about the runners in the races.

So many people, quite justifiably in my opinion, moan about the canned laughter on TV comedies, but the crowd noises on some of my voiceover boxing experiences would put some of those unfunnier comedy episodes to shame.

I mean, I've heard of a show travelling badly – which reminds me, I must stop for a moment and tell you the funniest true example of that that I've ever heard. Excuse the name-dropping, but one night I was having a drink with Eric Mashwitz, who wrote such evergreens as *A Nightingale Sang In Berkeley Square* and *Goodnight Vienna*, when he told me that he was driving past the

Lewisham Theatre in south London when it happened to be showing *Vienna*. Eric explained that he stopped the car and sought out the manager to ask him, politely, how the show was being received. The manager replied: 'About as good as *Goodnight Lewisham* would go down in Vienna.'

I'm not sure why, but I thought of that story every time I was pretending to be somewhere I wasn't. For instance, we were once showing a taped American fight from the *World of Sport* studio with yours truly pretending to be there live. It turned out hilariously when it was decided to dub in crowd noises from a recording of a big London fight. The sound naturally kept blasting out cries of 'Go on, me son' and various other Cockney exhortations and there was not one American voice to be heard coming over from the packed arena in Los Angeles.

It gets even sillier. We had our own bell in the studio but our man badly mistimed his clang to end the round while the two fighters in Los Angeles were still belting seven kinds of sweat out of each other. There was nothing for me to do, but start screaming. 'They haven't heard the bell, they haven't heard the bell!' When this went on for about a half a minute, with the 'Cockney' audience in Los Angeles hastily switched back on for effect, the crew in London were helpless with laughter.

When I later told the man responsible for the show, the American promoter George Parnassus, he threatened to kill me and my limey buddies for committing blasphemy. The real bell, he explained, had once timed a Dempsey fight and was nothing less than a boxing icon in his eyes.

Sillier still, was the incident when I was commentating on a Terry Marsh fight in a palatial hall in the posh principality of Monte Carlo with Prince Rainier himself present. While a minor preliminary bout bored everyone silly in that cathedral-like atmosphere, Jim Watt and I amused ourselves by watching a live American fight on our ringside monitors. Well, these two American heavyweights contrived to do something I had never seen before or since. They both landed pole-axe punches on each other's chins simultaneously and down they both went.

I was so shocked that I stood up in my seat and roared: 'Did you see that? Did you see that?' The two boxers in the ring above stared at me in amazement and the referee instucted them to 'stop boxing' while he asked me in French, 'what the hell are you playing at?'

If I did not know the lingo, I certainly knew the look and it was not an amused one. As I blurted out an apology Jim Watt, beside me, was laughing so much that he ducked under the ring apron in embarrassment. Still, the paying punters loved it. Well, I suppose they must have been partial to a spot of French farce in those parts, anyway.

That is not the only time the laugh has been on me, though. Oh dear no. Once, while I was in full flow in a studio voiceover commentary job I was repeatedly interrupted by a large Jamaican lady, who wished to know which refreshments I would prefer. I kept waving her away and pointing to the microphone, but she just kept urging me to make my mind up. Eventually, she said in a very loud voice: 'You've got to have something, man. You look like you need it.' Whereupon she thrust a banana into my mouth – leaving me momentarily speechless as her voice went out to millions.

Forced to flee between rounds, I sought sanctuary in a studio telephone box. It was a Bob Foster fight from

Florida. Bob was known as the 'Alberquerque Sheriff' and I was beginning to wish he was down here protecting me when the telephone in this box suddenly rang, midway through the next round. I stuffed the phone beneath my shirt hoping to drown the noise when a voice at the other end, which I recognised as belonging to my boss John Bromley, said: 'Hello, hello?' I snapped back: 'It's me in make-believe Miami. Bob Foster's just about to flatten somebody – that is if I don't flatten somebody first.' He had dialled the wrong extension.

I received some rough treatment from another lady once. I was rabbiting away at a live show, ringside, when a woman began clobbering me with her umbrella. She had mistaken me for my BBC counterpart, and some say lookalike, Harry Carpenter, who she was convinced had criticised her boxer son during a recent amateur broadcast. While boxing my ears with the brolly she relayed the nature of Harry's alleged insults all the time assuming that I was the villain of the piece.

Still, this time I did manage to get in a retaliatory verbal blast immediately after the round when I said: 'Madam, you are no better than your son at landing your shots on target.'

Another verbal blast I would far rather have left unspoken came when I used the dreaded 'F' word and it went out live in two regions, Granada and Central, before it could be edited out. I used this four-letter piece of industrial language when I was trying to interview Mike Tyson in the ring immediately after one of his many victories and a young interloper, who had evaded the security men and climbed through the ropes to join us, kept jogging my elbow and urging me to ask Tyson about Nelson Mandela.

The odds were that Mike had never heard of Mandela and would probably have asked what weight he boxed at. But as this kid nudged away at my elbow the microphone kept waving in front of Tyson's face like an unguided missile and, as I knew he was not very keen on ring interviews, I suddenly lost my rag completely and told this young pest to 'F... off!'

Although I was ashamed of that piece of unprofessional conduct, and Central and Granada received many letters reminding me of it, I think I would have been tempted to repeat it had I known that someone was picking my back trouser pocket during a similar interview with Muhammad Ali after he had defeated the British ex-paratrooper, Richard Dunn. Fortunately, I knew nothing about this little episode until an eyewitness recounted it to me afterwards and, better still, all the pickpocket got for his cheek was my comb.

CHAPTER TWENTY FOUR
DERRING-DO AND DOPEHEADS

'I've taken my fun where I've found it,
And now I must pay for my fun.'
RUDYARD KIPLING

When he was still a wide-eyed young novice and Britain's brightest heavyweight hope for years, Frank Bruno was taken to sit at the feet of the then long-reigning heavyweight champion of the world, Larry Holmes in July 1983.

Naïve Frank's mouth opened wider than his eyes in sheer astonishment, however, when the first piece of advice he was given by 'the guv'nor' was 'Lay off the coke, kid!'

Bruno had made the pilgrimage to Holmes's home in Easton, Pennsylvania with his brow furrowed in concentration. He had been expecting to be asked to digest priceless pearls of technical information from the great man.

Instead, what he learned was that the 80s was fast becoming the decade of the dope heads.

Among Larry's other considerable technical attributes, he had honed to perfection what many good judges reckoned was the most powerful left jab in the entire history of the heavyweight division. His opening verbal shot at Bruno was of the sledgehammer variety, too: 'There's no point in me advising you how to block a left lead or throw a right cross if you're going to go off and ruin it all by sniffing coke.' That was the first thing this wise old stager told our wet-behind-the ears Wandsworth boy. Also listening was another British hope, the then little known, Lloyd Honeyghan, who was a stablemate of Bruno's and destined to pull off one of the boxing sensations of the century.

These two young Brits had been taken on a learning curve to the States by their manager Terry Lawless. Fortunately, they took that warning to heart and instead of taking dope they indulged in deeds of derring-do on this country's behalf that brought them a world title each.

It could have been a close call for them. At that time, cocaine was sweeping through boxing in the USA like a self-induced plague. As Larry said then: 'The fight game is rife with cocaine these days. So many good kids seem to be getting into the stuff. They seem to think it's fun, but it's tragic.'

Several world champions admitted taking drugs, most pitiful of all being Oliver McCall, who was actually visited by his demons in the ring, the second time he fought Lennox Lewis. He quit in tears.

Many, many others were rumoured to prefer fashionable drugs and ghetto-blasting gymnasium music to the monastic rigours and discipline of long-haul training.

Fortunately for us, but tragically for him, on this side of the Atlantic only one young man publicly yielded to temptation. Yet, ironically, he had been the hardest trainer of them all. John Conteh, one of the most talented and determined fighters we have ever produced, fell prey to drink and drugs to such an extent that, by his own admission, he was just a shell of the champion he still aspired to be when he fought Matthew Saad Muhammad in Atlantic City on 29 March 1980 for the WBC light heavyweight title. And he was still only in his twenties.

The referee stopped the fight in the fourth round after John had been up and down like the proverbial yo-yo. He said afterwards that the only reason he was in the ring that night was because the money he was being paid was, temporarily, the most powerful drug of all.

Honest John even said that, as he prepared for that fateful night, his wife Veronica had to cradle him in her arms to quell his fears. It was not physical fear, but the fear of making a fool of himself in front of millions of TV viewers.

He had managed to kick the habit long enough to train for the fight, but, although his body was clean, his mind was still contaminated. This was the heart-wrenching way this once proud man described his fall: 'The fear of making a fool of myself in the ring overpowered all other emotions. As I ducked through the ropes, I wanted to keep looking at the floor. Falling about in a gutter in a deserted city in the early hours of the morning was one thing, but at least I did that in private. If I was going to have to fall about in this ring, with the eyes of the world upon me, I felt it was going to be impossible to live with the shame.

'Even as the fourth and final round began, I had still not managed to work up any sort of concentration. I found myself examining my surroundings. I remember thinking how shiny the canvas was, like one of those polished tables in the furniture vans I used to kip in as a kid in Liverpool. I thought crazy thoughts.

'As I backed on to the ropes, I was actually thinking about the texture of them, realising how rough they were as they scraped your shoulder blades. Up and down I went – five times inside two minutes in that final round. But Matthew Saad Muhammad was not knocking me unconscious, he was doing the opposite.

'I was conscious of trivial details. The audience, for instance, I began picking out their faces. I felt I could have counted the number of hairs on Frank Sinatra's transplant and Faye Dunaway's beauty spot danced on her cheek, as I gazed around me in a trance.'

This was the man whose tough old trainer, George Francis, made him break the ice on winter mornings on his daily swim in Hampstead pond.

Just as he had feared it would, the shame of that ignominious defeat did depress Conteh so much that he relapsed after the fight and made front-page headlines on every newspaper in England when he rampaged around his hotel naked and had to be overpowered by Francis and hotel security staff before being put under sedation.

As well as weeping for John that night, I nearly shed a little tear for myself. It happened to be my birthday and Frank Sinatra – himself an ex-fighter and an avid fan – had given my ageing ego the perfect present by spontaneously agreeing to do an inter-round chat for my commentary at the end of the next round, which just happened to be the fourth.

He was ready to leave his ringside seat and join me when the referee unwittingly upstaged him and stopped the contest, leaving me with more pressing needs to attend to than chatting up Ol' Blue Eyes. What an exclusive that would have made, eh? Still, by far the biggest coup to emerge from that nightmarish evening was John Conteh's decision to seek help for his addictions. I am proud to say that he has since conquered his demons one day at a time and has been clean and sober for a decade and more.

If it is admissable to make a joke about such a sad occasion, I can only say that Atlantic City is the kind of place that could make me go berserk every time I go there. I would rather be a lamp post in London than the Mayor of Atlantic City. Las Vegas is too tatty for my tastes, but this poor imitation with its famous boardwalk makes Southend-on-Sea look sophisticated.

Conteh's calamity brought the curtain down on one of the most eventful months in British boxing history. March of 1980 brought the old country a marvellous treble chance with three of our own topping the bill in America almost back to back.

This flurry of memorable action had begun in Las Vegas in triumph when Alan Minter became the first Briton to capture a world title on American soil since the fabled Ted Kid Lewis 65 years earlier.

Alan did it the hard way by beating Italian-American Vito Antofermo in a rugged, bloody, bruising battle that went the distance. When I interviewed him in the ring immediately after the fight, his first comment to me was: 'Is this going out live to my pals back home?' When I confirmed that it was, he suddenly said on air: 'On second thoughts, it doesn't really matter, 'cos they'll all be half pissed by now.'

That applied to his many fans who had travelled over to Las Vegas and helped themselves to the lopsided Las Vegas betting odds, which had this Cockney from the new town of Crawley in Sussex at an extremely inviting 2–1 against.

Incidentally, this history-making epic nearly turned into a double feature with an unscheduled bout between the rival Dads. Antofermo's father had been telling anyone who would listen that he used to win all the rock heading contests back home in his Sicilian village. Alan's dad, Sid, admitted that his experience with rocks only went as far as the ones on the Brighton front where he ran a drinking club, but he had been more than a little bit useful on the cobbles in his day. So there was plenty of pre-fight eyeballing between the two old boys every time they met up in the hotel. Still, just as their sons did, Antofermo senior and Minter senior respectfully shook each other's hands after the contest which was, of course, in keeping with the noblest traditions of the noble art.

Sad to say, this was not the case when Minter lost that precious title to Marvelous Marvin Hagler at Wembley, however. The great Hagler shredded Minter's cut-prone face and this time Minter's fans let him, themselves and British boxing down when they staged one of the most disgraceful riots in ring history. The ring was bombarded with plastic bottles while the victorious Hagler attempted to take his bow. He was bitterly disappointed when the ceremony to present him with his championship belt had to be abandoned. I was not too pleased, either, because as the missiles rained down, I was hit on the head with a hard back book. When I bent down to pick it up later, it turned out to be Alan Minter's autobiography. Needless to say, the events of this shameful evening were never published as a postscript.

Talking of postscripts, the most moving example I have seen featured the enforced retirement of that popular British welterweight Dave 'Boy' Green who hailed from the same Fens countryside as that earlier Chatteris legend Eric 'Boy' Boon.

Dave fits into the context of my story here because his fight against Sugar Ray Leonard in Maryland figured in the American trilogy I am recalling. It was on that night of my personal commentating nightmare, which I described earlier, when I had to cover four major fights more or less at the same time.

Anything I may have suffered was child's play compared to the effects of the perfect left hook with which Sugar Ray finished off our boy that night. Dave himself admits that whenever he replays the video he still says to himself: 'One of these days I am going to get up.'

Dave, who lost only four of his 41 professional fights, did eventually get up, of course. But he was never quite the same fighter after that experience. That moving postcript I referred to occurred after he lost again and his caring manager, Andy Smith, grabbed the mike and retired his beloved 'Boy' while he was still on his feet in the Royal Albert Hall ring.

I witnessed a scene that brought a lump as big as a boxing glove to my throat. Dave was both amazed and furious with Andy and screamed at him over and over again: 'You bastard'. He was only silenced when the entire Albert Hall crowd rose to its feet spontaneously and gave Green the most heartfelt standing ovation it is possible to imagine. He may not have been the greatest fighter they had ever seen, but, like Billy Walker before him, he had never given one iota less than his all.

Andy, who also trained and managed Joe Bugner, gave permission for his own son to become a pro and Smith junior, who was no mean comedian, captured all our hearts when he had the word 'Help' painted on the bottom of his boxing boots. That humble request must have acted as a lucky charm because he was never KO'd in his short career, which was ended by a recurring shoulder injury. He is now a paid and well-respected official of the British Boxing Board of Control.

As far as that august body is concerned, it must be wishing on a daily basis that it could resurrect the 1980s. From a British boxing point of view, that was a vintage decade.

It spawned Frank Bruno – more of him later – Barry McGuigan, Charlie Magri, Lloyd Honeyghan, Dennis Andries and Cornelius 'Boza' Edwards who all claimed world crowns. Talented entertainers such as Colin Jones and Tony Sibson who, sadly for them, only managed to become nearly men in the world rankings.

Ireland's McGuigan can lay claim to being the undisputed main man of the 1980s on this side of the Atlantic. Although on the wider world scene he could not help but be overshadowed by the four fabulous international stars of that era, namely Sugar Ray Leonard, Marvin Hagler, Tommy Hearns and Roberto Duran.

As my long life story becomes more and more up to date, I realise that reams have already been written in newspapers about the main protagonists so, with the occasional exception, I propose to ration myself to a brief comment here and there which has nothing to do with the esteem in which I hold them, nor are they in any particular pecking order.

McGuigan, who hailed from the border town of Clones, was so popular on both sides of the religious and political divides of his native land that he re-opened the King's Hall in Belfast, which had not staged shows for the previous 20 years.

More than 10,000 fans travelled to London's Queen's Park Rangers football ground to witness Barry wrest the world featherweight title from that dignified and much respected champion Eusebio Pedroza. The 27,000-strong crowd made it a throwback to the open-air shows of Jack Solomons when Mills and Turpin starred. As a

TV attraction its viewing figures won it the week's number one slot ahead of the soaps *East Enders* and *Coronation Street*. Barry's dad added a showbiz touch by singing 'Danny Boy' in the ring and, to reassure us that this was no amateur night, we were reminded that McGuigan senior had once finished third in the Eurovision Song Contest.

Barry fought like the proverbial man possessed for 15 exciting rounds that night. He successfully defended the title twice before succumbing to a Las Vegas heatwave and a mediocre opponent named Steve Cruz when the fight was staged during daytime, in temperatures of over 100 degrees in the ring, to meet the demands of TV. This was one of those rare occasions when I was somewhat ashamed of my TV livelihood.

Barry's life was soured by personal tragedy when his beloved brother committed suicide, his father died early and he fell out with his manager and mentor, Barney Eastwood, to such an extent that the pair finished up on opposite sides in court. With all that grief behind him, I am happy to report that Barry is now a well-paid pundit himself with Sky TV, a *Daily Express* boxing columnist and sought-after public speaker. He also formed the Professional Boxers' Association to safeguard the rights of his fellow professionals.

Stepney resident Charlie Magri sounds as Cockney as they come when he speaks, but he was, in fact, born in Tunisia and brought to this country as a baby. A product of the illustrious Arbour Youth Club, he was virtually unbeatable as an amateur flyweight. His long professional career was topped off triumphantly when he stopped Eleoncio Mercedes at Wembley, in 1983.

When he moved up a weight, however, Charlie retired after losing the domestic crown to Croydon's Duke

McKenzie. Cheerful Charlie never hurt a fly outside of business hours and he has recently started coaching and managing, and is doing well.

McKenzie, whose scientific but somewhat unspectacular style never seemed to excite the Press sufficiently, became the only British boxer this century to win three world titles at three different weights. A member of a supremely talented sporting family, he has several brothers who were boxers, one of whom, Clinton, was a British and European champion, and whose son is a very promising striker for Crystal Palace. Duke also earned recognition and respect outside the ring when he interrupted training for an important fight by pulling survivors out of a fatal train crash that occurred at the bottom of his Croydon garden.

It is a pity that Gentleman Duke had to bow out in his thirties with a first-round defeat at a show in Croydon promoted by his brothers in 1988.

When I first saw Dennis Andries as an amateur, I told his trainer Harry Griver that his boy would never make the big time in a month of Sundays. Now, that was the kind of tipping that would surely have earned me instant dismissal back in my dog racing days. Dennis not only won the world light heavyweight title but he actually regained it twice.

A Guyana-born Hackney man of honourable humility, he actually took the WBC boxing belt in a carrier bag on his lap by tube train for his first big London press conference. He was also so devoid of false pride that, after suffering a terrible beating at the the hands of 'Hit Man' Tommy Hearns, he went and asked Hearns' trainer to coach him full-time at the famous Kronk gym in Detroit. Dennis went on winning titles and tributes for what seemed an eternity.

234

I love the story he told me about the morning he unwittingly scared the life out of several Stamford Hill Jews when he was out roadrunning one morning. He was in a hooded tracksuit and the religious group apparently thought he was about to mug them so they hastily fled to a nearby synagogue with an embarrassed Dennis pursuing them and loudly protesting: 'Don't worry! I'm just a world boxing champion in training.'

This reminds me of another irresistible little 1980s anecdote concerning Frank Bruno and the late *Daily Mail* photographer, Monty Fresco. They were strolling down the strip in Las Vegas one morning shortly before Frank was due to fight there when Monty, who was notoriously mean, stopped a passer by, who was sporting a ten-gallon cowboy hat. Monty asked whether he could borrow the head-piece to put on his large companion's head for a fun photograph.

The 'cowboy' looked at them suspiciously for several seconds before declaring: 'Piss off, panhandler!' Monty, who stuttered, vigorously protested that this man was none other than the British and European heavyweight champion and that the proposed picture was for the *Daily Mail* in London, England.

Their cowboy perused them again then drawled: 'You still look like a couple of panhandlers to me,' and continued his morning stroll.

Which brings me to Bruno's one-time stablemate, Lloyd Honeyghan, who left Frank and their other Canning Town comrades at Terry Lawless' gym to team up full-time with Mickey Duff. Mickey made what everyone thought was the match from hell for Honeyghan when he pitched him against the immaculate Don Curry, who I then considered to be one of the best welterweights I had ever seen.

'Honey' astonished the world by out-boxing and out-gaming his man to pull off an amazing long-odds triumph in Atlantic City. A self-styled 'Ragamuffin Man' this Bermondsey boy became a big pal of Mike Tyson and is now branching out as a manager and promoter. He needs the money because he has a well-publicised stable of 'love children' by several different women.

CHAPTER TWENTY-FIVE
THE PRINCE AND THE PAUPER

'If you can meet with Triumph and Disaster
And treat those two imposters just the same.'
RUDYARD KIPLING

Left jab, right cross, left jab, right uppercut, left jab again, then, most difficult of all, a left jab followed instantly by a left hook ... That is known in the boxing trade as a combination. One punch begets another until you have fashioned a little creation of your very own.

It is the same, I have found, in the wordsmith trade. One word begets another until you compose what you hope is a passable article, commentary or – in this more ambitious case – an autobiography.

The reference to the mothers of Honeyghan's several children in the previous chapter prompts me to tackle the mother and father of all bar room boxing discussions. 'Who was the greatest heavyweight of them all?'

Contemplation of the meaning of 'greatness' could sidetrack us for several chapters, so I'll settle for talking about the most talked-about heavyweight I've had the privilege of knowing myself.

They have to be Muhammad Ali, who I have already discussed at great length, Mike Tyson, who I shall be covering later and, of course, Rocky Marciano and Joe Louis, the prince and the pauper.

Statistically, Rocky has to earn the epithet of 'Prince' because he still holds the heavyweight record of going an entire career undefeated. Joe was the 'Pauper' because he spent half of his life in poverty. I use the word 'poverty' guardedly, however, because, although Joe finished up without much money of his own, he was still known as 'America's Guest' and he never had to pick up a tab anywhere he went.

Better still, Joe Louis must be the only human being in the history of the world who has been paid to stand in front of his own statue, as was the case at Caesar's Palace, Las Vegas.

By one of life's endless little ironies, Larry Holmes, who reigned from 1979 until 1985 and ran the other four close in achievement but not in charisma, was attempting to surpass Rocky's record when he was deposed by Michael Spinks. The same Michael Spinks who was to become the only boxer I ever saw reveal naked fear in the ring when he later surrendered to Mike Tyson without striking a meaningful blow.

Even more ironically, the immortal Joe became a mere mortal for, one night anyway, when he watched Holmes defeat Trevor Berbick from a ringside wheelchair on 12 April 1981 and passed away a few hours later. So, just like my old grandfather, my dad and my uncle, old Joe died more or less with his boots on – except that he was wearing a yellow baseball cap at the fight, which, under the arc lights, resembled a golden halo.

My most astonishing memory of him was when I was in the company of a group of Brits who owned the Sportsman Club in London. We happened to be in

America during the bicentennial celebrations when Joe approached our group and said: 'I understand the Queen is in America right now.' 'She sure is,' said our spokesman, whose mouth fell open in embarrassment a moment later when Joe popped the question: 'Do you think she would come to Vegas while she's over here?'

In the face of much negative, incoherent mumbling from us, Joe picked up a house phone and asked the Caesar's Palace switchboard to put him through to the President.

A few minutes later, over the tannoy, came the *coup de grâce*. 'Mr Joe Louis, you have a call from the White House.' It was in shocked disbelief that we then heard Joe say: 'Would you mind putting me through to Gerry Ford, please?'

No wonder, then, that there was even a newspaper campaign in the USA to get pauper Joe buried in the world-famous Arlington Cemetery, which houses the graves of the most famous American heroes. Born in a dirt farmer's shack in Alabama and raised in a Detroit ghetto, Joe answered any worried questions about his financial situation, by saying: 'Ford's promised they'd keep my job open for me.'

When he died, a month short of his 67th birthday, he had survived two strokes, a heart by-pass operation and had been fitted with a pacemaker.

It was small wonder, then, that in those last years he was unable to carry out much more than the briefest of conversations, as the Caesar's Palace management had him wheeled to and from the ringside as a 'drawing card' for the punters. A few years earlier when I suggested that it must rile him to hear how much money modern fighters were earning, he simply said, philosophically: 'It would have made no difference to me. I would have gambled it away. Anyway, I made about $5 million and wound up broke and owing the government a million. Today, I would just have doubled or trebled the debt, that's all.'

When Marciano knocked out Louis in eight rounds in October 1951 it was an irrelevance as far as the 'who was the greatest' argument is concerned.

Rocky was in his prime and Joe was 36. Several comebacks and a spell of wartime inactivity had rusted him beyond recognition. With both of them at their peak, however, their contrasting styles ensured a classic. Our own Henry Cooper, who knows a thing or two about heavyweights, says of them: 'Louis was the most economical heavyweight ever. He would not move an inch to get away from a punch if half an inch would do. He could jab an opponent silly and then hook off the jab which is the most difficult manoeuvre any fighter can execute. As a kid, I aped him. So there can be no greater tribute than that. As for Marciano, he is the one I would definitely have tried to avoid. Rocky never threw a straight punch but he could knock you bandy with any kind of shot and you never knew where they were coming from. None of the guys Rocky fought were ever that good again.'

The two great men's lifestyles were just as contrasting as their boxing styles. Whereas Joe was one of the world's great spendthrifts, Rocky was mean to the point of being downright miserly.

A ditch digger before he became a boxer, he took up his former 'profession' after he retired and buried large sums of his money in tin cans. It is said, by the few people who knew him really well, that most of his missing millions have never been recovered. Perhaps that has something to do with the reason that his hard-up daughter went to prison for a minor offence.

When he came to England years after his retirement, Rocky did a quick radio stint with me for the British Forces Network. I offered him a nominal fee of £20 and he astonished me by taking it. The late Bob Waters, an old American boxing writer pal of mine, once lent Rocky his raincoat and it took months to get it back. When he did retrieve it, Bob found $300 wrapped in an elastic band stashed away in one of the pockets presumably for a rainy Rocky day.

That day came when he was killed in an air crash. He was about to attend a charity event and, rather than buy a plane ticket, Rocky cadged a lift in a private aircraft.

So, in the end, both the prince and the pauper were forced by destiny to treat those two imposters, triumph and disaster, just the same.

CHAPTER TWENTY-SIX
A SWING QUARTET

'But there is neither East nor West,
Border, nor Breed, nor Birth,
When two strong men stand face to face,
Though they come from the ends of the earth!'
RUDYARD KIPLING

I use this chapter title 'A String Quartet' advisedly. For there came together in the 1980s four men of similar weights but diverse skills whose styles and personalities blended so harmoniously that they turned the entire decade into a rhapsody to the sweet science.

In no order of preference, they were Sugar Ray Leonard, Marvin Hagler, Tommy Hearns and Roberto Duran. Just as heavyweights Ali, Frazier and Foreman thrilled us in the 1970s, this quartet galvanised boxing in the lower weight divisions during their prime time. None of them was ephemeral stars – just the reverse, they were all as durable as old boots.

There was one memorable moment of discord in their collective composition when Panamanian Duran suddenly turned away from Leonard in mid-contest and said: 'No Mas,' before walking headlong into ignominy.

As their careers became entwined they fought each other on a regular basis throughout their decade and provided sustained entertainment for fight fans that has never been surpassed. It is one of those strange quirks of sport that Mother Nature contrives to apportion her greatest heroes in terms of feast or famine – the 1980s were indeed a feast. At various times, one or other of these men reigned as champions at all weights from light right up to light heavy from 1972 to 1989.

Duran performed the overture to their show as early as 1972 when he dethroned our own Kenny Buchanan to take the world lightweight title. Astonishingly, he is still boxing at the age of 47. In his native Panama he is revered as a sporting icon. He was even exempted from paying income tax, and you can't get much more reverential treatment than that. They called him Mano de Piedra 'Fists of Stone', and they were not far wrong. Throughout the rest of the 1970s he was brilliant and unstoppable. He punched himself out of opposition, losing only one non-title decision in 70 fights. Then he vacated that title and took the welterweight crown.

Unfortunately, he was also an arrogant, ill-mannered man, who frequently made obscene gestures to opponents and often bragged that he would 'keel' them. In fact, he made our own controversial star Naseem Hamed look like a choirboy. Only recently it was reported from the depths of some small hall somewhere in South America that the now-bloated Roberto knocked out not only his opponent but his opponent's girlfriend when she jumped into the ring and attempted to scratch his eyes out.

I fear it would be of little benefit if Duran took advantage of the current fad for psycotherapy to sort out his problem personality. I mean, if he was told to let out his inner child, he would be even worse than he is now. His favourite boyhood pastime was to mug drunken sailors on the local beach that now bears his name. So why did a monster like this drop those hands of stone, and turn his back and refuse to fight on against a will o' the wisp such as Sugar Ray Leonard in the middle of the 8th round in New Orleans in November 1980?

For the answer to that question we must return to their epic contest five months earlier in Montreal.

Then Leonard had made the mistake of trying to mix it with a mixer *par excellence*. Not that Duran was totally crude, far from it. With the aid of expert tuition in American gyms, he became adept at hitting without too often being hit. He learned to slide expertly away from other boxers. Intrinsically, the man had the heart and soul of a warrior and was never better than when he went toe to toe.

Even so, the brilliant Leonard lost only by the narrowest point margin. Next time Sugar vowed to fight a very different stick-and-run campaign. Duran's Panamanian pride burst at the seams. If this fracas had taken place in an alley, there was no doubt that Duran would have killed his man by whatever means it might have taken to do it. Now, he reckoned that Leonard was trying to humiliate him by 'dancing like a girl' and he simply refused to have anything more to with him.

Duran went through the motions of obeying advice that suggested he should claim he had stomach cramps. Even as he was trotting this excuse out in the dressing-room later, he was sucking on an orange and wiping his hands on his sweaty crotch.

I have known Sugar Ray since the 1976 Olympics when he was still a kid. We struck up a friendship by chance. I happened to be the first Brit present when he carried his golden medal into an only half-filled press interview room in Montreal. It tickled his fancy that someone should have travelled halfway round the world to talk to him.

Half a lifetime later, when I was seriously ill in

hospital and he was a TV commentator, I am told that, just as the master of ceremonies was announcing a world title fight from the ring, Sugar shouted up at him: 'This fight is not official. Reggie's not here.'

Of all Sugar's many sweet moments, I suppose the sweetest came when he beat the seemingly unbeatable middleweight champion Marvelous Marvin Hagler and Hagler had it recognised by deed poll. It was Hagler's 67th fight and he had been unbeaten in 11 years.

Not that it was sweetness and light all the way for my pal, Sugar. Far from it. During the periods when Hagler was on top it was like watching Bambi being mugged. I had always marvelled at this friendly, handsome guy from North Carolina who greeted everyone he met with a wink and a smile. One moment he would resemble a beautiful stag at bay and the next he would summon up the power, strength and courage to overcome the likes of macho figures such as Duran, Hagler and Hearns.

Sugar won that Hagler epic on a split decision and Hagler retired, although he still finds time to brood angrily about the experience while he waits on set for his actor parts in Italian movies in Milan where he now lives. But he has abandoned his New Jersey accent and swears about it in Italian.

Sadly, unlike Marvin, Ray made a catostrophic comeback years later, which ended with him on his hands and knees on the canvas at the feet of a comparatively anonymous man named Terry Norris and had his millions of admirers feeling sick with shame for him.

'Why, oh why did you do it, Ray?' I asked him later. 'You didn't need the money. You're practically a billionaire!' 'It was the adrenalin, Reg,' he smiled. 'I am an adrenalin addict. It still is so hard to live without the buzz.'

Now, not a lot of people know this, but Thomas 'Hit Man' Hearns alias the 'Mo Town Cobra' came to England to box as a youngster. He was in the American amateur team that met the British amateurs and his opponent was George Gilbody of St Helens, Lancashire. Would you believe, he only beat George on a split decision?

When you consider that the Hit Man knocked out Duran and fought a draw against Leonard, that will be something for George's grandchildren to savour.

I saw that unheralded contest and Hearns was not showing any punching power at all. So you can imagine how staggered I was when he later became a poleaxing puncher. Tommy went on to win world titles at four different weights right up to light heavy. From 1980 until 1991 he was the holder of one world title or another.

He has kept most of his money and he loves the respect that the fight game has brought him, but he is in danger of losing it, if he continues to fight on as he is still doing now in his early forties.

CHAPTER TWENTY-SEVEN
CANNIBALS AND CLOWNS

'The Devil whispered behind the leaves
It's pretty, but is it art?'
RUDYARD KIPLING

One boxing colossus who has lost every last ounce of our respect is, of course, Mike Tyson. When he cannibilised Evander Holyfield he became, to quote Oscar Wilde, 'The unspeakable in pursuit of the uneatable'.

There was nothing pretty or obviously artistic about the way Tyson bit chunks out of his opponent's ear. But, like it or lump it – and as a commentator I'm afraid I found that pun irresistible – this was not an unprecedented act in the history of prize fighting.

Over the years, I have seen a man resort to biting in the ring on at least half a dozen different occasions. In each case, the only possible reason for it was frustration. Boxers have been bitten on the neck and the shoulder, but I must admit that Holyfield's ear was a first and, please God, a last.

Only recently, at the last Boxing Writers' Dinner, former British heavyweights Bunny Johnson and Billy Aird were laughing about the night Billy tried to take a lump out of Bunny's neck when he could find no other way past his defences. That was back in the days when Tyson was still a juvenile delinquent.

I am not for one moment suggesting that what Tyson did was a laughing matter, but I find some of the sermonising and moralising on the subject slightly hypocritical as well as patronising.

There will be queues stretching round the block for seats at his comeback fight and before too many well-educated citizens throw up their hands in horror I suggest they quickly check what made old Homer and his Iliad such a best-seller. I mean, Achilles and his mob were not too slow on the uptake when it came to a spot of old-fashioned blood letting, were they?

Minds infinitely more intelligent than mine have tried to understand what makes violence such an intrinsic part of man's nature and failed to come up with an answer. All I know is what Hollywood producers and boxing promoters also know and exploit, and that is that to have white hats like our own Frank Bruno you have to have black hats like Tyson.

Cannibals and clowns are all part of life's plot. What makes boxing such a compelling and, at times, repulsive sport is that it takes a man's inbred anxieties and exhilarations right to the edge. Like kids, many of us still find that Tyson in his embodiment of the bogeyman yet vulnerable bully is an irresistible spectacle even if we have to look through half-closed fingers at him.

Just as night follows day, where there's a Mike Tyson there will always be a Don King – but more of him later.

For the moment, far from exonerating mad Mike, and without claiming that two wrongs make a right, I just want to vent the anger I feel at some of today's moralising, sermonising media men and women. My trade seems to have degenerated from brilliant exponents of the descriptive phrase to opinionated manipulators with a so-called solution to everyone else's faults and problems.

Nobody ever claimed that boxing was ballet dancing. Nobody ever suggested that it could not be brutal, but I do insist that it is a realistic reflection of man's struggle through the ages. So maybe Tyson is an artist of sorts, after all.

That he was a rapist, there is very little doubt, either. And there can be very little surprise that he became one when you consider what his co-manager, Jim Jacobs, said about him when he was still just a novice. 'Mike is a highly sexed guy. The reason we like to keep him busy in the ring and in the gym is that it burns off that desire to go and get laid,' confided Jim.

He also had a desire to hit people very hard without – as it has now become apparent – getting hit back. Holyfield was the first fighter to know in his heart of hearts the truth about Tyson the bully. That is why he insisted to us before their ill-fated fracas: 'I don't know why you people keep worrying about me getting hit. It is Tyson who doesn't like being hit, not me.'

And when you consider Tyson's fall, I suggest that was more to do with karma than freedom of choice. Whatever. Enough words have been written on the man for me to have to bore you with thousands more. But in mitigation of Mike, I would like to add that, on a personal level, he showed me and old-timers like me, nothing but courtesy.

He was a boxing history fanatic who, before he put away childish things, pored long into the night at videos of the old gladiators. He even dressed like them in black shorts, no socks and no dressing-gown. Sadly, what seems to have escaped him is the ability to behave like those gentlemen outside the ring and not just learn to ape them in it.

When I made that reference to cannibals and clowns, I

did not intend it as a cheap shot at our own loveable Frank Bruno. Although, he did lead with his chin when he took up pantomime.

It was and still is Frank's innate ability to clown that has made him the mum's pin-up boy and the first TV sporting icon in this country.

Unlike Tyson, who appears to have shown little or no respect for his God-given talent and physique, big Frank has always had that quality most vital to the enjoyment of life – namely, gratitude.

His career was in jeopardy before it even got started. He won an ABA title at 18 but, on attempting to turn professional, failed to pass the Boxing Board of Control requirement of 6/18 vision at a distance of six metres. Only two surgeons, a Russian and a Colombian, were known to have arrested similar short-sightedness.

This strapping Wandsworth boy made the 6,000-mile journey to Bogota alone to prepare for a five feet tall surgeon named Jose Barraguer to operate. After Senhor Barraguer had done his work, young Frank had to wait alone for days in suspense in a darkened room before the bandages could be removed.

He still has trouble trying to describe his emotions during that make-or-break ordeal, but says it was a far more more fearful and demanding experience than taking punches in the boxing ring.

Obviously he eventually passed the eye test when he was 20 and went on to win worldwide fame and a considerable fortune. Due to a lack of suitable opponents and the way his career had been shrewdly mapped out for him, he never challenged for a British title.

He did fight three times for the world title, however, before being successful at the fourth time of asking when he had reached the veteran stage. He also had to endure another eye operation after sustaining several brutal beatings, two of them at the hands of Tyson.

This time, Professor David McLeod successfully repaired a detached retina. Like Joe Bugner before him, Frank had to suffer the slings and arrows of many macho fight fans discontent, because they felt that the Adonis-like physiques with which these two had been blessed should carry all before them. However, in boxing, muscles do not maketh the man. In fact, they can be a downright hindrance. As Bruno's wise old manager Terry Lawless explains: 'When you have biceps the size and weight of Bruno's it is like heaving a bag of cement around whenever you throw a punch. It can tire you as much as it damages your opponent, particularly if you miss a lot!'

Bruno also suffered from the constant pressure we put on him to bring back the heavyweight crown to these shores for the first time this century. When he did manage it after more than a decade of trying, and after titanic struggle with Oliver McCall, it proved well worth the wait for him when he was paraded around the streets of his native London in an open-top bus.

Honest Frank's most endearing quality was that he suffered no delusions about his ability. His courage, determination and fanatical dedication to physical fitness carried him on a long and lucrative journey that proved well beyond many a man of superior natural talent. Every penny he earned, he worked for. So it was with a great deal of pleasure that many of us who had criticised him over the years, attended the lavish party that he threw at his Essex mansion for the christening of his son, Frank junior, in 1997.

No expense was spared – there were dodgem car and helicopter rides for the kids and gallons of booze for the

600 adults. It was both tragic and heartwarming, though, to see the stricken boxer, Michael Watson, and crippled motorbike stuntman, Eddie Kidd, watching the Catholic christening ceremony from their wheelchairs.

An amusing little anecdote that puts Frank's popularity into perspective centres on the occasion when several thousand British followers travelled to Las Vegas for his second fight against Tyson. One Union Jack-garbed British fan spotted Joe Louis's statue in Caesar's Palace and mistakenly and somewhat drunkenly exclaimed: 'Blimey, they've built a statue to our Frank already.' A cynical American boxing writer quickly retorted: 'Nah, Bruno ain't that fast, buddy.' And big Frank's belly laugh echoed long and loud when I recounted the tale to him later.

CHAPTER TWENTY-EIGHT
NEW KIDS ON THE BLOCK

'If you can trust yourself when all men doubt you,
But make allowances for their doubting too.'
RUDYARD KIPLING

S omeone once said that TV has changed the world more than any other invention since the wheel. Well, no one will argue with the fact that TV has certainly made the planet a much smaller place by bringing it into our own living rooms. It has shrunk boxing, too. Where once old Jack Solomons used to bar Americans from appearing on other promoters' bills without his permission, British and American promoters have now become such buddy boys that they are going three-to-a-bed with TV.

Where Jack once studied dog race form every evening, today's leading promoters burn the midnight oil perusing audience ratings.

While there is no doubt that live TV has introduced a whole new audience to the fight game and moved it into prime time entertainment, it has also helped to devalue it as a sport by trivialising titles.

To cater for TV's voracious appetite for a top billing tag to be stuck on their main events, so many new boxing boards and new weight variations have come into existence that we are in danger of running out of letters of the alphabet to describe them all.

However many different ways the money men find to slice up the cake, they will never alter the ageless fact that fighters make fights – not titles. That the very best matches now add up to even bigger bucks than they ever did because of their novelty value.

In Britain, Frank Warren certainly burst, or more accurately, tip toed on to the promotional scene in the early 1980s. Learning the hard way, his first licensed shows at the Bloomsbury Crest Hotel in London resulted in huge losses and the old established promoters foolishly, quickly and wrongly wrote him off as a loser.

They could not have been more wrong. Raised in a council flat that overlooked the roof of King's Cross station in London, streetwise Frank raised his status to such an extent that he now lives in a King Henry VIII hunting lodge (circa 1598) in a 91-acre spread on the Hertfordshire-Essex border and runs his ever expanding business from luxury offices in nearby Hertford.

For a while, he teamed up with notorious American rival Don King. They formed a stunningly successful transatlantic partnership until they fell out and became involved in the litigation of which boxing promoters are so fond.

King then teamed up with the even newer British kid on the block, Frank Maloney, a man he once called a mental midget and now refers to as 'wonder man.'

If ever those words of Kipling's at the start of this chapter applied to anyone, they apply to King. Rather than make allowances for a doubting world, this convicted killer oozes so much self-satisfaction that if he was made of chocolate he would eat himself.

I have kept my contacts with him on a strictly

professional level and that usually means suffering from spells of grievous bodily harm to the ear while he rattles off his stream of rhetoric.

Frank Warren, on the other hand, I regard as a personal friend. Maybe I have a rapport with Frank because we were both born and raised in Islington and know where each other is coming from, so to speak.

I strongly disapproved of his earlier involvement with unlicensed shows, featuring notorious macho men and their supporting cronies and forcibly told him so. He says I was the only journalist in the country who at least went to a couple of them and checked them out for myself. The two I attended were well enough staged with a doctor in attendance and no mismatches.

He admits, however, that, although he made money from those knockabout ventures, he now regrets his involvement with them. He says it was the only way he knew how to break into this precarious business and get himself noticed.

Frank needed a reference to present to the Home Office for a work permit when he imported his first American to a British show. I was certain that the American in question, Tom Prater, was good enough for any of Warren's stars, as he had fought no less a man than Larry Holmes. So it proved because Warren's man was beaten.

Early on, Frank got himself the reputation of being a rebel. He explains away those years by saying: 'Promoting is the riskiest business I know and I resented petty restrictions by the Boxing Board.'

Today, the Board earn their highest income from sanction fees of Warren's TV shows.

Educated at the University of Life, Warren had been a bookmaker's clerk on racecourses, a printer with Robert

Maxwell's Permagon Press, a butcher and a partner in a nightclub with Frank McLintock, captain of the Arsenal double-winning team of the early 1970s.

His breakthrough came when he was courted by Independent Television to challenge the BBC who had boxing contracts with National Promotions, the company run by the 'old school' of Jarvis Astaire, Mickey Duff and Mike Barrett. From the very earliest days of TV boxing coverage, this had been a cosy arrangement whereby there were 24-hour delays on TV so that the live gates were unaffected.

Warren argued that attendances would not be unduly harmed by live coverage and he was right. Live attendances actually increased and the boxers themselves became TV celebrities. He prospered accordingly. But, being the gambler that all promoters are, he took a terrible financial tumble when backing for his dream venue, the London Arena in Docklands, collapsed when banks reneged on loans when the new safety precautions, introduced following the Bradford and Hillsborough soccer disasters, proved financially prohibitive.

Frank had all his assets tied up in this £36 million venture to transform an old banana and tomato warehouse and the disaster took him back to where he had started.

If that was not enough to finish most men, even worse was to come for this seemingly superhuman survivor. In a well publicised incident he was shot, at point blank range, at the entrance to the Barking Theatre where he was staging a show. One of the bullets to enter his body missed his heart by a millimetre.

Boxer Terry Marsh whom Warren managed successfully to British, European and world light welterweight titles, was charged with Frank's attempted murder and held in custody for nine months. However, he was acquitted and walked free. More than eight years have passed since those traumatic times and his physical and financial recovery has been little short of miraculous. He is a long way removed from the old Hollywood caricature of a big fight mogul in that he is an understated, smart-suited, blue chip city type, with no cigars and no coarse language. His is the ultimate comeback.

You could say that Don King has come a long way, too, since he was jailed for manslaughter in his days as a numbers racketeer in an earlier life in Cleveland. But what is increasingly debatable is in which direction is he travelling? As more and more revelations are printed about his activies his legal conflicts are becoming more frequent by the week.

As most of that side of his affairs are *sub judice*, I shall confine myself to recalling a few personal encounters with this outrageous character. He first entered my life when his famed hair was still low voltage and, would you believe, he was still softly spoken. He first entered the fisticuff fraternity by trying to become a commentator and asked me for advice on the subject. His crack at it was, at best, ordinary. I would remind of him of the repetition involved – ironic that, when I think how much he repeats himself now – how you have to keep referring to the weights and keep on identifying with the boxers. He acknowledged: 'I owe you a big favour' and then promptly threw the commentating towel in and informed me that he was going into the section of the boxing business where he could, to use his own words, bring his 'trickeration, wit and grit' into play.

Thereafter, he never said a word where ten would do.

Whatever reservations we may have about his morals and scruples or, indeed, his lack of them, no promoter has ever worked harder or more efficiently than King. PJ Barnum was a slouch by comparison.

King's chief American rival is Bob Arum, a lawyer by trade and by inclination. He steers well away from the legal problems of combining management and promotion – a trap that most of his contemporaries have fallen into at one time or another. Arum has never pretended to be a boxing expert, but he knows a box office winner when he sees one and has proved it on numerous occasions via his slick Top Rank Organisation, which operates out of Nevada. He is, of course, a sworn enemy of King's, but who in boxing isn't?

The current exception seems to be our own Frank Maloney. As a paid employee of Panix Promotions, Maloney is a percentage holder and official manager of the best card in the pack at the moment in Britain's Lennox Lewis.

He entered the 'heavyweight' side of the business a decade later than Warren, but looks set to replace Frank as King's British promotional partner. He earns top rating from me because of his involvement in the amateur game. A pint-sized Cockney, he has long been involved with the Fisher-Downside boxing club in Bermondsey whose vests Terry Downes and Lloyd Honeyghan once wore proudly.

The holder of an ABA coaching badge, Maloney still stays close to the amateurs and works tirelessly on their behalf. This tiniest new tot on the block has quickly blossomed into a top player with televised shows beamed to every boxing TV customer from Scandinavia to South Africa.

One other big-time Brit, who has gone off the boil a

bit, is Barry Hearn. He, like the sport itself, is simply suffering from the current dearth of top talent. A former overlord of snooker, he threatened to blow all his rivals off the map when he first got involved in the hardest game. It seemed to come easy to 'Barry Earner' as he was known in his former 'pot black' environment. He earned a fortune for Chris Eubank, was a partner in the lucrative Bruno-Bugner promotion and he helped produce terrestrial ITV ratings' toppers in the spectacularly successful years for British boxing just a few years ago.

This former accountant from Romford, in Essex, is still involved in our business, but I suspect he is currently getting more enjoyment, if not more material satisfaction, from latest sporting toy, Leyton Orient football club.

CHAPTER TWENTY-NINE
PAYING THE PIPER

'If you can fill the unforgiving minute
With sixty seconds worth of distance run'
RUDYARD KIPLING

This decade has blessed boxing with five super middleweights who have filled more British fans with more drama and excitement than at any other time in the game's history. Between them, men like Nigel Benn, Chris Eubank, Steve Collins, Michael Watson and Gerald McClellan pulled in once undreamed of audiences of between eight and fourteen million for a single scrap.

But Michael and Gerald were the ones fingered by fate to pay the piper for us all.

Their final minutes in a boxing ring were as unforgiving as it is possible to imagine when each of them were crippled for life after taking part in separate contests, which would have vied for the title 'fight of the century' had they not ended so tragically. Desperate moments such as these make even an incurable old enthusiast like me stop and wonder whether the game is really worth the candle after all. And I promise not to shirk the issue of ring deaths later.

For the simple expedient of chronology, I must record that those twin tragedies brought the curtain down on a period when televised boxing in this country boomed as never before or since. For Benn versus McClellan the viewing figures of fourteen million were higher than they were for the Grand National or the FA Cup Final of that year.

Having all these talented men around at the same time meant that, just as the boxing world had paid homage to the USA in the 1980s, with its star turns Leonard, Duran, Hearns and Hagler, so the spotlight switched to these shores instead.

This was the advent of the TV spectacular, with entrances and presentation gimmicks that were more staged and garish than some circus acts. So much so that dear old Henry Cooper eventually walked away from his long-standing radio commentating job complaining that the modern shows were too 'over the top' for him. Even more recently, just as the Beatles imported pop music to the USA in the early 1960s, so 'Prince' Naseem Hamed introduced pop boxing there in the late 1990s.

As an even more senior citizen than our 'Enery, I must admit that he had a point. Fighters these days seem to be more worried about colour co-ordination than cuts. I mean that bit about colour literally. They fret over the shades and the texture of their shorts and dressing gowns, to say nothing of their sequins and tinsel. As for the music, which is so deafening at today's shows, apart from making it harder for me to concentrate on describing the real action, I cannot comment on its significance, or otherwise – since Glenn Miller and The Ink Spots, I have been out of the game music-wise! On top of that, there are as many fireworks going off outside the ring as in it at some of the modern shows.

Mind you, fashion-wise, I was quite with it in my youth. When I was boxing it was my dream to own a pair of purple shorts just like the ones Joe Louis wore throughout his career, but I could not afford them then.

Yet, even if the sweet bird of youth had not long since flown and I had not lost a leg, I can't quite see myself in sequined shorts. Some of those old fogeys at the Board of Control must feel the same way as me because sequins have now been banned. Sequins can be picked up on a fighter's glove if he is knocked down and they could injure or even blind his opponent when he has to start boxing again. At least, that's the Board's story and, thank God, they are sticking to it.

But all this 'Nazmataz', as I now call it in deference to the most way out British boxer ever, means that more people are talking about boxing these days than ever before and, more importantly, more young people are doing that talking. It's just such a pity that more of them are not boxing themselves, but then TV has a lot to answer for there, too, with its modern mass production of couch potatoes.

Incidentaly, 'Naz' or Prince Naseem Hamed to punters like you and me, still had a glittering future, as did Lennox Lewis, when this book went to press. So more of them later.

Generally, like football, the modern game has become much faster than it used to be. Old-time fighters could hold and spoil and the fans even appreciated it. Many of them had learned to box at school or in youth clubs and they appreciated the finer points of defence more. Even dear old Len Harvey would not have drawn flies these days because he was a master of skilful yet negative tactics.

All the crash, bang, wallop stuff that goes on nowadays makes commentating a lot more straightforward, but I am still especially grateful when I can feast my eyes on a clever technical throwback of a fight, which evokes fond memories of consummate artists such as Welshman Howard Winstone and Scotsman Walter McGowan.

However, one relatively modern British boxer who came close to emulating that peerless pair was the defensive artist Pat Cowdell.

Enough of this Memory Lane meandering, though. Paradoxically, no one crashed banged and walloped more than the 'Dark Destroyer' Nigel Benn and no one enjoyed the spectacle of him in full flow more than me.

Benn is a moody man and it was changing moods rather than plans or tactics that determined his performances in the ring. Sometimes he could have the appetite of a hungry lion and at others he could lose interest completely. This blowing hot and cold personality of his was reflected in the way he was prone to change managers and trainers.

He served four years in the Royal Fusiliers, but the way he exploded his punches on target, I reckoned it would have been more appropriate if he had been in my old regiment, the Royal Artillery.

Benn's most memorable fight has to be the pulsating draw he fought with Chris Eubank at Manchester United's ground. The general concensus was that he would have won it had he not had a point deducted for a foul.

In my book, he won it anyway. I am old-fashioned enough to be totally opposed to drawn verdicts. The rules maintain that, when the points are level, the man who does more of the leading off should be the winner. In modern times that 'leading off' phrase has been wrongly interpreted as 'aggression.'

Now, when the Marquis of Queensberry framed the rules back in the days of *Boxiana* which happened to be the first sports paper ever, they did not differentiate from 'leading off' whether going forwards or backwards. 'Leading off while milling on the retreat' was the way our ancestors described it.

There was little doubt that the ever busy Benn did infinitely more leading off than Eubank that night.

If Manchester United's ground was the scene of one of the most memorable fight nights of the 1990s, Tottenham Hotspurs' ground was the venue for one of the most miserable.

That was the dreadful night when Michael Watson's life was ruined. Ironically, it was his opponent's courage that cost Michael so dearly. The tragedy came in the 12th and final round when he was well in front of Chris Eubank on points. Now, Eubank, who despite his eccentricities, was a very accomplished boxer, had unlimited bravery.

It was this courage which led to the fateful uppercut that felled Michael. Chris had been put on the canvas in the previous round and referee Roy Francis admits that he forgot to give him what, in recent times, is a mandatory eight count.

Eubank's courage got him to his feet at four and desperation sent him flying at Watson to land a full-blooded uppercut on Michael's chin. None of us, including Roy Francis or Michael's trainer Jimmy Tibbs, realised just how devastating the effect of that punch had been and, in hindsight, it was a mistake for Michael to come out for the 12th round.

As Sugar Ray Robinson always said, 'It is the punches that you don't see coming which hurt the most' and poor Michael was definitely not expecting that fateful uppercut. In addition, he had been in another gruelling world title just a few months earlier and he suddenly collapsed.

When I went to see him in hospital it was not to put too fine a point on it, gruesome. His brain was severely damaged and he was swathed in bandages.

I had a particular affection for Michael because he was an Islington boy like myself and we had both boxed in the London Federation of Boys' Club competition. Although he was the only one of the men I have been talking about in this chapter not to win a world title, he was the classiest boxer of them all.

It was so upsetting seeing him lying there that the only way I could deal with my emotions was to crack a feeble joke about the need for him to keep his eye on his bedside locker considering all the tea leaves around Hackney where the hospital was situated.

Somehow, he summoned up the tolerance to give me a slow smile and make a fist at me. I am happy to report that seven years on, he is now getting out of his wheelchair on a daily basis and is taking a few tentative steps towards recovery.

Sadly, there is not even that glimmer of hope for Gerald McClellan. In addition to being crippled, he has recently gone blind and is being cared for, round the clock, by his three sisters, Stacy, Lisa and Sandra, who are all married with families of their own to look after, too.

A trust fund has been set up for Gerald and contributions should be sent to The Gerald McClellan Trust Fund, PO Box 660, First Bank of Freeport, Freeport, Illinois 61032.

When disaster struck this brilliant young boxer in October 1995 it came during the tenth round of an epic ebb and flow contest with Nigel which, until that dreadful, unexpected moment when Gerald slowly sank down on one knee suffering from what was later diagnosed as a brain haemorrhage, was shaping up to be the fight of the century.

As I write these words, I feel flooded with so much irrational personal guilt that it seems almost criminal to continue with this narrative, but as a battle-hardened old soldier who has experienced his share of horror, I know that life has to go on.

And our show went on – I like to think with Gerald's blessing – with the arrival of a Celtic warrior who came from Dublin via America. His name is Steve Collins and he is an intelligent, articulate, engaging young man who took up the hardest game the hard way by going to America and asking the people who looked after Marvelous Marvin Hagler to teach him the ropes.

They did this to such good effect that he went on to lick both Benn and Eubank twice and to become one of my co-commentators after his retirement.

He also picked up some tips on psychological warfare out there, which had Chris Eubank screaming blue murder. I particularly enjoyed the incident which I shall relate because Eubank made me good and mad once when I was interviewing him and he suddenly said: 'I don't take any notice of boxing writers – they are all on dope.' When I took issue with him about that outrageous statement, he grudgingly amended 'dope' to 'coffee.'

When he had a row with Collins, however, he took it all the way by making an official protest to the Boxing Board of Control.

Steve had kidded him in the pre-fight publicity build-up by telling everyone that he had been receiving regular assistance from a hypnotist. And he entered the ring for their fight wearing earphones, giving the impression to Eubank that he was listening to a soothing self-help tape.

Chris carried on alarmed, claiming that Steve was taking unfair advantage of him and simply refused to believe this engaging Irishman when he revealed that he was, in fact, tuning in to his favourite piece of music.

CHAPTER THIRTY

OBITUARY

'To the legion of the lost ones,
To the cohort of the damned'
RUDYARD KIPLING

Boxing has claimed the lives of more than 350 men since I have been covering it in a professional capacity. There is absolutely no way I can box clever in trying to come to terms with that unforgiveable roll call. I could understand it if the bereaved families felt like lynching me if I tried.

So I will not even attempt to use that insulting excuse trotted out by so many about the number of fatalities in other sports. I can only plead guilty at taking my vicarious pleasure at their expense. And plead for clemency.

Defending the right of those young men to choose to sacrifice their own lives and to blight those of their loved ones into the bargain is something else, however.

I will defend freedom of choice to the death as I did during the last war and just as those young men do in the ring.

Now I happen to have no time for people who are always spouting their opinions, which is why I have kept my own to a minimum in this book. However, I will indulge myself here by stating my belief that to ban anyone's right to choose is to impose tyranny. I am aware that, taken to its limits, that philosophy could lead to unacceptable anarchy.

271

But in choosing to box, an athlete is attempting to fulfil man's God-given right to seek what that individual sees as the most noble means at his disposal for expressing himself. I have never encountered a psychopath inside that roped torture chamber, a masochist or two maybe, but never a man without feelings or conscience for his fellow human beings.

Among the big-name British boxers to have killed their opponents are Joe Bugner, Alan Minter and Barry McGuigan. At one time or another, they have all been stupidly asked the unanswerable question of how it felt to kill an opponent.

McGuigan gave the only sane reply possible when he said: 'The only way I could console myself was to say "It could easily have been the reverse. It could easily have been me."'

Two wrongs do not make a right. But they do add up to an adrenalin addict and addictions, whether legal or otherwise, sometimes ends with the addict paying the ultimate price. Few of them would want it any other way – dicing with death is a game that most of us have felt compelled to play at one time or another without knowing why.

These, in my opinion, are the cold facts of pursuing dangerous sports, not the moralistic certainties that boxing opponents are so fond of quoting, as if those morals were written in stone for those of us who they believe to have hearts of stone.

I say to them that those young men who died doing what they loved doing had a thirst for life that knew no bounds. Which of us can deny that challenging the Grim Reaper and beating him on occasions can be an irresistible game?

Not that boxing is a death wish. John Conteh, who

ruined his own career with the additional addictions of drink and drugs, puts his feelings for boxing this way: 'It is the ultimate clash of wills. A game of chess with gloves on. With pleasure and pain as the prize and the price.'

That truly great boxing writer, Hugh McIlvanney, summed up the inexcusable death of Welshman Johnny Owen with this unforgettable phrase about him: 'Boxing gave Johnny Owen his one positive means of self-expression. Outside the ring he was an inaudible and almost invisible personality. Inside, he became astonishingly positive and self-assured. He seemed to be more at home there than anywhere else. It is his tragedy that he found himself articulate in such a dangerous language.'

I make no excuse now, for using that most trite of all truisms: 'Life must go on.' And that is precisely what it is doing, in some style, for our two leading boxing lights of the moment, Lennox Lewis and Naseem Hamed.

Lewis lives a left hook away from me in a £3 million home in Hertfordshire. I often pop round there for a cup of tea with his mother, Violet. She and I became friends when I was commentating on one of Lennox's fights in Sacremento for a brand new cable TV outfit called Wire TV. The fight was a big hit for them but did not prevent their closure the very next week. At least the old *News* lasted a bit longer than that!

As for Violet, she climbed into the ring to berate one of the seconds of Lennox's opponent, Lionel Butler, who had been bad- mouthing her son. She was one feisty lady and I admired her spirit. It was quite a night for outspoken ladies: The defeated Butler's wife revealed that her husband had once sold Bibles for a living and recommmended to all and sundry that he was such a bad boxer that he would be better off back selling Bibles the following morning.

I first took serious notice of Lewis at the Los Angeles Olympics in 1984 when he was still a teenager and where he lost on a narrow points verdict to the eventual gold medal winner Tyrone Biggs. He was a good story for me because, although he was boxing for Canada where he had lived since he was 11 years old, he was, of course, born in London.

It was always a mystery to me that British managers never went knocking on his door to turn pro there and then. By the time they did sit up and take notice of him four years later, it was too late as far as they were concerned. This was when he came to the world's attention by beating Riddick Bowe in the 1988 Seoul Olympics.

By then Lennox was a big boy, and a laid back big boy at that. This time, he sent a lawyer to London offering his services. None of the established men had the bottle to put up the big bucks for which he was asking.

How they must all be kicking themselves now as Lennox notches up gross earnings of around $50 million to date and with an exceedingly good chance of becoming the highest paid sportsman of all time if his current handlers can persuade Evander Holyfield or Mike Tyson to share the ring with their man and unify the ludicrously carved-up world heavyweight crown – still the greatest single prize in all sport.

Instead Lewis accepted a deal, in which the percentages were heavily in his favour, from the boss of an insurance company. This character's name was Roger Levitt. He had no connections with the fight game and was not a Board of Control licensed manager. Independent Television, with plenty of encouragement from me, signed a dozen fight deals to launch Lennox's professional career.

No sooner had it started than Levitt's company collapsed and his employee's pension went down the drain with it. Levitt was convicted on a financial charge but escaped jail and was sentenced to community service. The famous *Daily Mail* diarist, Nigel Dempster, still refers to Levitt as 'The Ferret'. In our business, we use a shorter four-letter word to describe him.

Panos Eliades, a London-based Greek Cypriot, and a successful liquidator, soon stepped into the breach and began guiding Lennox up the greenback road with the assistance of the aforementioned Frank Maloney.

Now, after a scare or two – when he lost to Oliver McCall and laboured against one or two others – Lennox is looking increasingly like a licence to print money as far as these two are concerned.

When his new trainer Emmanuel Steward teaches him to deliver left leads that, at present, still look more like those of a painter than a puncher, there should be no stopping our man. You could be forgiven for thinking that, at 32, Lennox should be way beyond the learning stage, but heavyweights seldom reach their full potential before the age of 30, so time is still on his side.

Ironically, Britain had waited for more than a century to boast a world heavyweight champion to follow in the ancient footsteps of Cornishman Bob Fitzsimmons, and then we got two in double-quick time in Lewis and Bruno.

Lennox landed his, of course, without having to strike a blow in anger when they pulled Riddick Bowe's belt out of a London dustbin where he had thrown it in protest after refusing to fight our man for it.

At £50 million and still climbing, some piece of rubbish that turned out to be!

When I first saw Naseem Hamed getting up to his arrogant antics, I said in my commentary: 'Don't call us, we'll call you.' I did not fancy him one little bit.

I must confess that I have mellowed in my attitude towards him since then. However much members of my generation may object to his outward show of sportsmanship and courtesy, we just have to put it down to the generation gap and admit that he has the talent and the punching power to sustain his objectionable ego.

Early in Hamed's career, I was at ringside when I clearly heard that tough referee Roy Francis, who fought and beaten the best as an England amateur, threaten him: 'Do that again and I will personally throw you over that top 'effin' rope.' Roy had, like so many more of us, taken great exception to the way he was taunting and belittling his opponent. No less an authority on low life than the immortal American Budd Schulber, writer of epic films *On the Waterfront* and *The Harder They Fall* has said in print that our man was 'insufferable'.

Whether us old-timers like it or not, we have had to concede that Hamed has brought a brand new audience to boxing and that this younger generation has been reared on what they like to refer to as 'in your face' entertainment.

Hamed is coached by a veteran trainer in his home town of Sheffield. Brendan Ingle once fought Chris Finnegan and guided that other immensely talented son of Sheffield, Herol Graham, to within touching distance of a world title.

Irishman Brendan claims that he discovered Naseem when he happened to be passing a school playground where, as an eight- year-old, he was sensationally beating off a gang of school bullies.

Sometimes his flashy brashness undoes him temporarily, as when he was floored in Madison Square

Garden by Kevin Kelley and again when he was dumped on the canvas by Daniel Alicia. In each case, undefeated Hamed bounced back to knock his man out.

His reign as a nine stone, nine carat champion with millions in the bank and his own fleet of cars looks set to continue until he tires of telling himself how great he is, which is about as unlikely as me growing another leg.

CHAPTER THIRTY-ONE
THESE ARE OUR LIVES

'If neither foes nor loving friends
can hurt you?'
RUDYARD KIPLING

When Michael Aspel thrust his red book in front of my face and said: 'Reg Gutteridge, this is your life', the first thought to flash through my mind was: 'I could'a been somebody, I could'a been a contender'.

That line was, of course, the classic delivered by Marlon Brando when he played a failed boxer in my favourite film *On The Waterfront* which was written by my old mate Budd Schulberg.

I wondered what my old dad would have thought if he could have seen his only son's story being shown to millions. He probably would have said something like: 'Blimey, I breed a boxer and I wind up with a luvvie, instead.' But he would have been proud. I know that I was proud for him.

I was utterly gobsmacked when I realised what was happening to me, but more of that later. First, I have to confess that I was a cornerman twice before I topped the bill myself on what is regarded as one of the most popular ITV shows of all time.

On each of those two occasions I was a bit naughty

because the 'victims' are not supposed to have any foreknowledge of what is about to happen to them. The producers are so strict about this that they have been known to cancel the show at the 11th hour when they discovered that their subject had been tipped off in advance.

My cousin Jack Pallo was chosen at the height of his popularity as a wrestler when that game was all the rage on TV 20-odd years ago. Incidentally, he was known as Pallo simply because when he took up the 'grunt and groan' business, a family conference decided that Gutteridge was primarily a boxing name and we did not want it to be besmirched in the wrestling circus.

Now Jackie suffered from dyslexia to such an extent that his wife, Trixie, had to read his pantomime scripts and teach him the words. She also knew that he would be terrified if he forgot the names of any of the guests who were introduced to him during the show.

So with my co-operation, she tipped him off and begged me to keep mum. I was a walk-on guest and, as such, had to mark his card by filling him in on each guest as they came on.

Mind you, Jackie was a natural show-off so his acting skills earned him an Oscar-winning moment when it came to the 'surprise suprise' bit. The set was a ring at Reading where Pallo was performing and Eamon Andrews slipped through the ropes while Pallo was facing his own corner pad waiting for the bell before turning and facing his rival.

When he turned to confront Eamon and the famous red book, his phoney raised eyebrows even had me fooled.

A great one for publicity, he once managed to fool actress Honor Blackman and the entire cast of the 1970s hit show *The Avengers*. Playing a bit part as a heavy, Pallo did a wrestler's fall backwards into a freshly dug grave in a fight scene with Honor.

Jackie then feigned serious injury so convincingly that he was stretchered off to hospital where a bedside visit from Honor made the front page of the *Daily Sketch*. That was back in the days when real news items such as famines and threats of war featured in the papers unlike some of the sillier stuff today. Still I suppose the old devil earned his moment of glory because it certainly took guts to fall heavily enough to make it all look realistic.

Mind you, Pallo was so good at this kind of thing that there was a time when he was carried out of the ring looking so much the worse for wear that his wife rushed to the side of the stretcher in an extremely agitated state. It was only when he winked at her that Trixie hit him with her handbag.

He and Trixie are enjoying much quieter times in their retirement down in Ramsgate these days, although he tells me he is still suffering from the aches and pains of all those battles he had with Mick McManus and co. 'They may have been faked, but they still hurt plenty,' he says.

My other cornerman job was for Muhammad Ali. How's that for a throwaway line?

I was asked by the *This Is Your Life* team to contact Ali, who was then in early retirement, and ask him to come to London for an interview with me. My job, though, was to get Ali to the Royalty Theatre where Eamon Andrews was waiting to pounce from behind a door in the theatre foyer.

As we sat in a hired car driving towards our destination, Ali kept popping questions at me like: 'Why are you paying me for this interview? You never paid before. Are you keeping the money for yourself, you old rogue?'

I knew then, of course, that Ali was winding me up and that he must have been told about the surprise scam by his wife to save him any possible embarrassment. He kept on teasing me, though. 'What are you going to ask me about?' He demanded, 'And will there be an audience?' As the greatest ad-libber in or out of the business, Ali had never asked me questions like this before, but I wouldn't budge because I knew he would react better in front of the cameras if he thought he was fooling everyone instead of the other way around.

Ali kept this little game going all the way to 'curtain up' time. When we arrived at the theatre and the cameras were rolling, he deliberately pushed me through the door first even though I was trying to squirm sideways and out of range.

Having read Eamon's script, I was worried that Ali might not recognise the former American cop, Joe Martin, who encouraged 12-year-old Cassius Clay to take up boxing when he reported that his bike had been stolen.

Although his desperate illness was just starting to affect his short-term memory, I need not have fretted because Muhammad's long-term memory was still as sharp as a tack.

The show was a Christmas cracker and was later screened across the USA. Ali got his fake chat show cash and I got a vodka and tonic, a sausage on a stick and a free ride home.

As far as my own appearance is concerned, I would never have believed that I could have been hoodwinked as easily as I was. After all, as well as my involvement with cousin Jack and pal Ali, I had been a walk-on guest for Jim Wicks, Terry Lawless, Jim Watt, Charlie Magri,

Terry Marsh, colleague Dickie Davies and actors Bill Owen, a Boys' Club supporter and George 'Chuck' Sewell, who was my closest boyhood buddy.

I was set up by the show's scriptwriter, Norman Giller, who telephoned and asked whether I could rescue him with a 'voice- over' job at Teddington Studios (where the show was being recorded) for a sports production he was involved with at the time. I should have twigged when he asked me to wear a collar and tie, but even that hint went over my head.

On the evening in question, I was already booked to commentate for ITV at York Hall, Bethnal Green, and politely told Norman so. Norman then promised to lay on a car to take me to the boxing and then on to Teddington afterwards.

What he neglected to tell me was that I was being hijacked and taken straight to Teddington and that colleague Jim Rosenthal had been switched to York Hall to stand in for me.

It so happened that the only thing on my mind that evening was our lovely half-Persian cat, Tom. He had recently been run over outside our house and, that afternoon, he had managed, for the first time since the accident, to climb the stairs to the bedroom on his heavily plastered leg.

I was still celebrating Tom's recovery and was just deciding that he could stay in the bedroom to surprise Connie, who was due home within the hour. Instead, this bloody car turned up. It was a lousy journey, with the driver going in fits and starts and constantly answering the phone. This, I later discovered, was because some guests were late and the driver was being given instructions to slow down.

All this messing about had put me in such a bad

mood that when I saw Norman standing in the foyer, I was just about to swear at him. Fortunately, Henry Cooper and Frank Bruno suddenly appeared to lift me off my feet. I still thought it was some kind of a Giller gag until I saw the Red Book and then heard Las Vegas Master of Ceremonies, Michael Buffer, on a big screen and heard him shout his famous catchphrase 'Let's get ready to rumble! Reggie Gutteridge, this is your life.'

When Connie was introduced to me as the first guest, I was so nervous that all I could think of to say was: 'The cat is in the bedroom.'

CHAPTER THIRTY-TWO
YOUR GAME'S IN TROUBLE

'Yours is the Earth and everything that's in it,
And – which is more – you'll be a Man my son!'
RUDYARD KIPLING

As Her Majesty the Queen pinned a medal to my chest on 7 March 1995, she said: 'Your game appears to be in a bit of trouble.'

I was astonished. I loved her choice of the word 'game' but even in the split second that I desperately tried to think of an appropriate answer, I found myself wondering: 'Does she mean "game" as in way of life? Or does she mean it in the sporting sense, like her own favourite racing game?'

This was one well-informed, with-it lady. She was, of course, referring to the recent Michael Watson and Gerald McClellan tragedies.

Perhaps sensing my surprise at her use of the vernacular, Her Majesty paused and waited graciously for me to compose my response. It was one of those tongue-twisting moments – a bit like the one with General Eisenhower all over again. I mumbled an inappropriate: 'We seem to be able to overcome our troubles, Ma'am. But it is worrying.'

'How long have you been doing it?' That was the

Queen's next, more predictable, question. And when I replied: 'Longer than I care to admit, Ma'am,' she smiled to indicate that the presentation of my OBE was over.

As I once fought for King and country, this magical moment meant more to me than I can find words to express. Let's just say that I felt like doing a one-legged lap of honour round the red carpet.

I have never been able to discover where the recommendation for my award of the Order Of The British Empire came from, but it did bring so many congratulatory letters that I thought our regular 'postie' was going to get an hernia delivering them all. Yet he gave a double rap on our knocker to offer his best wishes, too, bless him.

The build-up to this unforgettable occasion came several months earlier when a brown envelope fell on to the mat one morning. I immediately thought it was another household bill.

When I opened it, the letter heading was 'Department of National Heritage'. What they wanted me to do was to tick the relative box if I agreed to accept an OBE in the New Year's Honours List of 1995.

Open-mouthed, I dropped the letter in the cornflakes, from where it was retrieved by Connie, who had to read it twice herself. The biggest mystery of all is that no one tells you why you have been nominated for a Royal tribute.

Connie and I agreed not to tell anyone, not even our daughters, until this bombshell had been confirmed. As I was already an Old Big 'Ead long before the Queen confirmed it, I could not resist showing off at the Christmas family lunch table and letting the girls in on this Gutteridge family secret.

It was two months before confirmation came and I spent a good deal of that time worrying whether I had ticked the correct box and whether my reply had got lost in the post.

On New Year's Eve, a news agency reporter telephoned to say that I was on the next day's Honours List and I make no apology for saying that, apart from family occasions like christenings and weddings, that was the proudest day of my life.

On the even prouder day of the investiture, there is no indication which member of the Royal family will be 'on duty'. I was lucky, I copped for the 'biggie'. Only three other guests are invited to attend with you and that, too, worked out neatly for me and for Connie and our two daughters, Susan and Sally-Anne.

When I was suitably suited and booted, my good pal Len Hatton insisted that the Gutteridges should be driven through the gates of Buckingham Palace in his white Rolls Royce.

At the gates, we were subjected to a security check, during which the police sergeant in charge, who obviously believed in equal opportunities, instructed a lady police constable to lie on her back beneath the car and check for hidden explosives.

Once inside the Palace, a high-ranking army officer lectures recipients on the required procedure. We were advised not to use what he termed the American 'Ma'rm' when addressing Her Majesty, but to make sure we enunciated it as the British 'Ma'am'.

I worried, with some justification, when I was informed that after the Queen had presented the medal and shaken my hand, I was to take a step backwards and march off. Now, artificial legs are not designed for you to walk backwards, so I inevitably stumbled during this maneouvre, but, luckily, I was not given the mandatory standing eight count.

With the lecture over, the waiting was the worst bit, football's Jimmy Hill and I flicked dandruff off each other's hired morning suit collars to take our minds off the nervous thirst we were working up, but there was no liquid refreshment available, not even water. The nicest touch of the entire ritual was that the band played softly thoughout.

When it come to awarding a few gongs of my own there are many I could dish out. First and foremost, they would go to all the boxers who went where angels fear to tread to provide my livelihood and marvellous memories.

They are all very special people, but the one I would like to single out – after our 20 years on the road together – is Jim Watt. Ours is a friendship that cannot be bought. Professionally, he is as sharp a commentator outside the ring as he was a champion in it – a great counter-puncher when it comes to punchlines and shrewd enough to have been one of the boxers who kept their money. If the new Scottish Parliament is in need of a Chancellor of the Exchequer, they should send for my man Watt. I must mention, too, that Jim bravely endured the almost unendurable loss of a son killed in a car accident as did my former TV boss, John Bromley.

Over the past 50 years, I have probably spent more time with my media mates than I have with my own family. My BBC rival, Harry Carpenter, has been a friend of longstanding, too. John Bromley always granted me the rare privilege of remembering my name. He addressed most other people as 'my old commander'. Gary Newbon gets a special mention. He has always played a 'blinder' for me. Most TV viewers know him as the guy who sticks microphones in front of sports personalities' noses and then has the guts to ask them the questions the fans themselves would like to ask. His day job is a seven-day-a-week stint as controller of sport for Carlton Central TV.

I really value the friendship of ITV presenters, Dickie Davies and Jim Rosenthal whose off-air personalities are not in the least bit affected by their TV popularity. Then there is Paul Doherty, whose famous father Peter could make a football talk. I miss that big man on the TV beat these days. He was as good as gold to me, although he would take no prisoners if anyone let him down.

Among the scribes I have scuffled around the world with, I owe thanks to veterans Frank Butler and Peter Wilson, whose words in those bygone days were respected by everyone in the fight game. They were like uncles to me in my salad days and it took a while for me to stop calling them mister.

Alan Hoby, the ex-Marine and Frank McGhee, the *Daily Mirror* successor to Peter Wilson, kindly fought their way into dressing-rooms for me after fights and collected the quotes.

Two younger pals, Colin Hart of the *Sun* and Alan Hubbard, who I nicknamed the chipmunks, both grew in stature and reputation until Colin became the best known Brit on the American boxing scene and Alan is now an executive on the *Observer*.

The three of us were once diverted from a boxing trip to cover the attempted assasination of President Ford in San Francisco and we all made the front half of 'the book' with our coverage. Mind you, both Colin and Alan had been newsmen in their time, so I was in good hands.

'Harty', who has an even broader cockney accent than me, often does inter-round summaries for radio. If the late Lord Reith can hear the pair of us in his studio in the sky, he is probably tempted to drop a couple of plums down for us to stick in our mouths.

Colin was given a much more important job by his boxing writer colleagues, however, when he was appointed chief cashier for our collective restaurant bills. He was only second in command under the *Daily Express'* dear old roly poly promoter's son, Sydney Hulls, who was not only a hero of the battle of Arnheim, but an heroic light eater – whenever it was light, Sydney ate. As such he was appointed chief culinary adviser and chief taster at five star restaurants worldwide, which had to be about the biggest perk this enviable job had to offer. The wages may not have been the biggest in the world, but the lifestyle wanted some licking.

This lifestyle owed much to the support of a long line of sports editors at the *Evening News*, the last and the best of these were my good friends Peter Watson and Vic Wakeling, who is currently head of sport at Sky TV.

A special vote of thanks goes to Norman Giller, who has always been there for me as a loyal and valued friend and troubleshooter in bad times as well as good. Norman was once our sports room office boy at the *News*. With a little bit of prodding from me, he branched out as a journalist in his own right and wrote for the *Boxing News*, before becoming a soccer writer for The Daily Express and then a sports TV critic for the *Sunday Express* and the *Sun*.

He was also a prolific ghost writer for the likes of Jimmy Greaves and Frank Bruno. The mention of Frank at this point leads me back to the beginning of this chapter and my OBE.

There is a story about the day he and Harry Carpenter were presented with their OBEs together. As they were waiting in line, side-by-side, the Queen was taking so long talking to the person in front of them that Bruno said, in what he thought was a stage whisper, but was in fact in a big, booming voice that echoed all round 'Buck House': 'Blimey, 'Arry if she don't 'urry up a bit, she's gonna have to drop us out!'

The loveliest Royal story I know concerns Mike Grade's grandmother. Now it so happens that I first knew Mike when he was not much older than a boy. He got himself a job as a sports reporter on the *Daily Mirror* where he turned up on his first day in a Rolls Royce and was promptly told to make the tea. He was also put on the amateur boxing beat where the programmes listed all the fighters by their initials. I have never forgotten how he would come up to me at every show and plead: 'Got any christian names for me, Reg?'

Mike went on, of course, to become Programme Controller of BBC 1, he's the head of Channel 4 and is, I understand, now one of the main men behind the Millennium dome.

I am sure he never came across a better comic line in all the scripts he encountered than the real-live one when his grandmother was presented to the Queen. Michael is the son of theatrical agent, Leslie Grade, whose two brothers were the most powerful men in showbusiness, Sir Lew Grade and Lord Bernard Delfont.

Their delightful Jewish mother was being presented to the Queen at a Royal Command Peformance one evening and when Her Majesty came face to face with her, Grandma Grade, shook the Royal hand, leaned forward and said: 'Thank you for all you have done for my two older boys, but do you think you could manage to do something for my Leslie? He feels a little left out'.

While I am on the subject of families, this is a good time to mention my own again. Sadly, the Gutteridge boxing dynasty appears to be over. I never had a son and although cousin Jackie Pallo had Jackie Junior who went into wrestling like his dad, he has no male heir, either.

I have been blessed with four lovely grandchildren, however, all of them boys. they are Jacques, 6, Robert, 4, Matthew, 2 and baby Alexander. Their mothers say that the chances of these lads following in my footsteps are nil. Still, they may have something to say about that themselves when they are old enough to decide. At least, when they are old enough to read this book, they will be able to see what their old grandpappy got up to.

Both my daughters went to university, which makes a working-class boy like me very proud indeed. Without any prompting from me, they both chose advertising as a profession. Their married names, Antonioni and Seneschall could bring a bonus at scrabble. Both husbands have kept a sporting touch in the family – Tony having boxed as an amateur and John having played rugby for the Scotland under 21 team.

My most guilty confession is that, having been away from home so much while pursuing my career, I spent less time with my own children than I am able to spend with the grandchildren. But better late than never, eh?

CHAPTER THIRTY-THREE
THE FAIR SEX?

*'And a woman is only a woman, but
a good cigar is a Smoke'*
RUDYARD KIPLING

Grandfather Gutteridge had better prepare to start spinning in his grave at this point, as I am about to mention what, to him and his generation, would have been the utterly unthinkable subject of women boxers.

That Kipling quote at the head of this chapter would just about have summed up old Arthur's views on this new controversy. Come to think of it, he probably started rotating years ago, what with women policemen, soldiers, sailors and air force wallahs and so on.

I must confess it was not until I started running an imaginary 'Who's Who' of modern women through my own head that the vehement protests I am about to launch started to sound more and more hypocritical.

Only a few chapters ago, I was defending the rights of men to choose serious injury or even death in the ring on the God-given grounds of freedom of choice.

So, pinned into a corner, I must confess that my revulsion towards women's boxing is an emotional rather than a logical reaction. I do have one advantage, or should I say disadvantage, over most people who have been sounding off on the subject lately. I have actually witnessed women box each other and it is not a pretty sight.

It is extremely sad for me to have to report that women box on a regular basis in this country at bleak venues, supporting kick boxing bouts and the like.

Regrettably, a lady named Jane Couch brought the matter into the full glare of the media when she successfully convinced an industrial tribunal that women boxers should be granted licences from the Board of Control in the same way that men are.

Leading columnist, Ian Wooldridge, of the *Daily Mail*, made the inarguable point that, if it is equality this woman and her compatriots are after, they won't get that until they fight against men. Perish the thought!

Another young colleague of mine, boxing writer Steve Bunce of the *Daily Telegraph*, put Miss Couch into perfect perspective for me with the following article in his paper, on 8 April 1998.

'Jane Couch lost her world title in January to a 37-year-old woman having just her seventh fight. Last week she beat the British Boxing Board of Control at an industrial tribunal and now she is suddenly the saviour of women's boxing.

'Couch, who has won four of her six recorded fights, claims to still be a world champion. She also claims to have the power to knock out men in the ring or on the cobbles. She is hard and tough and she is putting back the progress of the tricky issue of women's boxing.

'The Board should have embraced her and let her fall flat on her face. She is worth about £400 per fight, but she claims it is £20,000. If she is so good and her backers so confident, they should hire a hall, a doctor, print tickets and find an opponent. Couch does not have to be a board licence holder to fight. Anybody can box if they want to.

'Women box on a regular basis in Britain. Amateurs in small halls, away from the unwanted glare of publicity and professionals – yes, professionals like Couch – fight in bleak venues as supporting fights on nights of kick boxing.

'Some, like Lisa Houghton, a PE teacher at a school in Leeds, travel to Germany for fights. Couch is just the in-your-face part of the sport: Punching Spice, if you like.

'Couch went for glory and she won. The Board failed to listen to any advice and used the time dishonoured old chestnut that women are unable to box because of the menstrual cycle. When the Board try to explain their stance, it is like listening to Les Dawson in drag doing his girning act. They have made Couch a star.'

David Smith, of the London *Evening Standard* used a more emotive stance when he wrote 'Will families here now go to boxing for a good night out like they do in the States?

'Will you go? And, if so, do you know what you'll see? Let me enlighten you: you'll see women bleed, you'll see women's eyes blacken and painfully close beneath bulging bruises.

'You'll see a woman collapse beneath a rain of blows, her dignity drowning in the sweat that makes her singlet cling to her battered body.

'One day you may be there when a beaten woman fails to respond to the urgent attention of the referee or her trainer. You'll see the doctor climb in the ring, make a quick examination, then call for the paramedics. Later, you may learn from a newspaper or a news bulletin that the woman, who is wife, a mother, a sister, an aunt, is condemned to a useless existence in a wheelchair.'

The British Medical Association obviously had such a scenario in mind when they described the Couch findings as 'a demented decision of equal opportunities'.

When that day comes, God forbid, and don't think it is impossible because I had to commentate, against my wishes for Sky TV at the first Holyfield–Tyson fight when American star, Christy Martin, pulverized an opponent who fell around like a rag doll and could well have been critically injured that night.

As I said, when that day comes imagine the furore from the abolitionists then, especially with the number of women we have in Parliament today.

Wouldn't it be ironic – and I am aware that some would say poetic – if the sisterhood brings down the last male sporting bastion? I sincerely hope that I am not still above the daisies if and when that happens.

CHAPTER THIRTY-FOUR

A FUNNY THING HAPPENED ON THE WAY TO THE PUBLISHERS

'He's an absent-minded beggar
And his weaknesses are great'
RUDYARD KIPLING

The funny thing that happened to me was that I suddenly twigged that I had made a ricket with dear old Rudyard. For non-Cockney readers, I should translate that as: 'I suddenly realised that I had made a mistake with dear old Rudyard.'

I was virtually on my publisher John Blake's office doorstep when the survival instincts that have served me so well down the years, suddenly insisted: 'Take another look at Chapter Nine before you deliver the manuscript'.

Then, sure enough, the truth dawned. The Kipling quote that precedes chapter nine and is all about my wife Connie, was not Kipling's at all but Charles Kingsley's (1819–1875).

Just like Rudyard's 'absent-minded beggar' I had forgotten to check the heading on the page of the quotation book I was using and got my Kipling mixed up with my Kingsley.

But those Kingsley words so matched my feelings on that most personal of chapters that I decided to leave them in and plead guilty, figuring that one below the belt shot in 74 years of reminiscenses would not get me disqualified. If you, the reader, decide to deduct a point for foul play, so be it. The one true lesson my long life has taught me is that nobody is perfect.

And, as I am no exception to that rule, I shall take the opportunity that memory-jogging moment on my publisher's doorstep presented me with to begin rabbiting to you all over again.

Now, I would be the last one to suggest that people do not have moments of perfection. Indeed, I hope this book is full of illustrations of men who have scaled the heights of human endeavour. But to get the very best out of life. I have always needed to recognise the fine line between brilliance and banality, and perfection and pathos.

For me, no other human endeavour captures this precarious balancing act more accurately than boxing where men are putting themselves on offer, not only to their opponent, but to the demonic Gods of war. That is why a lifelong old 'wannabe' like me is still playing on the public's sympathies by hanging in there at ringside long after my sell-by date.

Maybe the good Lord was trying to tell me something on that prickly subject when I went to Hull on my 74th birthday recently to commentate on a fight for Sky TV. As I walked around the city memories came flooding back of the momentous events that were taking place the last time I visited Hull to see an aunt who lived there. I was eight years old and it was the first time I had been north of the Aldgate Pump. The streets were lined with cheering people to greet Amy Johnson, the famous pioneer woman flyer, who was being victoriously paraded around her home town after an historic flight to South Africa.

Another golden oldie, who thrilled the world in Amy Johnson's era was 'The Cinderella Man' James J Braddock, so-called because of his rags-to-riches rise from the dole queue in New York City to heavyweight champion of the world.

I have never worked so hard to crack a story than I did when James J visited England a few years back and asked promoter Mike Barrett's driver, Taffy Jones, to take him to Manchester where he told us he had been born.

James J also insisted that his late father had been a policeman in that city, which he poetically called 'England's pearl of the north'. Knowing that this would have given us a heavyweight champ that British boxing fans would have treated as a Second Coming, I enlisted the help of the then Manchester Chief Constable, Stanley Parr, whose officers scoured the city's ancient birth certificates to no avail.

Coincidentally, old James J's surname was borrowed by Jackie Braddock, a cracking Manchester boxer of the 1960s, who died only a year or so ago.

Eventually, we could only assume that this lovely old legendary pugilist, who enjoyed a drink or three in his long retirement, must have been a bit tired and emotional when he made his teasing claims.

This theory was reinforced a day or two later when that charitable veteran London cornerman, Denny Mancini, took James J to his brother's pub in Fulham. The old chap had a lovely time joining in with the locals at the dart board and being idolised by men who were young enough to be his great grandchildren.

When Denny dropped his guest back to the Hilton Hotel in Park Lane late that night he says that his instincts told him to go back and check on his wellbeing. 'I didn't want the champ to get mugged,' grins Denny, jokingly, but knowing that in these lawless times even such an unthinkable prospect was not so unlikely.

Unfortunately, this involved negotiating a one-way system and on the tortuous return journey to the drop-off point Denny kept getting glimpses of the old chap wandering about and getting himself more and more lost. The reason for this was that the Hilton had housed him in an overspill section that was not near the main entrance.

When Denny eventually caught up with him, the defiant old boy said: 'Hi Denny, am I glad to see you. Some bum with no sense of direction has just dumped me down in the wrong place.'

Another of boxings many great attractions is its irresistible impact on fight fans' universal love of nostalgia. Almost any conversation between a couple of boxing buffs involves booking a ticket on a time machine.

Another of the many human milestones along that journey is, of course, 'The Manassa Mauler' Jack Dempsey who reigned as king of the heavyweights during the roaring 1920s.

When I visited the great man's restaurant 20-odd years ago it was a major tourist attraction on Broadway. Three of us, all boxing people, were enjoying a meal with Jack when a man I can best describe as a Marlon Brando lookalike came in and started mouthing off at everyone in sight in a punch drunk voice.

Jack immediately left our table and marched over to this unwelcome visitor and began haranguing him: 'How many times have I got to tell you that I don't want your kind in here,' he bellowed.

I was squirming with embarrassment because I did

not relish one of my heroes talking and behaving in this undignified way. I was wondering why the hell he did not quietly get his manager to deal with the intruder.

As Jack was the archetypal version of the character who believes that actions speak louder than words, I was still fretting over the incident when the champ grabbed the man by the back of his jacket and trousers and ran him out of the restaurant door and on to the pavement.

Sensing how upset his British guests were, Jack apologised and then, grinning, he explained that the man was a well-known off-Broadway actor who begged Jack to let him indulge in this performance once a week. Then he shrugged and said: 'What the Hell, it doesn't hurt to do the guy a favour, but he still ain't made the papers with his little stunt yet.'

Dempsey's restaurant in those days was a favourite hangout joint for New York's most colourful characters and similar to the one Damon Runyan immortalised in *Guys and Dolls* and all his other wonderful short stories.

Would you believe that the London *Evening Standard* paid Runyan £500, which was a very impressive pay cheque in those days, to write exclusively for them on the Joe Louis v Tommy Farr fight, but neglected to inform him that they wanted it to be written in 'Ruyanese' which was very popular in this country then. To the paper's horror, the distinguished author sent them a blow-by-blow account, which they could have picked up from the agencies for next to nothing.

A similar commissioning exercise that went drastically wrong was the BBC's attempt to sign up Budd Schulberg for an inter-round summary job. They obviously had not done their research, so you can imagine their dismay when Shulberg, who suffered from a life-long stammer, came on the phone and stuttered that they must have the wrong man.

While on the subject of media deals that went wrong, one that went right for me and brought me a highly valued lifelong friendship, came when the *Evening News* decided to serialise that much-loved comedian, Norman Wisdom's, life story. He was 48.

It was not a hard decision for the then editor, Reg Willis to make because Norman had offered his story to the paper for nothing with one proviso – that I should ghostwrite it because he trusted me. In his youth, Norman had been a very useful southpaw flyweight and regularly drove me home from boxing shows at Earl's Court and the Empress Hall.

I did not have the heart to tell him that this task would be a big burden for me on top of my normal duties. He did not know, either, that the managing editor had chopped ten bob off my grand total of £20 in expenses.

Never mind, Norman was so pleased with the finished articles that he even offered to sell me his house for a knockdown £8,000, which was still way out of my league then. It doesn't bear thinking about what that same house would be worth now, but one material thing I still had to remember him by for many years was my upstairs loo!

This came about when Norman phoned Connie and asked me what kind of present I would like as a thank you gesture from him. She told him that it had been a labour of love on my part. Then when Norman went on to ask Connie where I was at that moment, she told him that I was helping a plumber to carry our old bath and toilet out of the house because we were fitting a new bathroom.

When we arrived at Bouldings in Bond Street to pay for the new toilet and bath, we were told: 'Mr Wisdom has already been in and paid for them.'

Many years later when that trusty old toilet had succumbed to wear and tear and a new one had to be installed, I posed for a photo of me demolishing it and sent it to Norman with a note saying: 'Sorry mate, but at least I don't have to think of you at least three times a day any more!'

Needless to say, I was delighted last year when the little fellow, now well into his eighties, travelled from his home in the Isle of Man to attend an ITV tribute dinner in my honour at the Café Royal, in London.

Another well-known comedian pal is Kenny Lynch. One of Kenny's off-stage one-liners that I shall always treasure came at a dinner show at the Anglo-American Sporting Club in the Hilton one night.

The old Marquis of Milford Haven, who made a name for himself in the 1950s as a ladies man and was regularly featured in the newspapers escorting busty beauties like film star the late Eva Bartok, was also a regular ringsider. His son and heir, incidentally, married George Walker's daughter, Susan, but they are now divorced.

Anyway, as I was leaving one particular Anglo-American show, I happened to be walking with Kenny just a few yards behind the Marquis, who, judging by his somewhat unsteady gait, had obviously been quite liberal with the port, when he tripped and fell headlong into the goldfish pond in the foyer.

Kenny shook his head and shouted down to the Marquis: 'God help us all. All it needs is for a dozen members of the Royal Family to be assassinated tonight and you'll be the King of England tomorrow!'

Those who know me best will be well aware that I fancy myself as a bit of a comedian, too, especially at the dinners and other functions I attend as a guest speaker. I was once given the opportunity to prove it by, of all people, that great, late comedy scriptwriter, Johnny Speight of *Till Death Do Us Part* fame.

I once had the pleasure of introducing the late great Bobby Moore to the guests at a *bon voyage* party for the England football team on the eve of their departure for the 1970 World Cup in Mexico. Johnny was one of the guests at this function. Also there was my old promoter pal, Harry Levene, whose large nose had been the making of that celebrated *Daily Express* cartoonist, Roy Ullyett.

I introduced Bobby's farewell speech by saying: 'Bobby, you will be delighted to know that Mr Levene will not be accompanying you to your high altitude destination. Otherwise, he would just have to take one sniff and he would nick all your rarified air.' Whereupon, Johnny approached me and asked whether I would be interested in supplying one-liners for a comedy show he was writing. I asked him what the show was about and he outlined the characteristics of Alf Garnett for me. I offered the considered opinion: 'It'll never go north of Watford, mate.'

With judgment like that, I suppose it is just as well I stuck to boxing, then.

So, right on cue, I have to confess that in just a few paragraphs from now, it will be time for the fat lady to sing. Before she does, I feel compelled to say that I have not deliberately neglected all the marvellous amateur boxers who have given me just as much pleasure as the professionals over the years. It is just that I have been saving their labours of love for my big finish.

One amateur night out that will always play a big part whenever I sit alone by the fire and sift through my precious memories came in Moscow back in the Cold War days of 1963 when, if you were unlucky enough to visit then God-forsaken city, you had to remember to take a supply of bangers and kippers for the expats there. For reasons known only to themselves, they craved them above all other gifts from home.

I was there with the British amateur boxing team for the European Games. And some team it was with the likes of Kenny Buchanan, Alan Rudkin and Johnny Pritchett in it.

Between the action we were all terribly bored with the non-existent social life until I discovered a comparatively lively little bar at the American Embassy staff club.

When the games were all over, I took the team to a farewell booze-up there where they, at least, had some drinkable imported American beer. I had not thought about asking the Embassy people how we were going to find our way through deserted streets back to our hotel in the wee small hours.

Anyway, as revellers do, we all piled out on to the pavement hoping for the best – which eventually arrived in the shape of a big open-backed lorry.

The team's heavyweight, ex-Guardsman Len Hobbs, waved the driver down and immediately hopped up into the cab beside him. Len somehow persuaded his new Russian mate in that instinctive half-sozzled sign language that has mysteriously transported me and so many of my my equally uneducated mates around the world and back, to give us a lift home wherever that happened to be.

Quicker than he could throw one of his lumbering left hooks, big Len was soon signalling for the rest of us to jump in the back. We did just that, only to land knee deep in wet cement. By the time we arrived at the hotel we almost needed a pneumatic drill to prize our ruined shoes and trousers out of that lorry.

So you can imagine how we felt when our ever

curious light heavyweight Dennis Pollard, who was then a sergeant in the Metropolitan Police and went on to make Chief Inspector, started to grill us next morning about what a cement lorry was doing on the streets at that time of the morning.

Exasperated, I correctly forecasted: 'You are a stone cold certainty to go all the way in that bleedin' old Bill of yours, mate. What's it got to do with you what a bleedin' Moscow cement lorry is doing?' Or words to that effect.

Just to round off with a tale of two cities, let me offer you this little gem from Rome.

During the 1967 world amateur boxing championships, me and my late *Evening Standard* mate George Whitingand I can't help thinking how fitting it is that dear old George should have almost the last word as he did so often when I was chasing his coat tails – had a rare afternoon off so we scanned the 'What to do in Rome' noticeboard.

'Perfect,' says I, 'English team wine tasting. Bus departs 2.30pm'.

Being newspapermen, we managed to miss the first bus, of course, but hopped on the second one which, as it turns out, was carrying the Irish team. Whoosh! Straight into the Vatican.

George and I looked at each other in horror. Twelve of us stood in a little room when in camePope Paul VI. Down the line he walked, shaking hands and welcoming us all in English. George muttered something about the 'bleedin' wine, or the lack of it', but I was too consumed with guilt to pay much attention to him. Millions of people would have loved to have met the Pope and there I was, a lapsed North London Protestant, chatting away with him like a good 'un slap bang in the middle of the Vatican.

You couldn't make it up, could you?